THE MAKING OF KINGS LYNN

KINGS LYNN ARCHAEOLOGICAL SURVEY

VOLUME I

The Making of Kings Lynn

Secular Buildings from the 11th to the 17th century

by

Vanessa Parker, M.A., Ph.D.
Senior Lecturer, Leeds School of Architecture

PHILLIMORE
London and Chichester

1971

Published by

PHILLIMORE & CO. LTD.
Shopwyke Hall, Chichester, Sussex.

SBN 900592 58 3

Thanks are due to the generous help of the Marc Fitch Fund in enabling this volume to be published

Text set by Phillimore in 11 pt. Press Roman
Made and printed by Eyre & Spottiswoode (Portsmouth) Ltd., at the Grosvenor Press

Contents

List of Plates

List of Figures in the Text

List of Figures in the Appendix

Tables

List of Primary Source Material with abbreviations used in text

Manuscript

Kings Lynn Muniments (K.L.M.)

- Hall Books (HB) Vols. I - X (1424-1731)
- Chamberlains Accounts: Rolls (Ea) Books of Entry (Ed.)
- Tolbooth and Town Dues and Tolls (Ee)
- Water Bailiffs Accounts (Dbl). (1574-97 and 1633)
- Common Staithe Accounts (Db27) (1595-1655)
- Mart Accounts (Dd) from 1581
- Surveys and Rentals (Bc)
- Deeds and Charters (Be)
- Gild Records (Gd)
- Town Charters (Aa)

Norfolk and Norwich Library: Archives

- Wills and Probate Inventories of the Norwich Consistory Court (NCC/INV)
- Wills and Probate Inventories of the Norwich Archdeaconry Court (NCC/A)
- Manuscripts from the collection of H.L. Bradfer Lawrence
- Miscellaneous Deeds and Charters

Public Record Office (P.R.O.)

- Exchequer:
  - Customs Accounts (E.122)
  - Depositions by Commission (E.134)
  - Port Books (E.190)
  - Special Commissions of Enquiry (E.178)
  - Subsidies (E.179)
- High Court of Admiralty: Examinations (HCA 13)
- State Papers: State Papers Domestic (SP 10)
- Chancery: Inquisitions Post Mortem (C 139)

British Museum (B.M.)

- Lansdowne MSS.

Bodleian Library

- Tanner MSS.

Somerset House

- Prerogative Court of Canterbury: Register of Wills (PCC)

Printed Primary Sources

The Red Register of Kings Lynn ed. Holcolmbe Ingleby

A Calendar of the Freemen of Lynn, 1292-1836 Norfolk Archaeology Original Papers (1913)

First Register of Norwich Cathedral Priory Norfolk Record Soc. Vol. XI (1939)

Public Record Office Calendars

- Patent Rolls
- State Papers Domestic
- Acts of the Privy Council

Acknowledgments

I should first like to express my gratitude to Professor W.G. Hoskins who initially encouraged me to undertake this work on Kings Lynn, and whose ready advice, and exhortation towards its completion, has been invaluable. Members of the Kings Lynn Museums Advisory Committee too have proved a constant source of stimulus, and I am particularly indebted to Professor E.M. Carus-Wilson for her helpful comments and criticism of the manuscript, and to Mr. W.A. Pantin for his advice on the investigation of historic buildings in Lynn. Professor Beresford has also kindly read, and commented on, the parts of the manuscript referring to the foundation of the new town, and I was much assisted by the criticisms of Mr. P.M. Tillott who read the manuscript in full. For errors and infelicities of expression I am, of course, solely responsible.

I should like to thank the Town Clerk of Kings Lynn for permission to use manuscripts in the borough archives, and to Mr. Leslie Hall for his kind assistance and co-operation in unearthing relevant documents for me. I am also grateful to Miss J. Kennedy, of the Norfolk and Norwich Record Office, and to the late Mr. H.L. Bradfer Lawrence, who gave me much valuable information on the history of Lynn families, and who allowed me access to his extensive collection of manuscripts. In Kings Lynn I have had the willing assistance of many people, but I should particularly like to thank Miss S. Mottram, Curator of the Museum, Mr. G. Holmes, the Borough Architect and Mr. Ridler, the Borough Surveyor, and their staffs. I am also profoundly grateful for the unvarying hospitality with which the occupants of old houses welcomed my intrusions with measuring tapes and other paraphernalia. Without their co-operation this book could never have been written. Visits to Lynn were a great pleasure largely owing to friends who kindly allowed me the freedom of their homes. I am particularly grateful to Miss Diana Bullock and the late Miss M.L. Keith for their hospitality at Greenland Fishery House, and to the late Colonel and Mrs. R. Otter, in whose sunny attic at Oxley House much of this book was written.

I have had assistance in preparing drawings for publication from Mr. A. Whittaker of the Royal Commission on Historic Monuments, York, and from Mr. John Waldron of the Leeds School of Architecture. Mr. R. Gocher of Kings Lynn spent a summer holiday helping me with measuring and surveying and I am grateful to Mr. P. Skinner for his work on the survey of No. 8 Purfleet Street.

Finally I acknowledge the financial support given to this project by the Douglas Knoop Research Fund, The University of Sheffield, the Society for Medieval Archaeology Colt Fund, the Kings Lynn Archaeological Survey, and the generous help of the Trustees of the Marc Fitch Fund towards the finance of publication.

Introduction

The Economic Development of Lynn and its Hinterland

THE TOWN OF LYNN was brought into being at the end of the 11th century by the Bishop of Norwich, who, at the request of a group of traders – perhaps already established on the western shores of their manor of Gaywood – decided to found a church and priory there and to regularise commercial activities by the grant of a market and fair.[1] In this way they laid the foundations for the rapid growth of a new port. The estuary banks above and below the settlement were lined by salt workings, a fact which in itself in this period was sufficient to guarantee a lively trade with its hinterland; and it stood at an important crossing where road, river and sea transport met on the southern shores of the Wash, linking the town to an extensive hinterland; to the cornlands of West Norfolk to the north and east, to the fertile eastern and southern fens, and by river to their surrounding uplands to south and west. (Fig.1.) It was thus in a commanding position to exploit the commercial possibilities of an expanding agricultural economy and its fortunes rose with those of its hinterland in the early Middle Ages. By 1377 the tax paying population was 3,217, indicating a pre-plague peak of 5,700 inhabitants in the early 14th century.[2]

Kings Lynn was a plantation town, one of the earliest in a great wave of new town foundation which spread throughout practically all Europe in the 12th and 13th centuries. In England during this period almost 200 towns were founded, some like Lynn, achieving instant success, others like Newton on the Isle of Wight, leaving only a name and a solitary farmhouse to commemorate the intentions of their builders.[3] New towns were intended at the outset to accommodate a given number of persons, sometimes over-estimated by the town's founder, but often accurately forecast from knowledge of local conditions. Thus many of these towns, Lynn among them, did not grow year by year from an already existing nucleus, a core containing an agricultural community, whose tracks and field boundaries determined the layout of the town's markets, streets and building plots.[4] Instead they were planned at the outset for an urban community and subsequent development was on lines determined by the needs of trade and industry rather than agriculture. In such towns it ought to be possible to find evidence in the buildings and their layout of the particular and unique purposes of the communities who built them. The land and water they manoeuvred and adapted to make a living for themselves, and the stone brick and timber they erected to house their families and their institutions, may indeed often be a better guide to the manner in which they lived than the writings they produced.

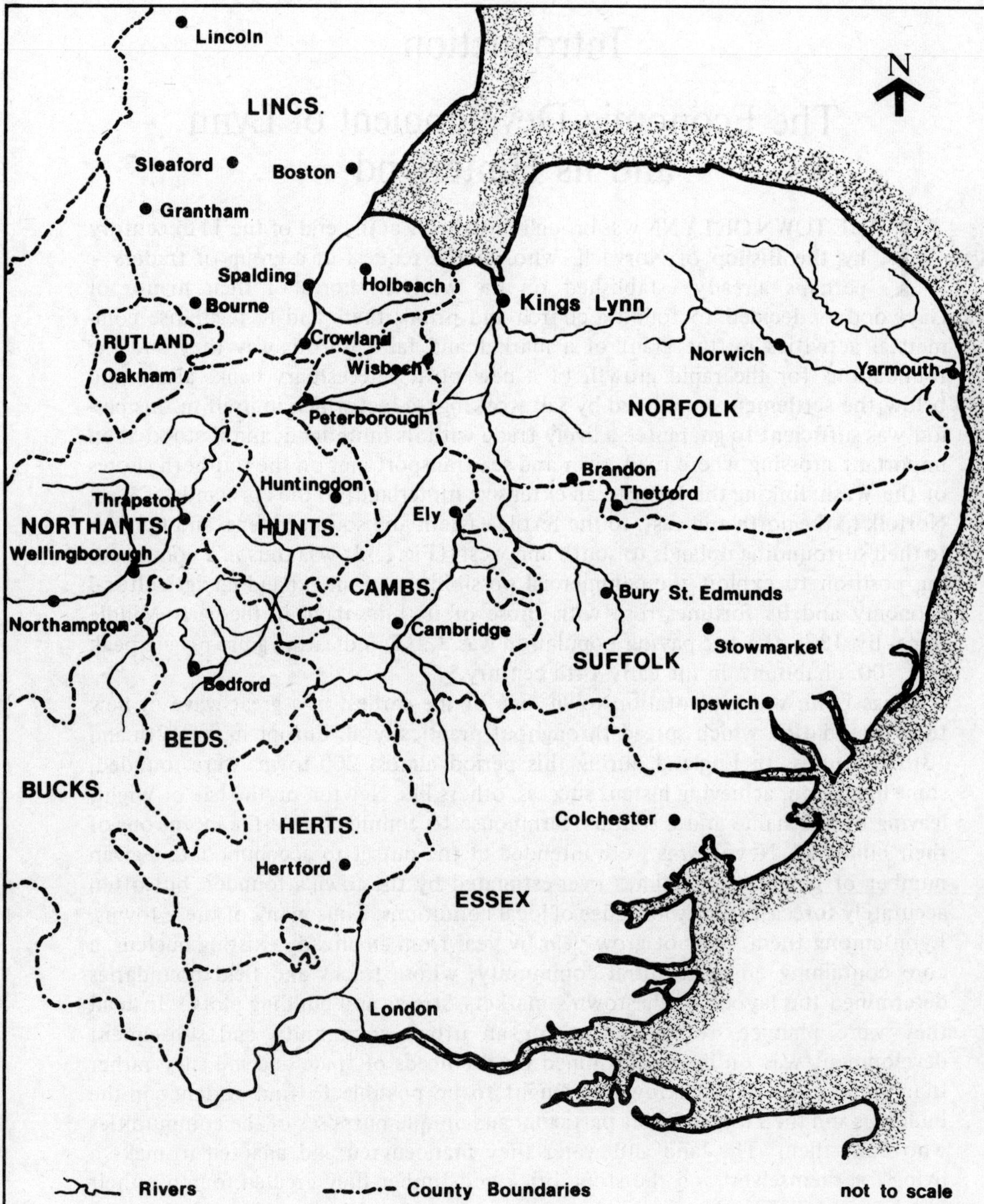

Fig 1 *Map of Kings Lynn and its trading hinterland*

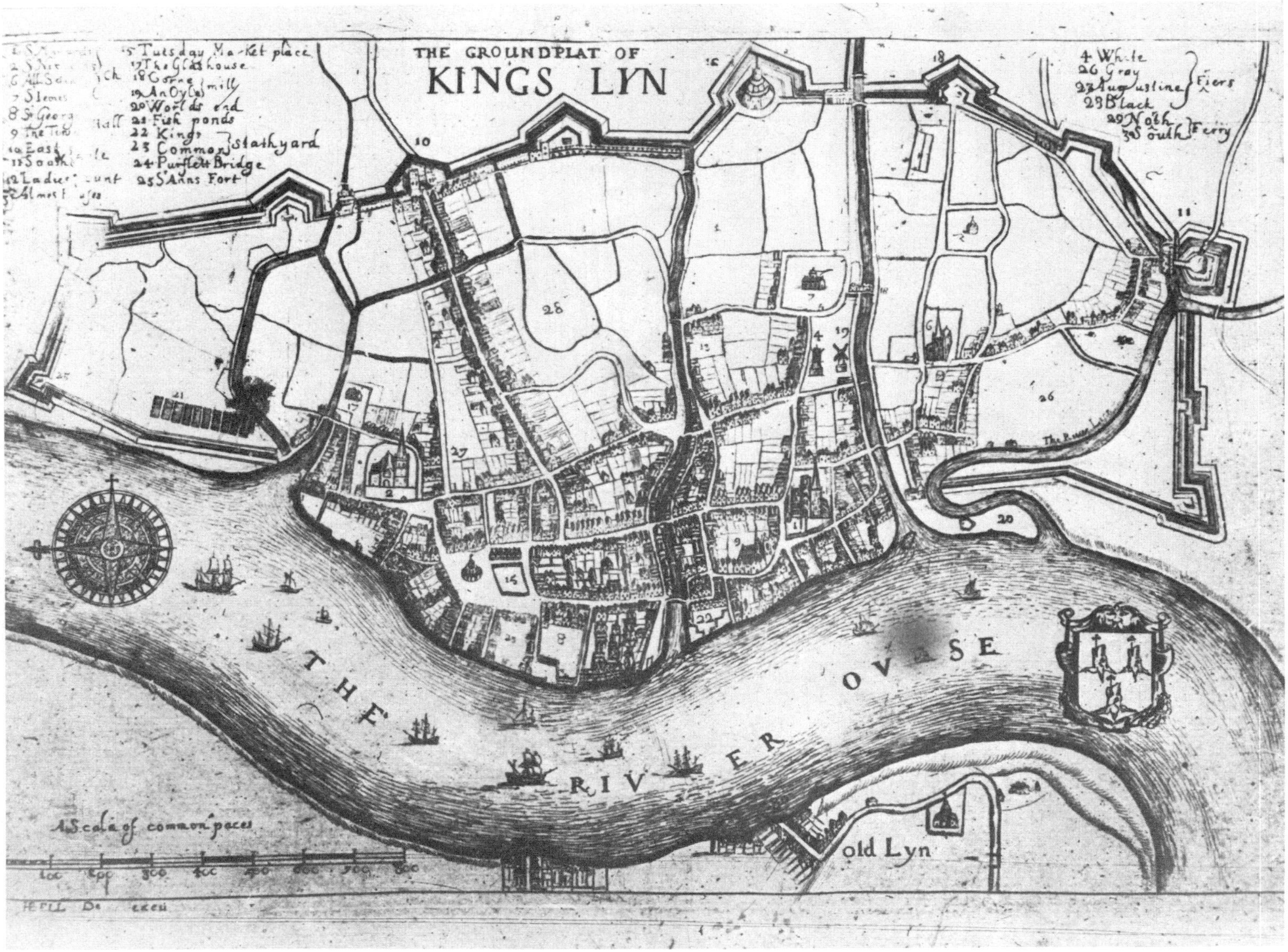

Plate 1 *The Groundplat of Kings Lyn; by Henry Bell, c.1680*

Plate 2 *Plan of Kings Lynn; by William Rastrick, 1725*

Plate 3A *The West Prospect of Kings Lynn, c.1725*

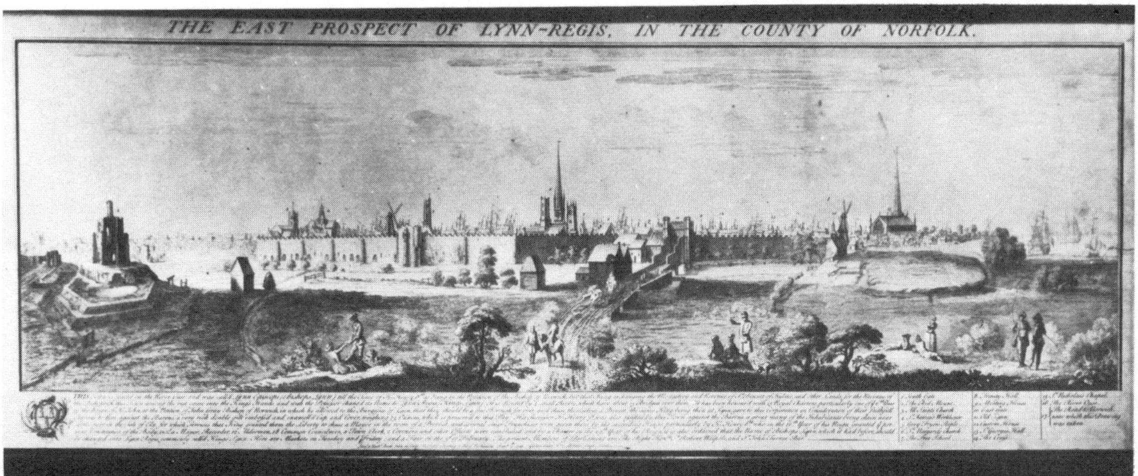

Plate 3B *The East Prospect of Kings Lynn, c.1725*

Plate 4A *Hampton Court, showing courtyard layout*

Plate 4B *Hampton Court, street range, c.1480*

Plate 5A *Hampton Court, south range*

Plate 5B *Hampton Court, warehouse arcade*

Plate 6A *No. 8 Purfleet Street; Hall range from east*

Plate 6B *No. 8 Purfleet Street; Hall crown post*

Plate 7A *No. 9 Nicholas Street; East elevation of Hall*

Plate 7B *No. 9 Nicholas Street; warehouse from north*

Plate 7C *No. 9 Nicholas Street; scissor braced trusses*

Plate 7D *No. 9 Nicholas Street; Hall crown post trusses*

The purpose of this volume is not to give an exhaustive account of all the many facets of an important trading town – the details of its economic, social, political and religious life for example are barely covered except where they have direct bearing on the main theme of this book. What is attempted here is the utilisation of a particular kind of historical evidence to help further our knowledge of the workings of an old settlement – the study of the built environment. An attempt has been made to reconstruct, both from archaeological remains above ground and from relevant documentary sources, a picture of Lynn as it was in various periods in the past, and to show how the life of the community both conditioned and was conditioned by the built fabric of the town. Such an approach to urban history becomes more difficult as each year passes: although many documents are now traced and preserved the older buildings in many towns are being steadily eroded by the need for redevelopment. Not only individual buildings disappear but often whole areas with an historic street pattern are done away with. In Kings Lynn redevelopment is now well under way; but at the time this research was carried out the town was in a most remarkable and indeed practically unique state of fossilisation. No major changes had been made either to buildings or to the street and waterway systems of communication since the end of the 18th century. And since, as will be explained, very little radical change had taken place in Lynn since the end of the 15th century, embedded behind 18th and 19th century facades was a complete medieval town.

The core of this book is concerned with the developments in the built environment of Kings Lynn. But to make this kind of study without reference to the context within which changes were taking place would obviate the whole point of such a study, the purpose of which is to throw as much light as this kind of evidence will give on the workings of the local community as a whole. The essential first step must be to establish the broad economic context within which people in the town of Lynn lived and worked. Once this has been established aspects of the built environment they created can be more fruitfully examined and explained.

The Economic Development of Lynn and its Hinterland

Kings Lynn lies in the south-east corner of the Wash, flanked to the east by the dry sandy loams of Norfolk, and bounded to the south and west by marsh and fen. Beyond the fenland the rich farming counties of Cambridge, Northampton, Leicester and Lincoln also came within Lynn's trading hinterland. Defoe, writing in 1722, claimed that Lynn 'supplies above six counties wholly and three in part with their goods'[5] and this had been the case since the 14th century and perhaps earlier. In 1373, when Lynn was constituted a staple port, it was claimed that it supplied the counties of Warwick, Leicester, Northampton, Rutland, Bedford, Buckingham, Cambridge, and Huntingdon with imported goods.[6] (Fig.1.)

The wealth of these counties was principally derived from agriculture and, except from a small corner of West Suffolk with whose clothiers Lynn had trading connections in the late Middle Ages, no great export industries were shipped through the town. Thus the fortunes of Lynn were closely linked to fluctuations in agricultural production. A good harvest, a large surplus of grain or wool over above that needed for local consumption, meant business for the port of Lynn, handling the trade and dispatching shipments coastwise or overseas. Sales of produce too meant rising incomes in the rural communities and market towns of the region, and as purchasing power rose so did the demand for goods of all kinds imported through Lynn.

Kings Lynn was at its most prosperous, in relation to other English towns, during the 13th century. The returns of King John's Custom in 1203-5, covering practically the whole of England with the exception of Bristol, show that after London and Southampton, Boston and Lynn were the most wealthy ports in the land.[7] By 1334, Lynn had dropped to 11th among the provincial towns, although the post-plague subsidy of 1377 shows a rise to seventh, maintained into the 16th century. The relative decline of Lynn probably did not set in until the beginning of the 17th century. The hearth tax of 1662 shows Lynn at 22nd, superseded not only by the ports of Bristol, Exeter, Ipswich, Hull and Plymouth, but by the provincial market towns such as Oxford and Cambridge, Canterbury, Worcester, Shrewsbury and Salisbury.[8] These changes in the economic status of Lynn reflect charges in the relative prosperity of its trading hinterland. In 1334 tax assessment per 1,000 acres was highest in the Holland division of Lincolnshire (£46.4), and in the counties of Oxford (£42.2), Norfolk (£38.9), Bedfordshire (£33.6), Berkshire (£31.4), Rutland (£31.4), Middlesex (£29.9), Gloucestershire (£28.0), Kesteven (£27.8), Huntingdon (£27.6), Cambridge (£26.9), and Northampton (£26.3), thus including the whole of Lynn's hinterland except Leicester among the 12 most wealthy counties in the land. By 1515 a comparable set of taxation returns show that East Anglia and the East Midlands had been superseded by counties to the south and west, by Middlesex and the Home Counties, and by the West Country. Not only had the former declined relatively, Norfolk to 12th, Cambridge to 21st, Northampton to 15th, Rutland to 22nd, and Holland to 19th, but they had also failed to increase in value at as fast a rate as many other parts of the country.[9] So that although the agriculture of these regions could hardly be described as stagnant in the 16th and 17th centuries the relatively great expansion of agricultural production, which in the 12th and 13th centuries had created the wealth of the port of Lynn, was not repeated in the centuries following the Black Death.

Nevertheless it should be stressed that this decline both in Lynn and its hinterland was relative not absolute. Although there are signs of an early halt to the expansion of the built-up area of the town there is no evidence of depopulation of streets and buildings. Rather the town remained at a steady level of prosperity from the 15th to the 17th centuries, and this is reflected in the improvement of an already existing urban fabric, rather than in renewal and extension.

In broad outline the economic development of Lynn and its hinterland falls into three main periods; the early medieval period of expansion to about the mid-13th century; a period of change as the main lines of trade altered in the 14th and 15th centuries; and a period of stability in the 16th and 17th centuries. The first period was the one to have the formative influence on the core of the town since by 1300 the main lines of the plan of Lynn as we know it today were already established.

Unfortunately there are still many questions concerning the early trading activities of Lynn to which no final answer can be given. One particularly important problem concerns the communications system of the 12th and 13th century fenland. (Fig.2.) Not only would a knowledge of this determine more precisely those areas with which Lynn actually traded in this early period, but, since points of transport interchange will be of cardinal importance in determing the plan of a trading town, it would also help clarify some of the questions about the way in which the early town was laid out. Inevitably, in the case of Lynn, it has often been assumed that her trade was carried mostly by water, with goods entering or leaving by sea, or by river. Although in the 16th century it is clear that the river/sea interchange was by far the most important one, this does not seem to have been entirely the case in the 13th century. Indeed the street-pattern indicates that a considerable volume of traffic by road had been planned for also.

The late medieval prosperity of Lynn clearly depended to a large extent on access to the Great Ouse which with its tributaries served Ely, the counties of Cambridge, Huntingdon and Bedford, and on the river Nene, which gave access to Peterborough and Northamptonshire. The problem of the early development of Lynn lies in the fact that both these rivers in the 12th and 13th centuries flowed into the Wash by the Wisbech estuary.[10] Only one river of any size, the Little Ouse, flowed past Lynn, connecting the town with Brandon and Thetford. However it is also known that, long before the 17th century drainage of the fens, considerable alterations had taken place at different periods in the outfall of the eastern rivers. Before the Romans colonised the fens even the Little Ouse had joined the Wisbech outlet, and the Lynn estuary had been joined by only a small stream flowing north from Stowbridge and a number of minor rivers including the Gay and the Nar from the east. Perhaps for drainage purposes, but probably for transport, the Romans altered the whole of the eastern fens river system, digging a cut to divert the Little Ouse from Wilton Bridge to Stowbridge, and another from Littleport to Brandon Creek, to divert the Great Ouse into the Little Ouse. A further cut to divert the Nene east as well was probably made along the line of Well Creek. All these cuts are clearly artificial since in places they go against the natural drainage of the area, while dredging has produced Roman finds which date their origin.[11] In early medieval times the only live channel remaining of Roman origin was the one which carried the Little Ouse from Wilton Bridge to Stowbridge and on to the Wash through the Lynn estuary. The Great Ouse cut

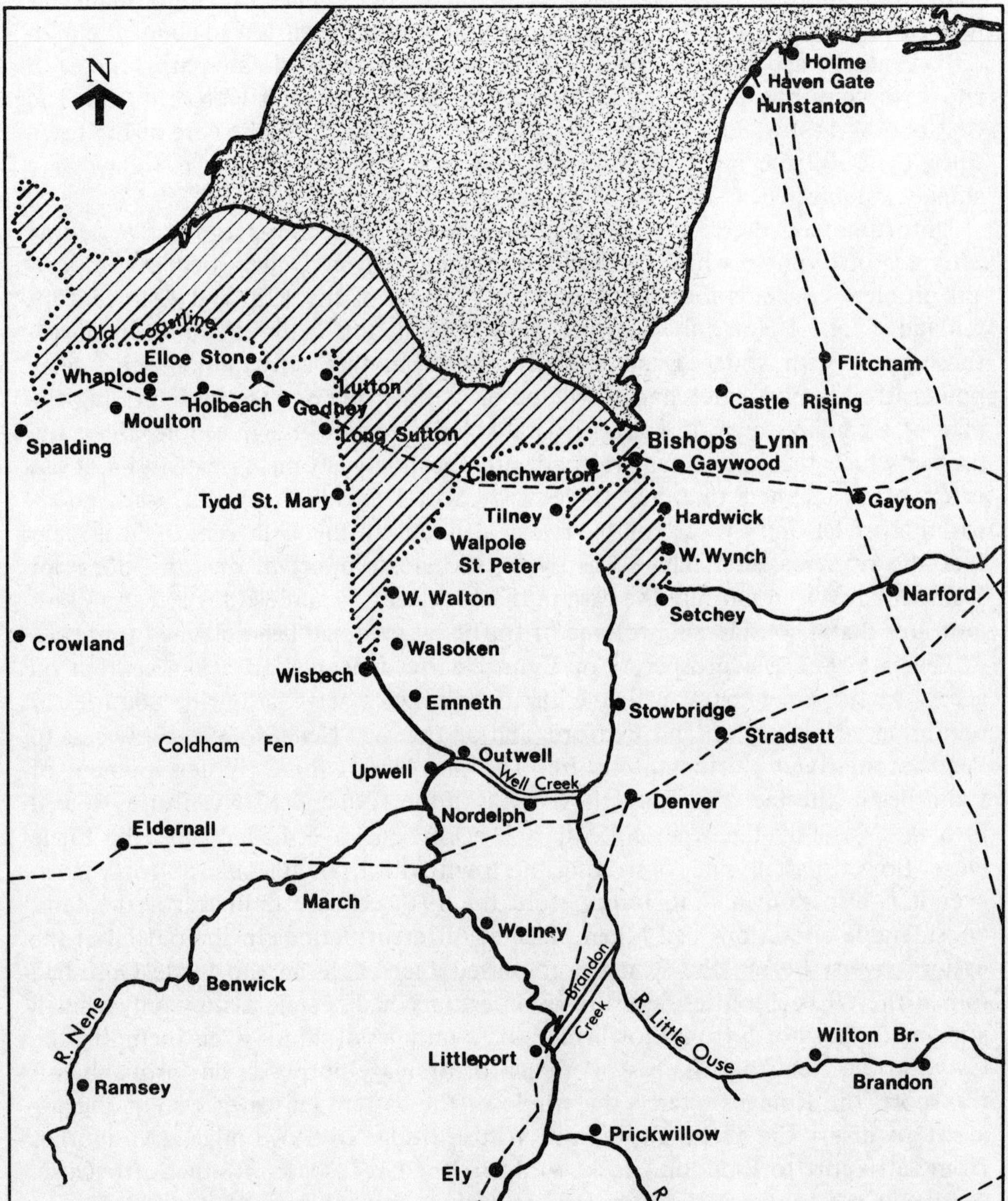

Fig 2 *Map of roads and rivers in the medieval fenland*

north from Littleport was silted up, as was Well Creek, and the course of the river has been conclusively shown to have flowed north-west through Welney to join the Nene at Outwell, at the head of Well Creek, and thus through Wisbech to the sea.[12]

If it were the case, however, that no shipping from Lynn could reach the Nene/Ouse system, Wisbech would surely have been a much more important medieval trading centre than, in fact, it appears to have been. Even allowing for the likely problems in getting sea-going ships up the estuary, or for the lack of the kind of institutional support given by the town's overlord by comparison with the activities of the Bishop of Norwich in Lynn, the lack of any evidence to suggest the wealth of Wisbech in the 13th century was in any way comparable to the wealth of Lynn suggests goods were diverted by some means to the latter.

Two possibilities here suggest themselves. The first is that Lynn, unlike Wisbech, was well served by roads as an alternative means of transport. The second is that a channel still existed in medieval times to link the Little Ouse with the Nene/Great Ouse outfall to the west. This second possibility was almost certainly realised, the channel, or channels lying along much the same line as that of the old Well Creek from Outwell to Stowbridge. That such a passage was open at least by the end of the 13th century is clear from the evidence cited in the case brought against the Bishop of Lichfield and Coventry in 1331 concerning a dam built at Outwell in connection with the drainage of Coldham fen.[13] The dam, it was said, had been built in the 1290's after complaints of flooding in the surrounding marshland in the previous decade.[14] The main objection urged against it was that boats bound for Lynn from Peterborough and other towns on the Nene had to travel 26 miles further via Welney and Littleport to Lynn, (this channel by now having apparently been re-opened) thus increasing the price of goods carried by this route. This suggests that the Bishop's dam at Outwell was part of a larger scheme, which had included the diversion of the waters of the Ouse into the Roman channel from Littleport to Brandon Creek, thereby providing a direct link between Lynn and towns on the upper reaches of the Ouse, and an alternative channel for Nene users beyond Outwell. This is supported by the evidence cited in Darby and Astbury of the complaints at the end of the 13th century by the men of Wisbech against Littleport men for diverting trade up their new cut to Lynn.[15] Thus it seems that it was after all possible by using channels parallel to Well Creek, or perhaps even Well Creek itself, for the men of Lynn to use the waters of the Great Ouse for shipping their merchandise. Indeed, in such a low lying watery area as the fens, criss-crossed as it was by drainage ditches and other channels, it would be unlikely that the passage of boats from one river system to another could not be effected somehow.[16]

The possibility, however, that the trade of Lynn was supplemented by considerable quantities of goods entering the town by road cannot be overlooked. Wisbech had no known early north/south land route within reach and lay directly between, but not on, the two major east/west road across the fens, the Roman Great Fen Causeway to the south, and the road on the ancient silt bank from Spalding to Clenchwarton to the north. Lynn, on the other-hand, lies close to the Peddars Way, a Roman road running from the north Norfolk coast at Holme through Castle Acre and southwards to Colchester, and a parallel section of the prehistoric trackway, the Icknield Way, running from a point on the coast to the west of Holme, through Gayton Thorpe to Thetford, Bury-St.-Edmunds, Newmarket and Cambridge. More important, however, passing through Lynn on the line of Damgate, (now Norfolk Street), was the east/west route across the northern fens. Starting at Spalding and linking the villages on the narrow band of silt dividing sea from fen on the southern shores of the Wash, it crossed the Ouse/Nene estuary by a ferry from Long Sutton, and the Little Ouse Estuary at Lynn by ferry from West Lynn, continuing through the town to Gaywood, Gayton and the junction with the Icknield Way.[17] Both the Icknield Way and the Spalding to Long Sutton road linked Lynn, in the absence of waterways, to two of the most prosperous farming areas in its hinterland, West Norfolk and the northern fens.

In 1334 one of the richest areas in England was the Holland division of Lincolnshire, containing the three wapentakes of Skirbeck, Kirton and Elloe. Elloe, bound on the east by the old sea-banks of the Ouse/Nene estuary, must almost certainly have marketed surplus produce through Lynn, as was the case in the 16th century,[18] villagers and traders taking the road with carts and pack animals for bulky loads, since only small boats of shallow draught could use the mud-filled creeks along the coast. By the time of Domesday Book the two and a half mile wide stretch of dry land between sea and fen was already densely settled; along it were some of the largest villages in England with an average of over 40 families apiece. Overpopulation then may have been the spur to the conquest of new lands, and the long narrow Elloe parishes indicate the directions in which they thrust outward, into saltmarsh on the one side and fresh water marsh on the other.[19] By the end of the 13th century, when the impetus towards reclamation seems to have been spent, about 50 square miles had been reclaimed from the fen and a lesser but still considerable amount from the sea. This was put to a variety of uses. Probably, however, stock rearing was the more important, particularly horses and the renowned fenland sheep with their heavy crop of wool. Arable acreage was also increased, which suggests, inspite of rising population, a surplus of grain for the market. But on the seaward side of the banks erected to keep out the waters, another crop could be harvested. Saltmarshes of up to half a mile in width formed in a few, perhaps 10 to 15, years, and from the salt impregnated peat and sand the salt itself was extracted by burning and evaporation.[20]

On the east side of Lynn too, trade was probably mainly carried by road. Although by the 16th century, when local tolls enable the extent of the port's hinterland to be established with some certainty, (Fig.3) west Norfolk had almost ceased to market produce through Lynn, in the early medieval period both corn

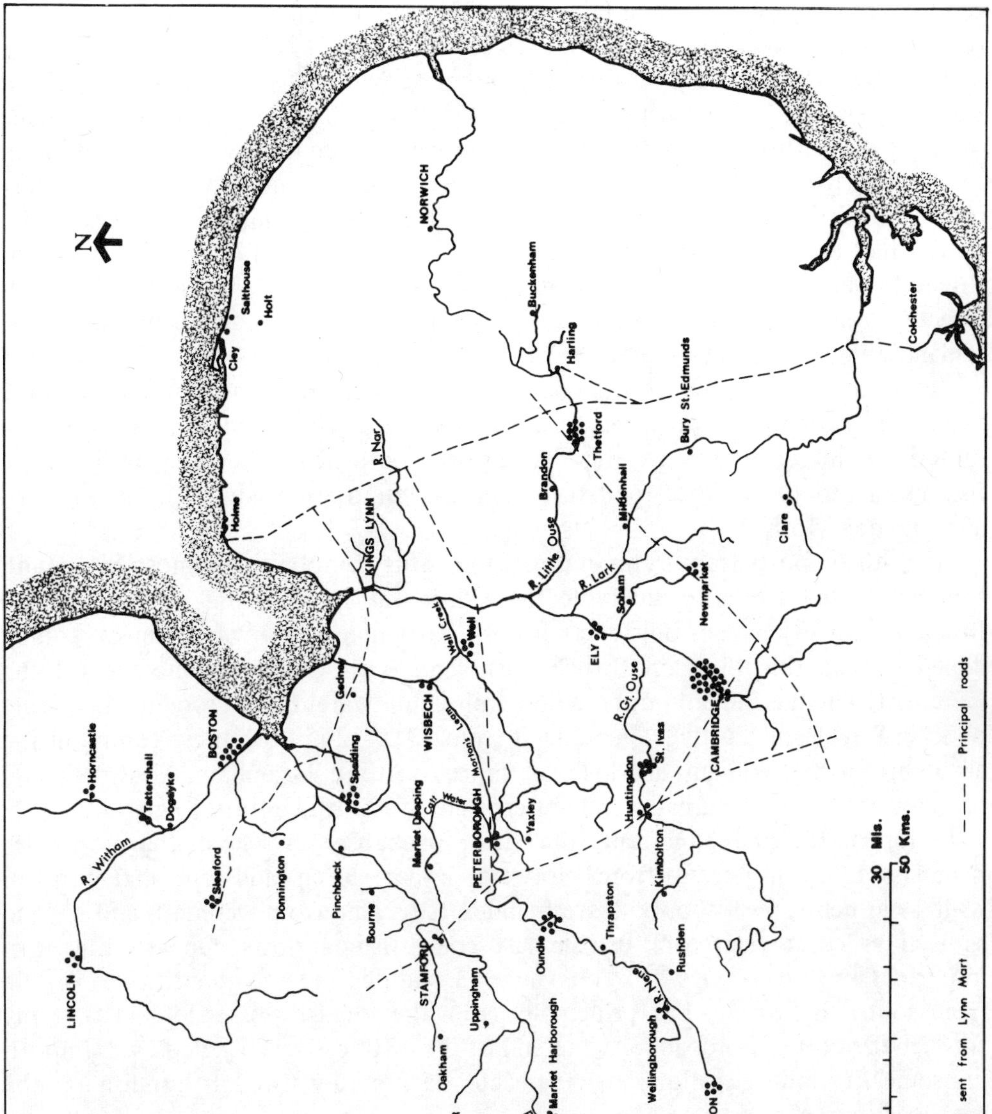

Fig 3 *Map showing destinations of goods sent from Lynn in 1585*

and wool from the 'good' sandy soils between Hunstanton and Castle Acre must surely have found an outlet there. The route from the east, through the East Gate and along Damgate, was lined with shops and wharves and was, until the 16th century, the site of the annual fair or mart. No records have been found, however, to point conclusively to trade with lands east of Lynn.

The early Middle Ages saw great gains in agricultural production throughout Europe, mainly as the result of colonisation of woodland and waste. By the end of the 13th century, when the impetus towards reclamation in the hinterland of Lynn seems to have been spent, the incomes of the great landowners had been very much increased. The Bishop of Ely, for example, whose main extensions to his estates had been in the fenland manors around Wisbech, had increased his income threefold between 1170 and 1300, 90 per cent of which came either from rents or directly from the profits of agriculture, while similar gains are recorded for the fenland abbeys of Ramsey and Crowland.[21]

The trade of Lynn before the end of the 13th century consisted mainly in the export of agricultural produce, notably grain and wool, and of salt, from the hinterland, in return for a variety of imports, both necessities like timber, iron, fish and a variety of other foodstuffs, and the luxuries of wine, spices, fine furs, and Flanders cloth.[22]

Of all the exports from Lynn in the 13th century wool was the most important, too, accounted for a considerable trade, not only with Flanders, Zealand and Brabant, but with the Baltic countries, particularly Norway, almost totally dependent at this time on British corn, and with Gascony. The great Lynn merchant, Thomas Melchbourne, whose house and warehouses stood at the corner of King Street and Purfleet quay, dealt from 1319-52 in both these commodities, as did his brother William, and his contemporary, John Wesenham. All three could be counted among the great merchant capitalists of 14th century England.[23]

In return for grain and salt, the latter probably for use in the North Sea fisheries, Lynn imported from Norway timber, pitch and tar, and furs for winter garments. Fish too, both fresh and cured, came from Denmark and Iceland as well as coast-wise from British east coast fishing ports. One of the most important inward cargoes to Lynn was wine, shipped in large quantities to Britain from southern Europe, but principally from the English possessions in Gascony through the port of Bordeaux. At the end of the 13th century England was importing some five million gallons of wine each year, mainly through London and the east coast ports.[25]

This account of Lynn's trading activities, however, is somewhat misleading since it ignores what was probably an extensive coastal trade through Lynn in early Middle Ages, for which there is little evidence, and the regional trade of Lynn itself. A recorded bargeload coming down the Nene in 1313 carried a variety of local produce, only some of which can have been intended for export.[24] Grain and wool, the most important commodities, were clearly intended for export through

Lynn, but timber, reeds, sedge and turfs were surely intended for a local market, as was the stone, so much of which, from Northamptonshire, was used in the public and private architecture of Lynn. Fish, herring, 'and other victuals' speak too of a coasting trade, while the murage grants to Lynn record a tax on coal in the 13th century indicating an early trading connection between Lynn and the north eastern coalfields.[26]

By the beginning of the 14th century, Lynn's great export trade in grain, wool and salt was already on the decline, and was to contract still further in the following two centuries. The reasons for this were threefold. The limits of agricultural expansion had in many places already been reached by the mid-13th century. On the Bishop of Ely's estates, as on the lands of the villagers of Elloe, there are no obvious signs of new assarts after about 1250, and with the onset of successive plagues after 1348 the retreat from marginal lands began.[27] Thus if there was no actual regression and there are clear signs, for example on the Ramsey Abbey estates, of a drop in farming profits, there was no expansion of production to increase Lynn's trade.

Secondly, the wool trade, running at between one and two thousand sacks a year from Lynn at the beginning of the 14th century had, after a period of renewed vigour at the end of the century, dwindled to practically nothing by 1420.[28] Largely because of increasingly high taxation on wool exports, raw wool was diverted at home to the rising domestic cloth industry and such as went overseas was sent mainly from London and Southampton. Boston and Lynn both suffered heavily from the loss of this trade, and whereas in some parts the trade in raw wool was replaced by trade in cloth, neither of the Wash ports was well placed in relation to the centres of the industry in the 15th century. Lynn exported small quantities of cloth during the 16th century, but not at anything like the same value as former wool exports. An account of local tolls of *c.* 1560 indicates that that time cloths were reaching Lynn from Suffolk, from the group of cloth working villages around Glemsford, Clare and Lavenham, from Stowmarket, and Needham and even from Ispwich.[29] It seems too, from reference in 1524 to an earlier exemption from toll granted to Kendal clothiers, as though they had once exported sufficient quantities of cloth through Lynn to make application for such a privilege worth while.[30]

A third reason for the late medieval contraction of Lynn's export trade was the growing encroachment of the German Hanse into the North Sea and Baltic trade, coupled with the increase in grain production in the Baltic region as an alternative source of supply to Norway and the Low Countries. By 1424 the Hanse had its own warehouses in Lynn, and much of the North Sea trade was controlled from similar stations in many important parts. Other changes were taking place too in the supply of salt to the North Sea fisheries. Salt produced more cheaply in Portugal and in the Bay of Borgneuf in France was superseding salt produced on the Lincolnshire and Norfolk coasts. Indeed, by the 16th century, salt was imported into the region and few of the old medieval salterns on the Norfolk and Lincolnshire coast seem to have remained in production.[31]

Nevertheless, in spite of the long-term contraction of Lynn's export trade, the 15th century may even have seen a rise in per-capita incomes in Lynn.[32] Certainly there is the evidence of a high level of investment in building both public and private. Both the largest merchant gilds, the Trinity Gild and the Gild of St. George built new gildhalls, begun in 1424 and 1406 respectively; St. Nicholas Chapel was rebuilt between 1371 and 1419, alterations and extensions were made to St. Margaret's and the Trinity Chapel, now demolished, was built in 1478; the walls and gates were repaired and the South Gate rebuilt and faced in stone. In addition, there was extensive rebuilding of houses in all sections of the community. By the early 16th century not only had this period of rebuilding come to an end, but there were great numbers of houses and other buildings in the town in a ruinous condition.[33] And it was not until the 1570's and 80's that there are signs that once again new building both of houses and warehouses was taking place.

From the mid-16th century the most lucrative branch of trade developing in Lynn was based largely on coasting, and on two principal commodities, corn and coal. A distribution map of the destinations to which goods were sent after the February Mart in 1585 shows that Lynn's agricultural hinterland, far from contracting since the 14th century, included all the principal towns and villages served by the Ouse, the Nene and the Welland and their tributaires. (Fig.3.) In all of the counties ringing the fens to south and west, sheep-corn husbandry was extensively practised in the 16th and 17th centuries.[34] The fens too had a mixed arable-pasture economy, but there stock rearing, particularly, as in earlier times, horses and sheep, with dairying in the vicinity of towns, was more common than the production of grain for the market.[35] Camden (1610) found in the marshland near Lynn, 'a soile standing upon a very rich and fertile mould, and breeding an abundance of cattle; in so much that in a place commonly called Tilneysmeth there feed much about 300,000 sheep'.[36] Lynn merchants owning farms in the Norfolk fens often carried flocks of up to 200 sheep, and many had horses and cattle in addition.[37] The average fenland farmer, however, was likely to have kept on average about 20 sheep, 10 head of cattle, six horses and four pigs.[38]

The main outward cargo from Lynn in the 16th and 17th centuries was grain – wheat, rye, oats and barley, the latter often malted, with small quantities of rape-seed, buck-seed, and peas and beans. Some animal products, butter for example, and hides, were sent mainly to London, but neither wool nor cloth found its way in any quantity through Lynn in this period. The greater part of the very considerable quantities of grain shipped through Lynn went not for export over-seas, although some certainly went to the Low Countries, but by the coasting trade to the north of England – to Yorkshire, Tyneside, and Berwick, and to London. During the 16th century well over half of Lynn's total grain export in normal years was carried north to Newcastle, and even in the 17th century, when the proportion shipped to London began to rise, Newcastle and Hull together usually received around one third of grain shipments.[39]

The return cargo from Newcastle, Sunderland, and to some extent from the Scottish port of Kirkcaldy, was coal, imports of which began to increase in the 1530's and grew steadily to 1700. In 1561-2 Lynn handled 4,955 chalders, in 1586-7 this had increased to 9,582, and a century later this had more than doubled to 22,683 chalders in 1683.[40] Practically no coal was re-exported from Lynn. It was all absorbed both in Lynn itself and in the towns of the hinterland where it replaced peat and wood as the main domestic fuel.

Coal, however, was not the only commodity imported through Lynn, although it was the most important. In a memorandum of about 1655, preserved in the Lynn Muniments, it was claimed that before the draining of the Bedford level, Lynn supplied 10 counties not only with coal, but with fish, salt, Norway timber, wine, pitch, tar, hemp and iron.[41] Wine in the 16th century came from Spain, Portugal and the south of France in return principaly for grain. Timber, pitch, and tar, and iron were brought from the Baltic in the two or three ships which sailed annually to Danzig or Bergen, or purchased in the Low Countries, the great emporium of Western Europe for goods of all kinds from all over the known world.[42] Indeed, although Lynn ships did venture into distant waters, both the necessities and the luxuries they imported could all be obtained in Rotterdam, Middleburgh, Einkhuisen, Amsterdam, or in many of the Dutch ports to which Lynn ships sailed. Thus in the year ending 17 September 1621, Lynn imported from the Low Countries native cordage, cloth, hops and paper, and a variety of goods brought there from overseas:- Spanish and French wines, salt, timber and naval stores, sugar, prunes, raisins, pepper, cloves and West Indian ginger.[43] Even millstones, brought to Dordrecht from the Cologne region, were imported from thence to Lynn, until superseded by the gritstone stones from Derbyshire in the 17th century.[44]

One important commodity handled in Lynn at all times of the year was fish. The trade in each of the different types of fish was, of course, a seasonal one, but the degree of specialisation among the fishing fleets of the east coast ports menat a sizeable coasting trade throughout the year. The Lynn fishing fleet had, since the 15th century, made an annual voyage to Iceland in February, returning in August or September with cod and ling, while the main centre of the herring fisheries was Yarmouth. Much of Lynn's trade in fish was conducted at the February mart, when quantities in barrels or cases were distributed inland for consumption during Lent.[45]

Although the broad lines of Lynn's trade in the 17th century were already established at the end of the 16th, the fen drainage schemes, both before and after the Civil War, while they had no easily quantifiable effect on trade, seriously disrupted for a time the fenland economy. Although it was claimed that passage along the main waterways was never actually stopped, the volume of complaints from Lynn indicates that there were many times when it certainly became more difficult.[46] And for those who lived and farmed on the fens the disappearance of fenland common and marsh, meant the disappearance too of part of their means of subsistence. Drainage schemes, however, were intended in the long term to raise the productivity of the land, and by 1674 the returns of the Hearth Tax do indeed indicate rising land values in the drained areas of Ely.[47] From this then, in the long term, the merchants of Lynn clearly benefited, and at the end of the 17th century the town was still thriving. When Defoe visited it in 1722, he described it as a 'beautiful, well built, well situated town', a tribute no doubt to the fine, recently erected, Custom House, and the elegant classical facades of the houses in the waterfront streets.[48] It was not until the coming of the railways in the 19th century that the collapse of Lynn's trade set in as its hinterland shrank to the immediately adjacent fenland.

Although the Freemans Register[49] has survived in Lynn, and lists enrolments from 1300 onwards, (Table I), the occupational structure of the town cannot be reconstructed from it before the end of the 15th century, and even then only with a good deal of uncertainty. Even in the period 1491 to 1520 the occupations of almost half of those registered were unrecorded, and the same is true of the next 30 years. When, after 1551, a far greater number of recorded occupations survive, it is clear from local acts concerning the registration of freemen that the system was beginning to give way, and, except for merchants, many people were ignoring registration altogether. Nevertheless, from such incomplete evidence as we have, we can draw some conclusion as to the general characteristics of the occupational structure of Lynn.

First, Kings Lynn clearly remained from 1300 to 1700 a town where trade and traders dominated its economic and political life. The development of exports industries, by processing raw materials as they passed through the town in trade, seems to have failed. The last recorded attempts to start relatively large scale industrial activity seem to have been made in the 16th century, particularly in the 1560's, by offering protection to protestant refugees from abroad, and by financing clothiers from other English towns in the setting up of businesses in Lynn.[50] The Freemans Register gives no indication that there were craftsmen working other than for local market in Lynn and its immediate vicinity except at this time. The relatively large numbers in the clothing trades in the period 1551 to 1580 is an indication that an industry was in the making, but the attempt was abhortive.

A second general characteristic of Lynn, as of many well established local market towns, was the tendency in the 17th century to act as a focus for the social as well as the business life of the surrounding country gentry.[51] From 1640 onwards gentry were enrolling as Freemen of the borough in increasing numbers and stimulating both the provisioning and the manufacturing trades. Their impact on the built environment of the town in this period is discussed below.

Table I

Occupations recorded in the Freeman register of Kings Lynn
1300-1700

	Merchants	Food & Drink	Clothing	Local Industries	Build-ing	Misc.	Unspecified
1300-5		5	14	11		2	62
1342-70		6	9	12		1	238
1371-1400 (less 1395-8)		9	10	16	1	8	211
1401-1430 (less 1403-11)	23	8	10	22	1	3	139
1431-60	46	45	53	134	17	7	163
1461-90	25	41	46	79	8	22	53
1491-1520	35	51	48	37	4	21	152
1521-1550	44	35	55	44	8	10	168
1551-1580	186	67	101	112	8	20	20
1581-1610	212	30	59	83	10	26	18
1611-1640	98	45	60	91	21	45	82
1641-1670	57	105	85	132	35	150	41
1671-1700	34	131	47	231	58	220	14

NOTES

Occupations in each category cited above.[54]

1 Merchants

2 Food and Drink: baker, brewer, butcher, cook, fishmonger, grocer, innkeeper, oatmeal-maker, spicer, vinter.

3 Clothing: capper, clothier, draper, glover, hosier, linnen-draper, mercer, shoemaker, woollendraper.

4 Local Industry: anchorsmith, barker, bladesmith, brazier, cooper, cordiner, chandler, dyer, fisherman, furbisher, fletcher, fuller, glassmaker (1837), gunsmith (1650), hair-weaver, lister, locksmith, miller, nailman, oilmaker, pinmaker, pewterer, potter, roper, sadler smith, shipwright, spurrier, skinner, sherman, tanner, turner, soap-boiler (1647), tobacco pipe maker (1655), wax chandler.

5 Building: Bricklayer, carpenter, glazier, housewright, joiner, mason, painter, tiler.

6 Miscellaneous: apothecary, barber, clerk, customer, chapman, goldsmith, jeweller, mariner, organmaker (1518), musician (1644), sailor, shipmaster, surgeon, tobacco seller (1653), waterman, Gentleman.

After 1500, when the lists seem to have been kept more systematically, there were three broad categories into which most of the recorded occupations fell. The smallest group in terms of size was of merchants but it was by far the most powerful in the community, both economically and politically. The merchants dominated the governing body of the medieval town through the Holy Trinity gild and after 1524, in the newly reconstituted corporation, formed themselves into a self-perpetuating oligarchy.[52] The second largest group were industrial craftsmen, working not for export, but for local and regional trade. It was these people who provided the merchants with their packing cases and barrels, who built their ships, and who made domestic utensils, clothing and shoes for the inhabitants of the town. Approaching this group in size was that of the food and drink trades including the cooks, who had their own quarters off the south-east corner of the Tuesday Market. Although most merchant households had their own bakehouses and brewhouses, there seems to have been sufficient public demand to make baking and brewing extremely profitable. On the rare occasions when the mayor of Lynn was not a merchant he was usually a member of this group. Two further groups appear in the Register; the building trades; and a miscellaneous group comprising goldsmiths and jewellers, non-industrial occupations which cannot be otherwise classified, and service occupations including the watermen and mariners. The small numbers recorded for these groups are unlikely to be a genuine reflection of the numbers actually engaged in such occupations.

The Freeman's Register is, however, no guide at all as to how the majority of the people of Lynn lived and worked. Professor Hoskins has calculated that, in the 16th century, at least one third of the population of a town the size of Lynn were wage earners, most of whom lived barely above the subsistence level.[53] These in Lynn were employed mainly in the service industries, as porters, mariners, carters, cleaners and labourers, without whom the busy life of the waterfront would have halted. A further third of the population of Lynn may have lived more or less permanently on a minimum subsistence level. Such people leave no written record of their way of life, nor is there evidence above ground of their houses.

Notes to Introduction

1 *First Register of Norwich Cathedral Priory,* Norfolk Record Society XI, (1939), 51.

2 M.W. Beresford, *New Towns of the Middle Ages*, (1967), 265-7 and M.W. Beresford, *Lay Subsidies and Poll Taxes,* (1963).

3 M.W. Beresford and J.K. St. Joseph, *Medieval England, an Aerial Survey,* (1958), 255-6.

4 See for example M.R.G. Conzen, 'Alnwick, Northumberland, a Study in Town-Plan Analysis', *Institute of British Geographers Research Papers,* No.27 (1960).

5 D. Defoe, *A Tour Through the Whole Island of Great Britain,* ed. G.D.H. Cole (1927), 73.

6 H.C. Darby, *The Medieval Fenland,* (1940), 98 n. 3.

7 N.S.B. Gras, *The Early English Customs System* (1918), 221-2.

8 W.G. Hoskins, *Local History in England* (1959), 176-7.

9 R.S. Schofield, 'The Geographical Distribution of Wealth in England 1334-1649', *Ec.H.R.*, Second Series, XVIII, (1965), 481-510.

10 W. Dugdale, *The History of the Imbanking and Draining of Rivers, Fens and Marshes* (Second ed. 1772), 394-6; A.K. Astbury, *The Black Fens* (1957), 138-47; H.C. Darby, *The Medieval Fenland* (1940), 96-100.

11 A.K. Astbury, *Black Fens,* 138-47; Gordon Fowler, 'Fenland Waterways Past and Present', *Cambridge Antiq. Soc.*, XXXIII, 1933, 108-32 and XXXIV, 1934, 17-32.

12 Dugdale, op cit. 394-6.

13 *Cartularium Monasterii de Rameseia,* Rolls Series (1893), III, 141-57.

14 *Calendar of Patent Rolls,* (1292-1301), 24, 159, 218, 287, 458, 465.

15 Darby, *Medieval Fenland,* 96; Astbury, *Black Fens,* 140.

16 See for example the map of pre-Drainage water courses in the eastern fens in Dugdale, *Imbanking,* 144-5.

17 I.D. Margary, *Roman Roads in Britain,* (Second Ed. 1967), 243-64; H.C. Darby, *Domesday Geography of Eastern England* (1952), 134-5; E.M. Beloe, 'The Pedders' Way and its Attendant Roads', *Camb. Antiq. Soc.*, IX, (1894-5), 77-95.

18 Joan Thirsk, *Fenland Farming in the Sixteenth Century,* University of Leicester, Department of English Local History, Occasional Papers, No.3, 1953, 12.

19 H.E. Hallam, *The New Lands of Elloe,* University of Leicester, Department of English Local History, Occasional Papers, No.6 1954, passim.

20 A.R. Bridbury, *England and the Salt Trade in the Late Middle Ages,* (1955), 10-21.

21 E. Miller, *The Abbey and Bishopric of Ely* (1951) 94-8; J.A. Raftis, *The Estates of Ramsey Abbey* (1957) 115; F.M. Page, *The Estates of Crowland Abbey* (1934).

22 For a more detailed discussion of the medieval trade of Lynn, see E.M. Carus-Wilson, 'The Medieval Trade of the Ports of the Wash', *Medieval Archaeology,* VI-VII, (1962-3), 182-201, *passim.*

23 N.S.B. Gras, *Evolution of the English Corn Market,* (1926), 172-3.

24 *Cartularium Monasterii de Rameseia,* 155.

25 M.K. James, 'The Fluctuations of the Anglo-Gascon Wine Trade during the Fourteenth Century', *Ec.H.R.,* 2nd Ser., XII, 1951.

26 J.C. Tingey, 'The Grants of Murage to Norwich, Yarmouth and Lynn', *Norf. Arch.*, XVIII, (1912), 147.

27 Miller, *Bishopric of Ely,* 100; Hallam, *Newlands of Elloe,* 41.

28 E.M. Carus-Wilson and Olive Coleman, *Englands Export Trade 1275-1547,* (1963), 134-5.

29 K.L.M./Db3.

30 K.L.M./H.B.3/152d. A 'Kendallman' was registered as a Freeman of Lynn in 1520-1, *Freemans Register,* 82.

31 P.R.O. E 178, 2951.

32 A.R. Bridbury, *Economic Growth, England in the Later Middle Ages,* (1962), ch. V. *passim.*

33 See below p.166.

34 Joan Thirsk, 'The Farming Regions of England', in J. Thirsk (ed), *The Agrarian History of England and Wales,* Vol. IV (1500-1640) 40-49, 89-99, passim.

35 Thirsk, *Fenland Farming,* 26-8.

36 Quoted in H.C. Darby, *The Draining of the Fens* (1940), 24.

37 See for example the wills of Edward Baker (d.1549), P.C.C. 19 Bucke; Thomas Thorisby (d.1510), P.C.C.34 Bennett; and Thomas Guybon (d.1569), P.C.C. 14 Lyon.

38 Thirsk, *Fenland Farming,* 28.

39 Gras, *English Corn Market,* 305-9.

40 N.J. Williams, *The Maritime Trade of the East Anglian Ports, 1550-1590,* (unpubl. D. Phil. Thesis, University of Oxford 1952), 163; T.S. Willan, *The English Coasting Trade 1600-1750,* (1938), 210; J.U. Nef, *The Rise of the British Coal Industry* (1932), Vol.2, 156.

41 K.L.M. in bundle, Ee.

42 For example see P.R.O. E 190, 425/3, 429/1, 430/5, 431/2, 6, 432/5, 433/6.

43 *S.P.D.,* XXII, 132.

44 A good series of the accounts of Lynn's millstone trade are in K.L.M., Db.27, with gaps 1553-1700.

45 K.L.M./Db1 *passim.*

46 T.S. Willan, 'River Navigation and Trade from the Witham to the Yare 1600-1730' *Norf. Arch.,* XXVI, 1938, 296-7.

47 Darby, *Drainage of the Fens,* 49-58, 83-94, *passim.*

48 Defoe, *Tour,* 73

49 'A Calendar of the Freemen of Lynn 1292-1836', *Norf. Arch.* Original Papers, 1913.

50 K.L.M./H.B.V/60, 61, 67, 70, 77, 83, 86, 105, 132, 133, 139.

51 Alan Everitt, *Change in the Provinces: The Seventeenth Century*, 25-6.

52 Sir W. Savage, *The Making of Our Towns,* (1952) 74-5.

53 W.G. Hoskins, 'English Provincial Towns in the early sixteenth century', *Trans. R.H.S.,* Ser. 5, VI, (1956), 18.

54 For many reasons the Freeman Register is an unreliable guide to an exact knowledge of the occupational structure of towns.

It is clear both from Local Acts recorded in the Hall Books and from excessive numbers of particular crafts registered in particular years that some occupations had periodically to be persuaded to register at all.

In Lynn, as in other towns, merchant status conferred the right to trade wholesale, and many craftworkers also found it to their advantage to pay the extra fine and register as a merchant. This almost certainly accounts for the inflated number of merchants registered after the Local Act of 1547 (see below p.158). many, indeed most, of whose names do not occur in the Port Books, Customs Accounts or Accounts of Local Tolls of the late 16th century.

The increase in the number of freemen in the 'Miscellaneous' category during the 17th century is mainly accounted for by the numbers of local gentry registered, and also by the increase in numbers of semi-professional and professional occupations, lawyers, clerks, and 'surgeons'.

I

The Topography of Lynn from the 11th to the 17th centuries

KINGS LYNN, although admirably placed to take advantage of trade, 'standing', as one writer put it, 'at the gateway of the Ouse as though it were turnkey of it',[1] must nevertheless have faced almost insurmountable difficulties when it came to laying out a town on the site allocated by the Bishop of Norwich. (Fig.4.) This site had actually lain within the estuary lake or 'len' through which the Little Ouse, the Nar, the Gay and two small streams from the east flowed into the Wash.[2] The lake itself was defined on its western side by a bank, a continuation of the pre-conquest sea bank along the southern shores of the Wash which turned south to Setchey from Clenchwarton protecting the eastern shores of the marshland villages of Tilney and Wiggenhall St. Mary. The eastern bank seems to have followed the line of the present road from Setchey through West Winch and Hardwick to the site of the South gate of the present town of Lynn, and to have continued northward from thence on the line followed later by the town ditch and bank to the point at which it was crossed by the Purfleet river. North of this line the bank has entirely disappeared, although that is not to say it did not once exist. When no longer needed, banks were often taken down and the earth spread on the nearby fields.[3] In Lynn that may well have happened when the stone wall north of the Purfleet was built in the 12th century.

The estuary banks enclosed an oval shaped lake with a narrow neck to the north, on one side of which was Clenchwarton and West Lynn, known as Old Lynn, and on the other, the site of the new town. So two factors might well have disposed the Bishop towards the choice of this particular site on the estuary for his town: first it was the point at which a ferry carried the road from the fens across the narrowest part of the estuary, and secondly, only at this point can the river have scoured out a deep enough channel to take sea-going vessels. (Fig.4.)

Whether or not the site was still under water when the Bishop decided to build there can only now be a matter of conjecture, but several factors would suggest that dry land had already formed to the seaward side of the bank by the end of the 11th century. Unless there is unusual turbulence in the water, salt marsh of up to half a mile in width can form in the Wash area from deposits of silt within about 10 to 15 years after the building of a sea bank.[4] The salterns on the site mentioned in the grant of Lynn priory to the monks of Norwich Cathedral in 1101, indicate that some salt marsh had indeed formed by that date,[5] and the siting of the Priory itself some half mile to the west of the bank at Gannock suggest a site chosen right on the edge of whatever dry land could be expected to form without further

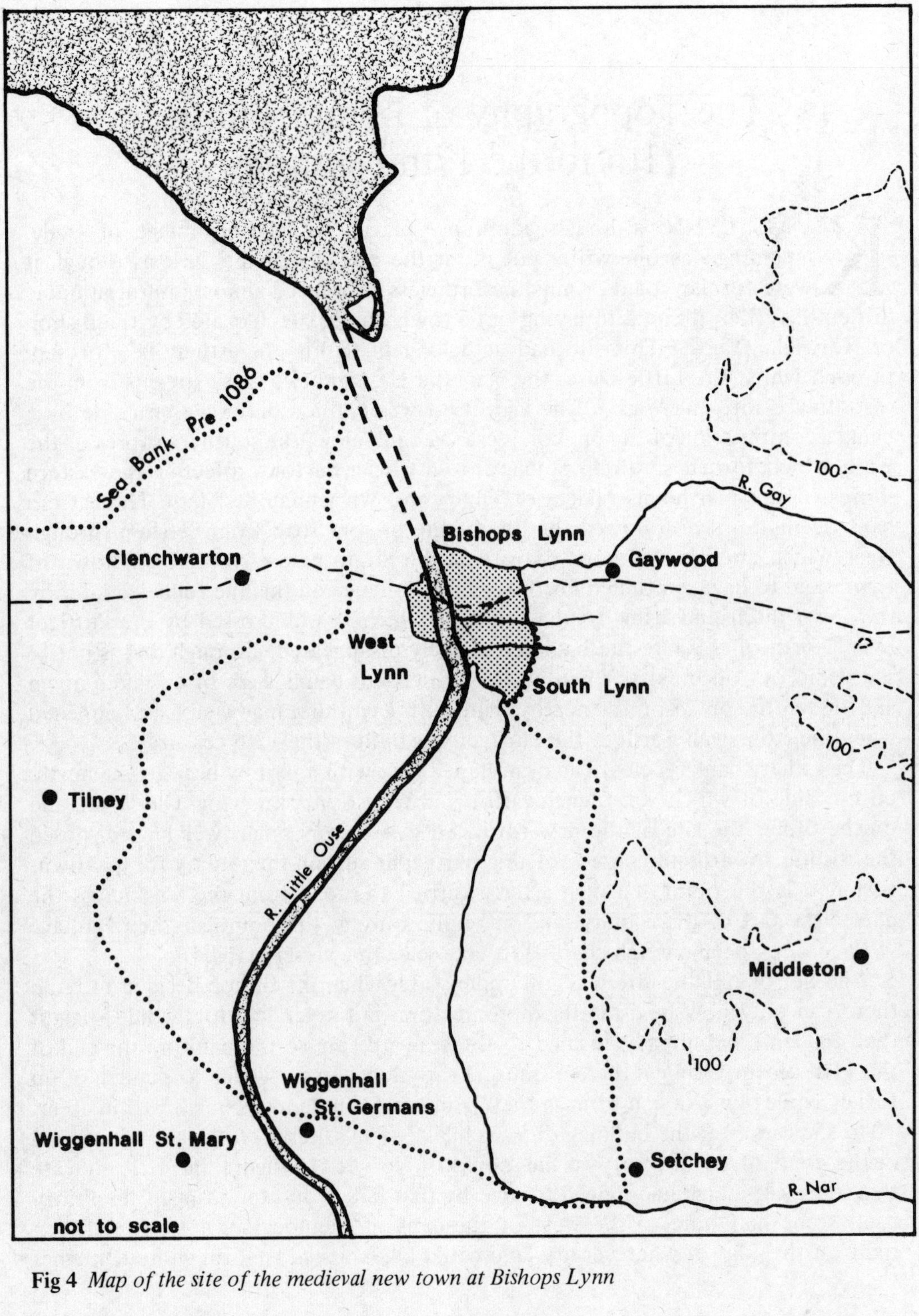

Fig 4 *Map of the site of the medieval new town at Bishops Lynn*

reclamation and drainage. (Fig.5.) In addition there was a village with a church at South Lynn by the end of the 11th century,[6] and it is unlikely that this site would be dry, while the one a few hundred yards to the north was still covered with water. Even so, salt marsh was by no means ideal building land, and much work would need to be done to dry out the site and protect it from floods.

According to the Domesday survey, the 'len' or estuarine lake was divided into four sections, which became respectively, North, South, West and Bishop's Lynn. In 1085, settlement was recorded on all parts of the 'len' except that belonging to Bishop of Elmham (later Norwich) as part of his manor of Gaywood.[7] However, unrecorded in the Domesday Survey, there was, in fact, a small group of traders already established there by that time. They paid tolls to the Bishop,[8] and it was at their request that he founded the Priory in 1095 and obtained for them a market and fair. But although the *settlement* at South Lynn may well not be much older than the settlement on the Bishop's manor, the *church* is certainly older than St. Margaret's since it is recorded in the grant of 1101 when St. Margaret's had only just been begun. This grant, transferring his Lynn Priory to the monks of Norwich, was made soon after the Bishop had transferred his see from Elmham in 1101. It included 'land, marsh and people' between Possfled, later Purfleet, to the north, and the lands of the church in South Lynn lying on the south side of 'Sewoldsfled', later Millfleet, to the south, the right to the 'sand market' weekly on Saturdays, and to an annual fair on the feast of St. Margaret.[9] Thus the first town of Bishops Lynn lay between the Millfleet and the Purfleet, on a half mile stretch of marsh running back to the sea bank at Gannock. But within 50 years the town had already outgrown its original boundaries. During the time of William Turbe (Bishop of Norwich, 1146-1174), an extension north of the Purfleet was built. This, however, was over land not included in the original grant to the monks and it came under the direct lordship of the Bishop. The extension was treated like a new town and was granted privileges similar to those of the original settlement to the south. It had its own market, held on a Tuesday, a fair and its own chapel, that dedicated to St. Nicholas. These two towns remained separate until the beginning of the 13th century when the Bishop, by granting the monks similar privileges elsewhere, was able to buy back his original grant of land in Lynn. With both settlements again under his lordship, he obtained a charter for the town in 1204,[10] expecting, no doubt, rich rewards from the further commercial growth of the port.

Any account of the topography of Lynn then must take into account not only the physical features of the site, but also the administrative and judicial areas into which it was divided. Of the physical features, the watercourses particularly seem to have dominated the town plan from the beginning, largely, of course, because of fixed crossing points, and their use as highways, sewers, sources of power to drive mills and other machinery, and of fresh water. The northern boundary of the Bishop's town was fixed by the river Gay, and the southern boundary of South Lynn by the Nar. Between these were two smaller streams, already mentioned, flowing into the estuary from east to west, the Millfleet, formerly known as Sewoldsfled, and Purfleet. A multitude of smaller channels also existed at least until the 16th century. These, however, were for the most part man-made. A second physical feature to influence the town plan was the ancient sea bank to the east. This determined the limits of expansion of the town on this side, and provided the foundations of the later defences. But above all, it was the communications of the site, the already existing roads raised on causeways above the marshes, and the location of river and fleets, which determined the points of interchange from one system of transport to another, and thus created nodal points in the town plan. (Fig.5.)

In the 12th century when the main lines of the town were laid out, Kings Lynn was, in an administrative sense, not one town, but three. There was, first of all, the monks' town with its market between the Millfleet and the Purfleet, a second self-contained extension with its own market and chapel to the north under the lordship of the Bishop, and a third town in South Lynn. The latter was separately administered until as late as 1555.[11] When compared with either of the two towns to the north, the extent to which medieval towns might be dependant on the support of feudal overlords immediately becomes evident. This southern area was outside the Bishop's jurisdiction and the settlement seems never to have received the necessary market grant or charter to enable it to grow in competition with Bishops Lynn. As a result, South Lynn, lying as it did downstream of an area of considerable commercial activity, seems to have remained mainly agricultural, though by the 15th century it had its own merchant gild and a small but wealthy group of traders.

Finally, since Lynn was a plantation town, a word must be said on the subject of medieval town planning. It has often been assumed that in the less advanced stages of European civilisation, a more pragmatic approach was adopted towards the problems of design, and that both architecture and town planning could be expected to demonstrate the system based on the idea that 'form follows function'. Nothing, in fact, could be further from the truth. A belief in empirical knowledge is an aspect of much more recent advances in scientific philosophy. Medieval society built and planned by using more abstract systems of design, and in planning and laying out towns used simple geometric forms, aesthetically satisfying and simple to set out on the ground. In practice a pragmatic approach was adopted only as it were, by default, for those new towns where a relatively small number of 'takers' were expected, and the overlord would only commit himself to setting out the market and allowed streets and other elements of the plan to develop without the imposition of an overall scheme.[12] Large towns, however, were planned at the outset using a rectilinear grid form of layout involving only the use of simple rectangles combined in various ways to form open spaces, building plots and a rectilinear mesh of streets.[13] Lynn undoubtedly falls into this latter category in

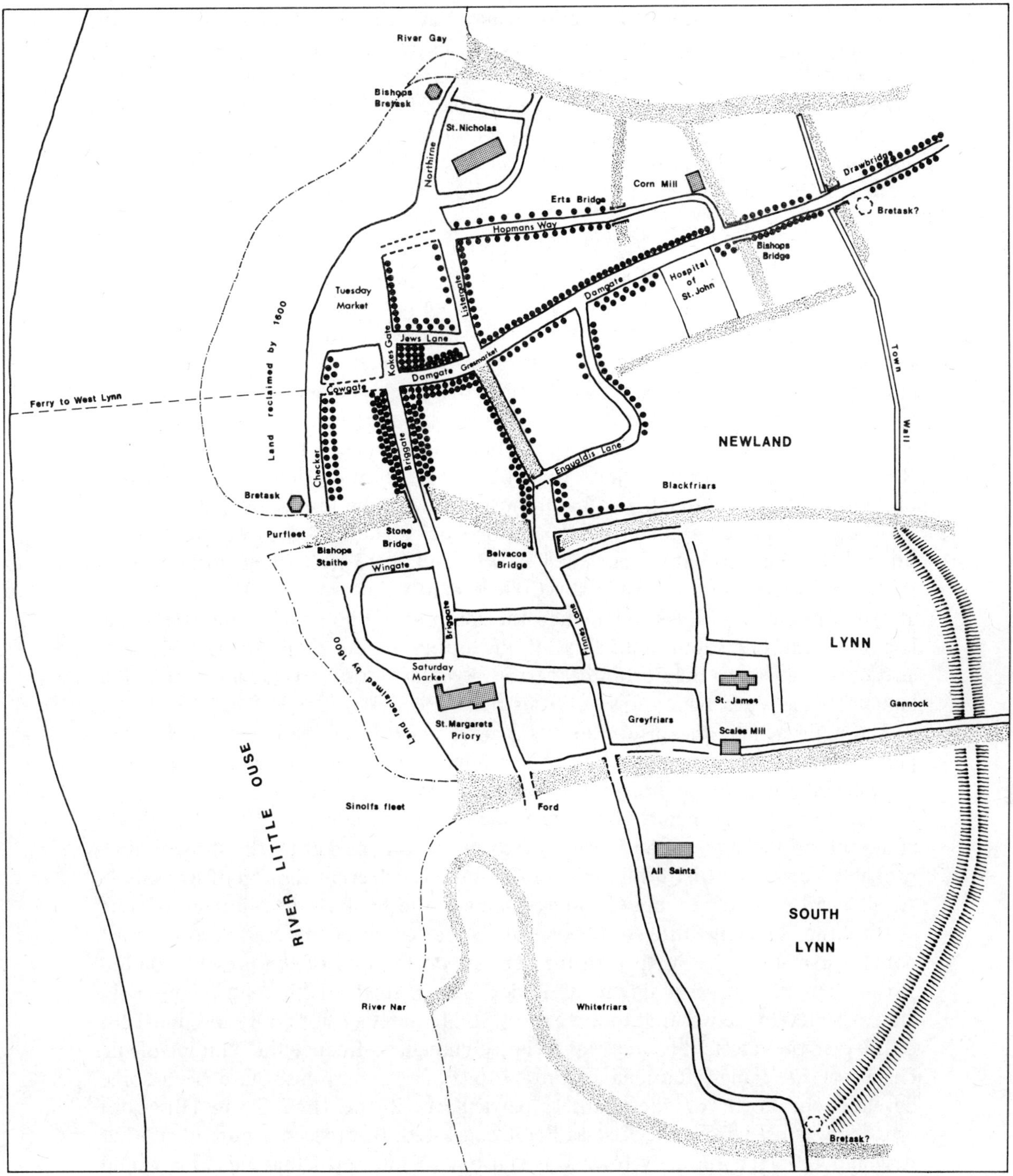

Fig 5 *Map of 13th century Lynn incorporating the Survey of the Newland c.1250 for the part of the town to the north of the Purfleet*
• *one tenement in Newland Survey*

some respects. But while the intention may have been to impose a completely regular layout, in few towns was the site sufficiently flat and well drained to make this possible. Almost all the gridded medieval new towns make some concession to the difficulties of the terrain, and in Lynn the plan seems to have been designed to take account more often of the difficulties of the waterlogged site and its communications. The grid was used, however, to order secondary, residential or craft working streets.

The Medieval Town

The earliest planned settlement at Lynn was built on the 'land and marsh' between Purfleet and Millfleet, the area later granted by the Bishop to the monks of Norwich Cathedral Priory. (Fig.5.) St. Margaret's church occupied the most westerly position on this site and the town developed to the east between the church and the Gannock bank. The church, with the conventual buildings on its south side and the 'sand market'[14] on its north, stood right beside the waterfront, and probably occupied the whole of the bank southward to the Millfleet. Even in Red Register deeds of the 14th century, there is no mention of a street on the line of Nelson Street, although by that time there were buildings along the line of St. Margaret's Place as far south as Hampton Court. The bank westwards from the priory was thus probably reclaimed slowly and a 13th century timber wharf found in the courtyard of Thoresby College marks the progress of consolidation at that time.[15] It is not known when the southern section of Nelson Street was laid out, but the south boundary of the priory in the mid-16th century was already some way to the north of this road. Evidence of it survived in the line of a lane known as Vicar Lane shown on Raistrick's 'Plan' of 1725.[16] (Plate 2.)

The approach to the priory and its market place from the landward side was perhaps originally from Gannock where there was an ancient gate in the town defences, although Beloe thought the main road from Gaywood crossed a causeway to the site of the later East Gate and turned south to approach the monks town along the north bank of the Purfleet, crossing to the market by the stone bridge, probably across the first bridgeable point on the Purfleet, at the top of Briggate.[17] At all events, the road from Gannock followed the bank of the Millfleet, turning north either at Lady Bridge up Stonegate Street to enter the market at the east corner, or making the north turn further east up the line of the present London Road, then turning west down St. James' Street. In the 12th century the main area to be developed was that to the east of St. Margaret's Church. By the mid-12th century at the latest, this area was wealthy enough to finance the building of the chapel of St. James, founded before 1146.[18] There may also have been some development north of the market, particularly if the High Street (Briggate) crossing was used from the first as Beloe suggested. But it seems more likely that it would be when the new town was laid out to the north that this area would begin to expand. By the early 14th century, when the Red Register deeds cover this part of the town, the stone bridge in the High Street (Briggate) was clearly a key factor in the development of this part of the town. From it, the street ran direct to the Saturday market and a second road, known as Wingate, (now Queen Street), wound west along the Purfleet bank on the line of the present Baker Lane to the Bishop's staithe (later King staithe), then turned southward to the market. Further west a second bridge, probably not built until the Newland was laid out, was by the 14th century exerting a similar pull northward. Finneslane, now Tower Street, ran north to it from St. James' Street. Linking the two bridges along the south bank of the Purfleet was Sedgeford Lane, and Mad or Mor Lane now Union Lane joined the two roads further south. To the east of Finneslane was an area which even in the 16th century was crossed by open water-courses. Along the Purfleet was Fullers Row, on the line of the present South Clough Lane, and to the south a network of smaller lanes and streets which have since disappeared.

The mid-12th century extension of the built-up area north of the Purfleet was laid out as a complete new town, with its own market and fair, a chapel and its own system of fortifications. Fortunately more is known about the topography of this section of the town in the early stages of its development because a survey was made of the area in the first half of the 13th century. The survey, most of which has been preserved in a 15th century copy,[19] lists tenements street by street, and, with the exception of a small area around St. Nicholas Chapel, covers the ground from the Gaywood river in the north to the north bank of the Purfleet where it marked the southern boundary of the new town. (Fig.5.)

The main routeway of the new town was the street known as Damgate. This entered the town at the East Gate and followed the line of the present Norfolk Street as far as the junction with High Street. In the 12th century it continued westwards to the river bank, where there was, and is, an ancient ferry right to West Lynn. Ferry Lane today is a continuation of the line of Norfolk Street, and the missing section between High Street and King Street was known as Cowgate in the late 14th century,[20] and still existed as a foot path on Raistrick's 'Plan'. (Plate 2.) Even today there is still a public right of way through Woolworths, who have built across this line. This important street was linked through Gaywood to the Great Fen Road and the other medieval routes, including the Peddars Way, which skirted the Fens to the east, and across the estuary to West Lynn, Long Sutton, and the silt-bank road to Spalding. (Fig.4.) It was thus at this time the route along which most of the town's trade by land was probably carried. In the 13th century survey it was densely built-up from end to end, and even in the 16th century when its heyday as a main routeway was passed, it was the site where by tradition the annual fair of the town was held.[21]

The trade of medieval Lynn was not, of course, carried entirely by road, and the geographical situation of the town gave it potential for the development of a far more extensive trade carried by water. Nonetheless, an interchange between road and waterborne traffic was clearly essential, and in the new town certain parts of the layout were specifically designed to accommodate this. In the 13th century there were four points in the northern part of the town at which road and waterborn traffic connected. The most important was, of course, the Tuesday market place, but the Survey also indicates three staithes in the eastern part of Damgate: at the East Gate, at Littleport, and, just off the main route, a staithe in Hopmans Way (now Austin Street).

In the Survey the Tuesday market place was a large open space built up only on the east and south sides and, therefore, presumably set out to the waterfront on the west and north. The southern boundary of the market was the line of the now almost lost continuation of Norfolk Street (Damgate) from High Street to the waterside, so that where the road met the Ouse bank a space of about half an acre on its north side had been laid out where goods could be exchanged. The Survey does not mention this, but presumably at this time all the western side of the market place was a public landing stage, which by the 16th century had been reduced by encroachments of private individuals to the area of the present Common Staithe.[22] Similarly, even by the 13th century, encroachments on the southern side had reduced the area of the market by about one third; the short street north from the end of Damgate to the market was known as Kokesgate where permanent buildings seem to have replaced what were probably the temporary booths of the medieval cooks, catering for travellers at the point where they set down their loads.

Even with an area as large as the Tuesday market place and its quays, it may have been difficult to accommodate the vessels of all the merchants who wanted to use the port. An alternative was to use the navigable sections of those fresh-water fleets which flowed through the town, the river Gay in the north and the Purfleet in the south. Unfortunately, neither fleet touched Damgate at any point, and it seems to have been necessary to dig artificial channels to bring boats to staithes on the line of the road. In the survey there were clearly three such canals bringing boats from the river Gay to Damgate. The most easterly joined Damgate at the East Gate; a second and much more important canal crossed Damgate at Littleport bridge then known as the Bishop's Bridge; and a third canal was not cut right through to Damgate but its staithe was reached by a short section of road branching off to the north-east from Chapel Street, then known as Listergate. Canal-building using the waters of the Purfleet to bring vessels to Damgate does not seem to have been attempted, perhaps because the amount of water in the fleet was not sufficient to fill the canals at low tide.

Apart from the navigable canals there must, in the 13th century, have been a whole network of drainage ditches on the site of the new town which are not mentioned in the Survey. Only one such channel, known as Colwensfleet and flowing down the centre of Webstar Row, a street on the site of the present Broad Street, was sufficiently important to be mentioned by name, but traces of the others are to be found in 16th century records and even then these were extensive.[23] They were at least as extensive as those to be found in medieval Salisbury, but in the main they seem to have been dug parallel to the lines of the streets and not along them, and to have functioned as open sewers, carrying waste collected at the backs of tenements out to the estuary.[24] There is no suggestion that Lynn was once laid out as a fully developed water-town on the same lines as the Dutch water-towns where water and road transport within the town were of equal importance. The street pattern seems to have developed independently of the drainage ditches, and the waterways brought to certain key points at a later stage.

The principal routes so far described on the Newland catered for movement of goods from east to west, but north to south communications had also to be laid out on the new land to link up with the old settlement south of the Purfleet. In the 13th century there were two main crossings over the Purfleet, and it was these which determined the lines of the principal north-south routes in the new town. The bridge in High Street was one of these crossings, and the line of the street on the south side was continued northward into the Tuesday market, determing the line of its eastern boundary. A second crossing was made at the top of Tower Street (Finneslane) by Belvaco's bridge (later Baxter's bridge), marking the starting point for another north-south route up Broad Street (Webstar Row), beside the fleet, to Chapel Street (Listergate) on the other side of Norfolk Street (Damgate), and round the west end of St. Nicholas Chapel to cross out of the town over the river Gay, later known as Fisherfleet, at Dowshill bridge. These parallel runs of north-south routes were linked occasionally by lanes running from east to west like Surrey Street (Jews lane) and Market Lane (Pillory Lane) from the Tuesday market to Chapel Street (Listergate), and New Conduit Street (Fincham Street), linking High Street north of the bridge with Broad Street along the north bank of the Purfleet.

In the 13th century there was no crossing place where Purfleet bridge now stands at the top of Queen Street (Wingate). There were, however, the beginnings of a route north-south, the early history of which is obscure. This was the waterfront route from the Purfleet to St. Anne's Fort, which, in the 13th century, was only in existence for a short section south of the Tuesday market. North of the market the main route out of the town by Dowshill bridge ran round the east end of St. Nicholas Chapel and this suggests that the chapel itself was built right on the waterside as was the Tuesday market, and that the laying-out of a street round the market and along St. Anns Street (North End) took place only as the bank was consolidated and the line of the waterfront pushed further west. This must have happened soon after the 13th century Survey was complete, for 31 tenements are there recorded along the line of the river bank, all of them in King Street (Checker Street) on the east side of the line of the street and facing directly on to the waterfront. When the Red Register[25] was compiled at the beginning of the 14th century not only was the line of waterfront streets north of the Purfleet complete, but in some cases buildings had already spread to the western side.

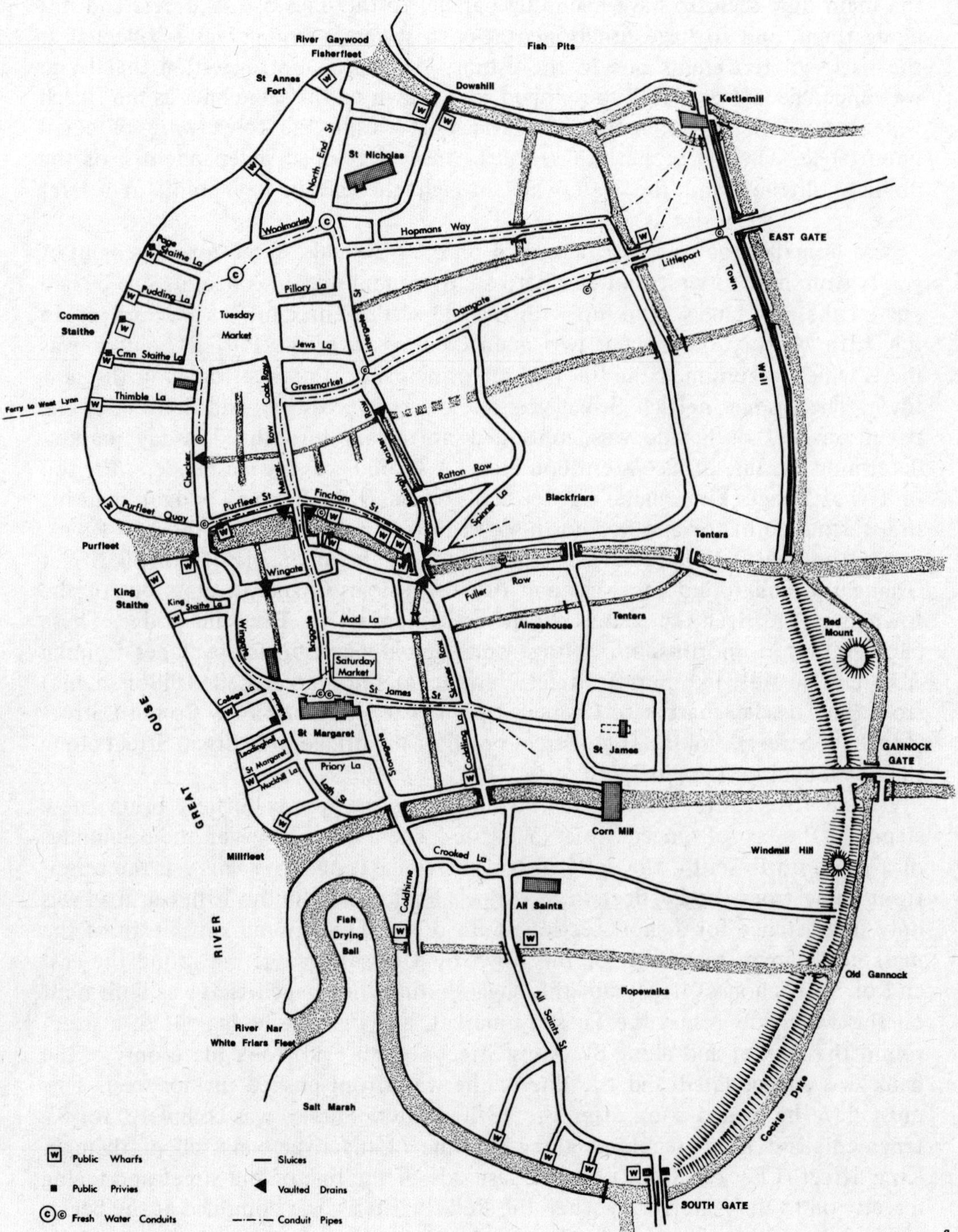

Fig 6 *Map of Kings Lynn in the mid-16th century*

Kings Lynn, then, in the 13th century, was a town whose layout was developed in such a way that goods entering the town from east or west by road could be transferred to water transport for shipment overseas. Damgate, the market place and the staithes, both on the waterfront and inland, were the nodal points of the plan, around which secondary development took place to accommodate the non-merchant sections of the Lynn community. The layout of streets in the latter sections gives every appearance of a planned grid. When the Friars came to the town in the 13th century, the main streets of the town north of the Millfleet were already densely built. Only the Austin Friars acquired a site in the mid-13th century near the Tuesday market, on the east side of Chapel Street (Listergate Street), bounded on the north by Austin Street (Hopmans Way). The Black Friars, the Grey Friars and the White Friars, the latter in South Lynn, all occupied extensive sites between the built up area to the west and the town wall on the east. Plenty of land was available there since the line of the wall, determined not by the extent of the town, but by the already existing sea bank, enclosed an area at least three times as large as the built-up part of the whole town.

16th and 17th Century Lynn

From the mid-14th century to the mid-16th century the documentary evidence for detailed changes in the topography of Lynn is very slight. But in the mid-16th century the town received the grant not only of the fee farm of the Bishop's manor of Lynn, but a good deal of monastic land and gild property in the town,[26] and several surveys and rentals survive from this period as the new acquisitions were recorded and assessed.[27] These surveys reveal a town plan which was in many respects unchanged since medieval times. (Fig.6.) One important aspect was the apparently increased importance of the Ouse waterfront, and of those other parts of the town to which access could be had by boat, shown in the growth in the number of staithes on the Ouse and the navigable fleets. There are two possible reasons for this change. The increasing use of the Ouse bank, and the reclamation which took place there, which will have given access to deeper water, may well be linked to the increasing use of ships with deeper draughts from the 15th century onwards. Secondly, this may also reflect the gradual disappearance of road traffic from the trade of the town, and an increasing volume of waterborn trade both by river and sea. The accounts of tolls from 1557 onwards, where they record the destination of goods and the form of transport used, indicate that very little traffic was using the land gates by this time. (Fig.3.)[28] Waterborne trade in the 16th century was accommodated at public and private quays, not only along the Ouse bank but also along the navigable fleets far into the built-up area of the town. (Fig.6). Apart from the great public landing stages laid out in early medieval times, the Common Staithe to the west of the Tuesday market and the Bishop's Staithe (later King's Staithe) on the south bank at the mouth of the Purfleet, there were 27 public quays in Lynn in 1557.[29] Six of these were south of the Millfleet, 11 were located on the Ouse bank between Millfleet and Fisherfleet and the remaining 10 on the fleets. The Purfleet particularly was choked with river traffic. The chief landing stage was at Baxter's Bridge where a spacious market place had been laid out at the south end of Broad Street (Webstar's Row). It was possible, moreover, to take barges further up than this and there were both public and private quays even in South Clough Lane (Fuller Row). On the Fisherfleet the ancient staithes at Dowshill bridge, Hopman's Way bridge, Littleport bridge and East Gates were all still in use and even on the Millfleet, where navigation was uncertain owing to the stopages caused upstream by the town's watermill, there was a staithe at Bevers bridge at the foot of Greyfriars Street (Codling Lane). By the mid-16th century, it is probable that waterborne traffic in the fleets had passed its peak, since there are repeated complaints of silting and other obstructions. A century earlier, many merchants had been attracted to their shores and they were lined, as the Ouse bank was, with their houses and warehouses.

Probably the most striking change along the waterfront of Lynn between 1350 and 1550 was the development of the Ouse bank as a residential and commercial area by Lynn merchants. By 1400 a street had been laid out in two sections, one between the Millfleet and the Purfleet, along Nelson Street (Lath Street) and Queen Street (Wingate), and another from the Purfleet northward to St. Anne's Fort. The bridge linking these two sections across the Purfleet was probably built during the 15th century. To the west of the roadway much of the river bank had been reclaimed as merchants extended their properties into the haven. The old points of public access along the waterfront had many of them been preserved and, as the merchants' tenements extended, lanes were laid out from the street to the receding line of the bank. In 1557 there were 12 such lanes between Millfleet and St. Anne's, most of them with a wharf at the foot.

As the waterfront area was extending, so the area around St. James' Chapel was contracting. In 1557, it was recorded that 'St. James' End street containeth many old fleets and lanes decayed whose names not known'.[30] Today, the once thriving centre around its medieval church has entirely disappeared. The chapel, recorded as ruinous in 1561, was converted into a workhouse and finally demolished in 1910. The decline of this area probably started soon after it was built when the new town to the north diverted along Damgate the merchandise formerly using a route from Gannock to the waterfront quays through St. James'. Thus migration northward was probably the first cause of the decay of the St. James' area, to be followed by migration west as the waterfront was further developed in the late middle ages.

One further change in the 16th-century topography of Lynn remains to be examined: the impact on the town of the dissolution of the monasteries. With the exception of the Benedictine Priory of St. Margaret, all the religious foundations in Lynn were located on the outskirts of the medieval built-up area. When they were abandoned the buildings were pulled down and the stone and brick robbed, leaving only the towers of the Greyfriars and the Whitefriars standing to act as seamarks from the Lynn channel. The sites were not developed again until the 18th century. St. Margaret's Priory, however, occupied a site in an important commercial area. All the conventual buildings to the south of the present Priory Lane were pulled down and the land redeveloped. Priory Lane itself was built by 1589, when the remains of the priory buildings there had been converted into cottages,[31] and the area between Priory Lane and the church became the burial ground. For the most part the extensive properties of the monasteries elsewhere in the town merely changed their ownership and fell into ruin. Even by the 19th century only the site of the Blackfriars and the Austin Friars had been redeveloped.

When the first accurate map was made of Kings Lynn in the late 17th century, (Plate I), it showed a town which was the same in all important respects as the one described in the 16th century surveys.[32] The built-up area had not been extended and the main interest of the trading community was still centred largely on the waterfront and the two market places. The town plan of Lynn before 1700 was thus built-up in three stages; the first was the building of the monastic town beside the priory church of St. Margaret in the early 12th century; the second was completed by about 1200 when the new town had been laid out to the north of the Purfleet; and the final stage was probably reached by the mid-15th century with the further development of the waterfront area. The size of the built-up area seems to have remained relatively cosntant after the building of the northward extension in the 12th century, the decline of the area around St. James' being compensated for in the extensions westward along the line of the river bank.

Notes to Chapter I

1 Quoted in T. Badeslade, *The History of the Ancient and Present State of the Navigation of the Port of Kings Lynn* (1725), 6.

2 E.M. Beloe, 'Freebridge Hundred and the Making of Lynn', *Norf. Arch.*, XII, 1895, 311-35; Astbury, *Black Fens*, map.

3 Hallam, *New Lands of Elloe,* 15.

4 F.J.T. Kestner, 'The Old Coastline of the Wash', *Geog. Jul.*, CXXVIII, 1962, 462.

5 *Reg. Norwich Cath. Priory,* 51.

6 See below p.21.

7 Charles Parkin, *Topography . . . of the Borough of Kings Lynn,* Blomefield's Norfolk, VIII 1808, 419-20, 479-80.

8 Ibid, 480.

9 *Reg. Norwich Cath. Priory,* 51.

10 K.L.M./Aa; See also Parkin, *History of Lynn,* 482-6.

11 H.M.C. *Eleventh Report* Appendix, Part III, 208.

12 M.W. Beresford, *New Towns of the Middle Ages,* (1967), 153.

13 M.W. Beresford, *New Towns of the Middle Ages,* (1967), 146-53.

14 *Reg. Norwich Cath. Priory,* 51.

15 H. Parker, 'A Medieval Wharf in Thoresby College Courtyard, Kings Lynn', *Med. Arch.,* IX 94-105.

16 William Raistrick, A Plan of the Borough of Kings Lynn, 1725, in *Blomefield's Norfolk* VIII, 476.

17 Beloe, 'Making of Lynn', 330n.6.

18 Beloe, 'Making of Lynn', 332 n.6.

19 K.L.M./Bc 1. Although the heading to the Terrier is missing, the original survey must date from before 1270. The Austin Friars, whose conventual buildings were laid out to the east of Listergate by that date, are not mentioned in the detailed survey of that part of the town, and the 22 tenements outside the East Gate were destroyed in the Barons War.

20 Charter temp. Richard III cited in H.J. Hillen, *History of Kings Lynn,* I.

21 K.L.M./H.B.IV/488, 501, 507; H.B.V/135.

22 In Salisbury the Bishop authorised traders to build on one side of the market place in 1367 K.H. Rogers 'Town Plan of Salisbury' in M.D. Lobel, (ed) *Historic Towns,* I, (1969).

23 K.L.M./Bc.7/71, See Appendix I.

24 K.H. Rogers, 'Salisbury' in M.D. Lobel, (ed), *Historic Towns* I, (1969).

25 *Red Register,* eg. Vol. I, 15, 56, 60, 61, 191, etc.

26 K.L.M./Bb 1, Bb3.

27 K.L.M./Bc 7, Parts 1, 9, 10, 11; Bc 8; Bc 9.

28 K.L.M./Db1, 1574-5, 1580-1, 1581-2, 1583-4, 1586, 1597.

29 K.L.M./Bc 7 Part 1, 72 (Appendix I).

30 K.L.M./Bc 7 (Appendix I).

31 K.L.M./Bc 9 /17d. See Francis Shaxton's holding in Priory Lane.

32 H. Bell, *The Groundplat of Kings Lynn, c.*1680.

II

Tenements and their Layout

BEFORE 1700 a building plot in Lynn was developed more often than not to provide a townsman with both his home and his workplace. Its size and shape might vary but generally in Lynn plots were rectangular with the shorter side abutting on to the street and some were serviced from the opposite end by a road or navigable waterway or drained by an open sewer. (Fig.7.) The siting and grouping of building plots was determined by a number of factors arising from the different needs of different occupations. All basically required access to communications either by road or river or both, but some occupations made special demands. Dyers and fullers were drawn to areas where there was running water, shopkeepers and innkeepers to the streets likely to be crowded with travellers, fishermen to areas where there were safe moorings for their boats, and, of course, merchants to those parts of the town where goods changed hands at the points of interchange between one system of communication and another. A characteristic feature of the layout and use of building plots in Kings Lynn was the rather generalised pattern of zoning by occupation which emerged from the rational exploitation of the site of the town and its communications. This is not to say that whole streets were given over exclusively to one occupation, but that there were certain clearly defined *areas* where tradesmen, or merchants, or craftsmen were most likely to be found. Lynn is apparently at variance with some other medieval towns in this respect, perhaps because of keen competition for waterfront sites by merchants.[1] At all events this pattern was not a static one and underwent several changes in the course of the town's early history. Alterations to it were the result not of a major change in the occupational structure of the town creating new requirements within the built-up area but primarily of change within the town's communications system. Thus there were two periods when the zoning of occupations altered, the first around the end of the 14th century, by which time the town had probably begun to receive and send more of its goods by water than by road,[2] and a second when both the river Ouse and the navigable fleets began to silt up causing increasing problems for shipping from the mid-15th century onwards.

Unfortunately, there is very little detailed documentary or archaeological evidence beyond that given in the 13th century Survey of the 'Newland'[3] for the layout of the town's building plots before the beginning of the 14th century, and by this time a changed pattern of land use was already beginning to emerge. In the earlier period it is clear from the Survey that in the northern part of the town the

Fig 7 *Map of building plots and their occupants in Damgate Ward, 1568-1579*

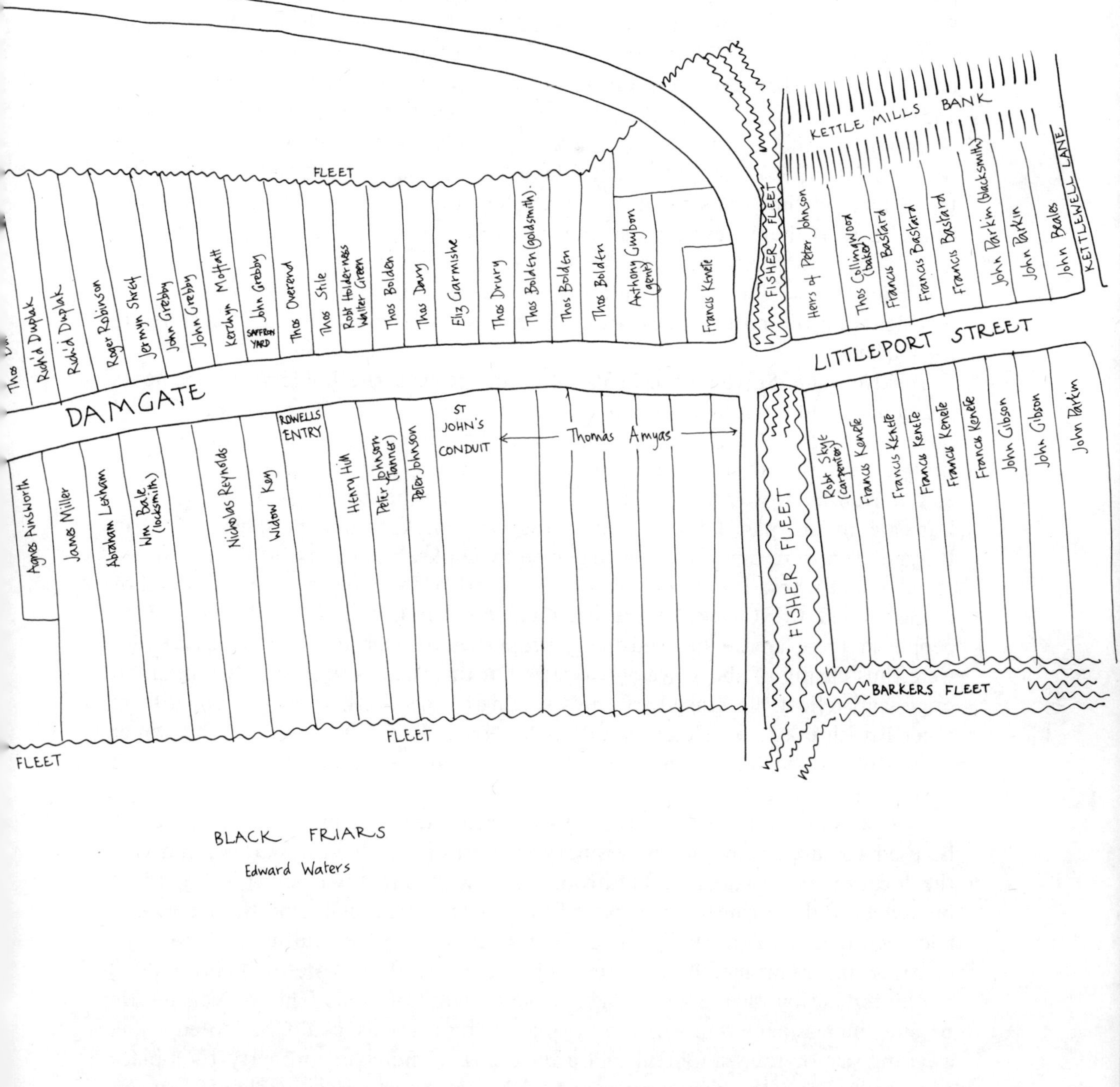
FLEET
Thos
Rich'd Duplak
Rich'd Duplak
Roger Robinson
Jermyn Shret
John Grebby
John Grebby
Kerchyn Moffatt
John Grebby
SAFFRON YARD
Thos Overend
Thos Stile
Robt Holderness Walter Green
Thos Bolden
Thos Davy
Eliz Garmishe
Thos Drury
Thos Bolden (goldsmith)
Thos Bolden
Thos Bolden
Anthony Gmybon (gent)
Francis Kenele
FISHER FLEET
KETTLE MILLS BANK
Heirs of Peter Johnson
Thos Collingwood (baker)
Francis Bastard
Francis Bastard
Francis Bastard
John Parkin (blacksmith)
John Parkin
John Parkin
John Beales
KETTLEWELL LANE
LITTLEPORT STREET
DAMGATE
ROWELLS ENTRY
ST JOHN'S CONDUIT
Thomas Amyas
Agnes Ainsworth
James Miller
Abraham Letham
Wm. Bale (locksmith)
Nicholas Reynolds
Widow Key
Henry Hill
Peter Johnson (tanner)
Peter Johnson
FISHER FLEET
Robt Skyle (carpenter)
Francis Kenele
Francis Kenele
Francis Kenele
Francis Kenele
Francis Kenele
John Gibson
John Gibson
John Parkin
BARKERS FLEET
FLEET
FLEET
BLACK FRIARS
Edward Waters

most densely built streets were Norfolk Street (Damgate), the northern end of High Street (Briggate) and the east side of King Street (Checker). (Fig.5.) No standard plot size can be identified here, as it can in Stratford-upon-Avon and other medieval new towns.[4] In Briggate the average width of the building plots was only 13 feet, and in Damgate and the Checker it was on average between 20 and 25 feet wide. Elsewhere in the north part of the town average widths of plots varied from between 30 and 40 feet on the east side of the Tuesday Market and in Jews Lane, to 50 feet on the east side of Listergate. On the west side of Listergate, (now Chapel Street) there were only six tenements where today there are 24 and other roads were also barely built-up. Webstar Row, (now Broad Street) for example, had only two or three tenements on its eastern side and there were only five tenements on the north side of Fincham Street (now New Conduit Street) beside the Purfleet.

The Newland Survey of *c.*1250, although it lists the holders of tenements individually, does not mention occupations except in a very few cases. Fullers and tanners were found where access could be had to supplies of water, as at Dowshill Bridge, on the north side of Damgate near the Bishop's mill race, and at the south end of Webstar Row near the Purfleet. Shops were mentioned at the west end of Damgate in the part later known as the Gressmarket, and in Briggate; and in Briggate also were inns and plots occupied by cooks, particularly at the north end of the street where it entered the Tuesday Market. Probably both the east end of Damgate and the Checker were occupied by merchants. Not only were there people in these areas who held many properties through out the town and who were thus clearly of above average wealth, but their names suggest a cosmopolitan origin and reflect the range of Lynn's trading connections. There were men from other British ports like Hedon and Berwick, from Walsingham, Wells, and Cromer in Norfolk as well as from overseas, from Spain, France, Bruges, Bergen, and Easterlings from the Baltic.

It is only at the beginning of the 14th century that documentary evidence can be used to supplement an increasing wealth of archaeological material and that the location of building plots throughout the whole town and the layout of buildings on them can be investigated in any detail. By that time the river Ouse had been diverted from Wisbech to Kings Lynn, fenland agriculture had begun to contract and Lynn merchants were probably distributing more of their goods in the hinterland by river, abandoning the old network of roads. Thus a riverside site became increasingly important as a place where goods could be stored while awaiting sale or trans-shipment and a re-zoning of merchant property took place as a result. From the beginning of the 14th century onwards merchants laid out their houses and warehouses on the banks both of the river Ouse and of those navigable fleets to which access could be gained from the main river. Damgate seems not to have been depopulated but to have maintained about the same density of settlement (Fig.7): by the 16th century its tenements were occupied not by the merchant aristocracy but by industrial craftsmen, particularly those of the building trades. Also by this period the pattern of zoning elsewhere had been somewhat altered. Fullers, who presumably once occupied sites on the south bank of the Purfleet in the lane known as Fuller Row, had been replaced there by merchants using the fleet for access to their warehouses; and cloth workers had also been replaced by other craftsmen in Webstar Row, perhaps because the fleet was already drying up – by the end of the century it was partly covered in. This development seems to be part of a general intermingling of industrial craftsmen of all kinds who, by the 16th century, could be found scattered – apparently at random – in all the less sought after areas of the town. Whether this was also the case earlier in the town's history is not clear, although it has been found that wherever zoning existed, the gilds tended to promote it in the interests of organisation and supervision of work.[5] By the 16th century the gilds in Lynn had become very weak and only five of the 30 or more that existed in the 15th century had possessions worth recording in 1562.[6] Thus one possible barrier to earlier intermingling of craft workers may have been removed, permitting a new pattern of settlement at this time. This intermingling was not, however, common to all occupations in Lynn as it appears to have been in other towns in the 16th century. The markets, the routes to them and the routes between them were still occupied predominantly by shopkeepers and innkeepers, particularly in High Street (Briggate); in the north a clearly defined area around the mouth of the river Gay was occupied by the fishermen who kept their boats in the sheltered harbour in the mouth of the fleet and jealously excluded the merchants from their quays;[7] and in South Lynn there was a farming community with a dairy herd and sheep in the marshlands.[8]

Only one alteration to this basic pattern was to take place before the end of the 17th century and that was caused by the silting of the waterways of the town in the 15th and 16th century. By 1600 most merchants had abandoned the sites both on the Purfleet and the Millfleet and around the Saturday Market and were concentrated to a greater extent in the northern part of the town around the Tuesday Market where navigation was not so badly affected. The extensive properties they had once held in the most southern parts of the town were then adapted in a variety of ways. Many of them were taken over by the growing numbers of professional people who seem to have been coming into the town at this time, and by gentry from the surrounding countryside, and were subsequently not much altered. Others seem to have been divided into a number of smaller units and let as rooms, and others again were occupied by shipmasters, mariners and those who had business on the waterfront.

Because of the zoning of different occupations, albeit on a broad scale in Lynn, certain areas of the town have a kind of homogeneity still visible today and deriving from both the quality and kind of building to be found there. This is not unique in English towns but it is somewhat unusual and is completely lacking in a place like York for example, where there seems to have been only slight occuaptional zoning pattern in the town.[9] One such area in Lynn is the waterfront including both the Ouse bank itself and the banks of the once-navigable fleets. Another area, now unfortunately completely gone and largely unrecorded, was that of the fishing community at the mouth of the river Gay; and a third area included most of the streets away from the waterfront where building plots were developed in similar ways although in this instance there were undoubtedly differences of detail that have subsequently been lost in later rebuildings.

Waterfront property was probably developed and laid out for the most part by merchants, although we have little evidence as to the details of this process until the 14th century. By that time the Red Register deeds show that merchants had spread out along the whole of the Ouse bank from the Millfleet in the south to St. Anne's Fort at the mouth of the Gaywood river in the north, and had also occupied sites on the banks of the Millfleet and the Purfleet – at that date navigable for some distance inland. The development of waterfront tenements in Lynn was not a simple matter of laying out a building plot to a fixed line, but of taking into account the continuous process of reclamation and consolidation of the banks. Building plots were thus continually altering in size and form, at least until the end of the 16th century. In the early stages of the development of all waterfront sites, holdings were split into two parts with a road lying between the landing stages on the bank and the houses opposite. Clifton House in Queen Street and Hampton Court in Nelson Street, however, were clearly undivided properties and they represent the earliest archaeological evidence for a different and later form of layout, only made possible as the line of the waterfront receded substantially from the line of the road.

In the early stages of the development of waterfront sites, Kings Lynn probably followed the same pattern as the Dutch dyke towns.[10] There the roads were laid out on the high land of the river banks. In Kings Lynn, too, with its low-lying marshy site, the firm banks of the rivers and fleets would offer the best lines for roads and pathways. Along the river side of those bank-top roads some areas must have been set aside for public access to the water, but private berths must soon have been laid out, perhaps initially with steps and a tying up place for boats such as William Glover was still leasing to fishermen in the Fisherfleet in 1606.[11] In the earliest Red Register deeds for waterfront areas, properties comprised two parts, house and quay, the house being laid out on the opposite side of the road. To begin with all the river banks including the Ouse bank must have been laid out in this way, as divided tenements with the house facing the quay across the bank-top road.

Where the watercourses still flowed close to the line of the banks this layout persisted into the 17th century, but in some areas of the town, particularly along the Ouse bank and for part of the Purfleet, land could be reclaimed from the rivers and consolidated to form not only a berth for ships but waterfront space for buildings. By the 14th century some of the quays in these parts of the town were obviously landing stages of some size, often equipped with warehouses and shops. Nevertheless, many tenements were still divided at this stage, with the house on the opposite side of the road. This kind of layout is clearly documented in the Red Register. For instance, in the details of a property devised by Alice, widow of Robert Chape, in 1349, the main tenement and buildings faced west on to the street, which was not named. The 'adjoining' quay faced east on to the street and west onto the haven, (i.e. the Ouse) and was bounded on the south by a public 'watergate' or lane called Tinnerslane giving access to a public wharf.[12] Another similar property was devised in 1340 by Joan, the widow of John of Thornegge, to John of Massingham. The capital tenement faced west on to the 'common way', again not named, the quays and buildings on them faced east onto the street and west onto the haven.[13] In Purfleet Street the property boundaries today still run across the road to include land on the bank of the Purfleet with land on the north of the street. The bank was used as a quay in 1610 when John Basset, merchant, left to his son his capital messuage where he lived with the warehouse 'over against' (i.e. opposite) the same in Purfleet Street;[14] and all along New Conduit Street (then Fincham Street) the chamberlains noted this kind of layout in their survey of 1579. (Fig.7.)

Although Raistrick's map of Kings Lynn made in 1725 (Plate 2) shows Purfleet Street and New Conduit Street still laid out with divided tenements, houses and quays being on opposite sides of the road, the layout along the Ouse bank had by then undergone further changes. The early stages of a different kind of layout of building plots on parts of the Ouse bank are documented in mid-14th century deeds in the Red Register, and it seems as though the first stages of the transition to the final form of layout on waterfront sites was made in this part of the town during this period. In some descriptions of property all the buildings of a particular holding, including the dwelling house, lie between the roadway on the east and the haven or river Ouse on the west. John of Swerdstone, for example, in his will of 1349, left jointly to his wife and his son John his 'capital messuage and quay' which all lay to the west of the road. Fronting the street were shops with solars above; behind them was the hall and beyond that the quay on the river bank.[15] It was this kind of layout on an undivided tenement, where all the buildings lay between the road and the waterfront, that became typical on the Ouse bank, and it is one for which there is ample archaeological evidence today.

This later development became possible as additional land was reclaimed from the river. Excavations at Thoresby College in Queen Street have shown, by uncovering a timber wharf, that the early course of the river ran appreciably to the east of the present line, and deposits found in front of the wharf suggest that rubbish tipped into the river was the main cause of the slow movement of the river bank westwards.[16] As the river bank receded from the line of the old road (now Nelson Street, St. Margaret's Place, Queen Street, King Street, Tuesday Market, St. Nicholas

Street and St. Anne Street) the length of the tenement between road and river increased. Thus there was room on the waterside not only for the quay and warehouses but also for the dwelling houses and shops which were moved over the street to bring the whole complex together.

At points where the river continued to flow close to the line of the road, as by the Purfleet and the Millfleet and as it did for instance along Nelson Street and in parts of the North End and St. Anne Street, the old, divided pattern of house opposite warehouse persisted even along the Ouse bank. It was only where the bank had been substantially consolidated that the pattern changed to one of undivided properties. Thus, even at the beginning of the 17th century there were still some divided tenements in these areas.[17]

A typical undivided holding on the river bank was long and narrow, up to 400 feet long in places towards the end of the 15th century, and about 20 to 30 feet wide. An entry passage usually ran down one side, giving access to the house at the street end and then to successive ranges of warehouses and out-buildings down to the river. The house was L-shaped with the front range running the full width of the plot bridging the passage. Demand for land was apparently never strong enough to force people to build high so few buildings exceed two storeys; some had cellars for additional warehouse space and perhaps also to raise the hall above the level of the floods. There was also a good deal of open space left between individual buildings – the yards, gardens and orchards mentioned frequently in deeds and wills. Usually buildings were strung out down the side of a long, narrow plot, but there were some undivided tenements where the plot was almost as wide as it was long. In that case (as for instance at Hampton Court in Nelson Street), the owner took the greatest possible advantage of the river frontage by laying out a warehouse parallel to it, and the rest of the buildings were arranged around an open courtyard, entered in the centre of the street range. (Fig.8.)

The building of an important medieval merchant consisted of a house, a quay, a warehouse, usually a shop or group of shops, a kitchen separate from the house, and possible also part shares in a privy or 'wardrobe' over a nearby fleet.[18] One almost complete group of a medieval merchant's buildings – on an undivided plot – has survived: Hampton Court, which lies between Nelson Street on the east, and the river on the west, bounded on the north by St. Margaret's Lane. (Fig.8; Plates 4-5.) Since the site is wide in relation to its length, the buildings are laid out round a courtyard with the warehouse, arcaded at ground level, across the west end. In the street range were shops, where a part of a shop window still remains, and above them a solar; the hall lay at right angles behind this, along the south side. The north side of the court was probably closed with some building in medieval times, but the present one dates from the 17th century. No trace of a detached kitchen has survived but in this particular case the hall had a hearth with a brick chimney, an unusual feature at this date, and this may have sufficed for cooking.

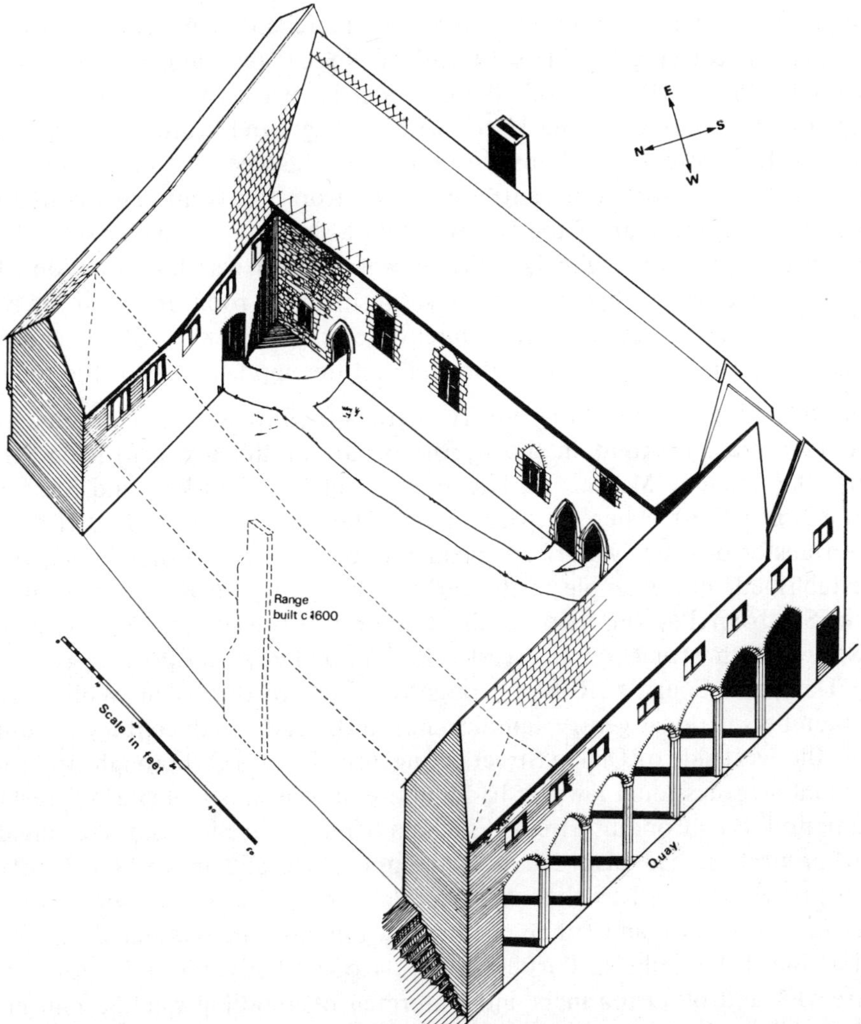

Fig 8 *Hampton Court, Nelson Street: reconstruction*

Of the undivided tenements on the long narrow sites in King Street and Queen Street none survives without major rebuilding. At Clifton House, on the corner of Queen Street and King Staithe Lane, archaeological investigations have revealed a medieval house with a hall containing an open hearth lying at right angles to the street, and an adjacent building, the vaulted undercroft of which still survives, also lying at right angles to the road. (Figs. 43-5; Plates 21-2.) No. 9 King Street also contains substantial evidence of a house lying at right angles to the street, but in neither case have other buildings such as warehouses survived, nor is there any evidence of shops.

Buildings that probably belonged to medieval merchants have also survived at No. 8 Purfleet Street (Fig.11; Plate 6) and at No. 30 on the east side of King Street. (Fig.23; Plates 10-11). Both these properties, which were of the divided kind, had houses fronting on the street with high ground storeys which in the case of No.30 King Street was almost certainly open between the timber supports and protected by a pentice roof cantilevered out from the front. This contained the shop. Access to the rear of the site was by passageway down the side of the buildings but only at No. 8 Purfleet Street was there a warehouse beyond the house, perhaps because at that time there was insufficient room for it on the river bank opposite. There is no trace of a warehouse at No. 30 King Street and this would almost certainly have stood on the quay on the opposite side of the road.

By the beginning of the 16th century merchant properties had become concentrated to a greater extent in the northern part of the town, in King Street (Checker), the Tuesday Market, St. Nicholas Street (Woolmarket) and St. Ann's Street (the North End). Where the occupants of tenements can be identified after 1500 the transfer of other waterfront property to gentry and professional people can be established. For example in the early 17th century Sir Robert Bell and his son-in-law Sir John Peyton, two of the Cambridgeshire gentry, had houses in Nelson Street (Lath Street) on the west side; Sir John Peyton's house was almost certainly Hampton Court.[19] Robert Houghton, Edward Baker and William Hoo were all members of local gentry families and in the early 17th century occupied houses on the west side of Queen Street (Wingate). Thomas Oxborough, the town Recorder and a professional lawyer, had a house in Nelson Street (Lath Street) in the same period. New Conduit Street (Fincham Street), once laid out with divided merchant properties, had also declined in importance and in 1579 four of its largest properties belonged to Nicholas Wynter, another local landowner. (Fig.7.) Other tenements in this and other declining waterfront areas were occupied by shipmasters like John Duke in Purfleet Street, Robert Ladyman in Nelson Street (Lath Street)[20] and other mariners and watermen of middling wealth. The great merchant families, the Millers, the Revetts, the Somes, and the Claybornes all had their properties near the Tuesday Market.

There is no evidence, either documentary or archaeological, to suggest that waterfront property was much altered by these changes in the 16th and 17th centuries. All the gentry families so far mentioned, with the possible exception of Nicholas Wynter, carried on some trading activities in the town, although clearly not on the same scale as the professional merchant. Thus, warehouse accommodation seems to have been retained; indeed Robert Houghton, who acquired Thoresby College at the Dissolution,[21] made a warehouse out of the College dining hall which happened to be located near the quay. Others occupying medieval merchants' premises seem to have utilised what was already there, rather than begun major rebuilding on different lines.

Merchant properties themselves were not entirely rebuilt but only modernised and extended in the 16th and 17th centuries. This was no doubt because the techniques of trade were changing only very gradually and many merchants were quite content to carry on the same kind of business from the premises occupied by their medieval ancestors. In the 16th century a merchant in Lynn was still involved in many aspects of commercial activity which, in the 17th and 18th centuries, were gradually to become the concern of specialists. He owned, and sometimes even sailed, his own ships; he provisioned them from his own bakehouse and brewhouse; and he sold his goods retail as well as wholesale. His household economy, too, was much more self sufficient than might be expected in view of the degree of specialised economic activity possible in the town. His property thus included not only the basic requirements of landing-stage, warehouse, house and shop, but bakehouses, brewhouses, mills, yards, gardens, and orchards, dovecotes and fields to graze his animals.[22]

But, however large a complex establishment might become, there were still, until the end of the 17th century, certain essential buildings which had to be accommodated on the merchant's plot, and these were substantially the same as in the medieval period. There was first of all the house, still located at the street end of the plot with the main living rooms in a range at right-angles to the street; there was the warehouse lying between the house and the quay and the quay itself on the river bank. The quay was particularly important. Lesser merchants, if their houses lay away from the waterfront, seem to have had some plot of private ground, even if only at the top end of the navigable stretch of the Purfleet, where they could land cargo from a boat. For the greater merchants, the bigger his business the larger number of ships' berths needed. There were public landing places along the Ouse where cranes and other facilities for handling bulky cargoes were provided, but merchants with waterfront property also had their own landing place at the end of their yards. In many cases this was known as a watergate. An engraving of the waterfront of Lynn in the early 18th century (Plate 3A) shows warehouses fronting directly on to the river, as they do today along the stretch northward from Purfleet to the Tuesday Market. Watergates were openings with steps, often in the gable ends of warehouses, where small boats could be handled inside and unloaded under cover. (Plate 31A) Some merchants may even have had their own arrangements for unloading larger vessels on their own property. John Burdy, who died in 1528, owned a private crane;[23] and in 1647 'one hoisting crane and two crane ropes, one iron hook and two slings' were part of the equipment of a large property leased to John Lucas in Lath Street.[24] In 1580 two men were licensed by the Corporation to build 'bridges'. One of them, built by William Pinder in Lath Street, was to be 'without the watergate of his house where he lives into the hove there 20 feet in length and 7 feet broad', for which he paid the Corporation 2d. a year.[25] This appears to have been some kind of jetty where a larger ship could be unloaded, perhaps a similar construction to the 'new timber bridge at

College Muckhill' erected by the town chamberlains in 1578, from which periodically the Muckhill 'Fowers' cleared the College Muckhill.[26]

Warehouses in the 16th and 17th centuries often stretched in a continuous line from quay to house so that goods could be moved under cover between street and waterfront. As most merchants dealt in miscellaneous cargoes, warehouses were rarely purpose-built to house a particular commodity. An exception in the sixteenth century seems to have been made in the case of fish and coal, and grain seems to have been stored in the first floor 'corn-chambers' which were plaster rendered inside. The juxtaposition of house, warehouse and quay is still the characteristic feature of building layouts along the Ouse bank in Lynn.

Another necessary part of a merchant's property was open ground. Away from the house, often in the town fields, he had land for livestock, horses for the journeys he had to make by road, cows for dairy produce, and sheep. Nearer home, open ground was used for a variety of purposes, from growing fruit to stacking timber and other bulky wares. Yards could be used for this latter purpose, and the warehouses seem often to have been arranged round a series of such spaces. Where additional space was available among the warehouses, gardens were laid out, and if the area was not sufficient, extra plots of 'garden ground' were bought or leased elsewhere in the town. When Michael Revett died in 1636 he left to his wife the garden near his house 'to bleach and dry clothes, to take herbs, and to recreate herself'.[27] Herbs and vegetables were grown within the built-up area of the town and fruit as well. There are references in the 17th century to both pear trees and apple trees growing in the town's orchards.

One effect of specialisation in the 16th and 17th centuries was the gradual disappearance of the merchant's shop. In some towns wholesale merchants were specifically debarred from retail trade, but this kind of restriction did not operate in Lynn. Here the loss of the retail shop was a normal part of the slow movement towards specialisation in trade found in all commercial towns in this period. The evidence for this in Lynn is mainly archaeological. Along the whole length of the Ouse bank only one shop window survives today in Hampton Court, and this dates from the 15th century. All the other house fronts have been rebuilt, the greater number of them in the 17th century, subsequently modified in the early 18th century by the removal of ornate gables and the addition of plain rectangular sash windows and pedimented doorcases. The brickwork of many of these front walls, however, dates from the 17th century, when timber framed buildings had their front walls 'latched'[28] an alteration for which the council granted licenses and which involved the rebuilding of the timber ground storey in brick to a line which was flush with the first floor jetty. There are a few such houses in Nelson Street to the south of Hampton Court. A number of houses seem to have been completely rebuilt during the 17th century, like No. 29 Queen Street, (Plate 22A) and Nos. 23 and 25 King Street, and others had their front walls completely reconstructed and redesigned. In no case is there a trace of a shop window, or of the additional door openings in the front of the building to give access to shop units independently of the house.

The change which left large trading businesses without shops probably did not really get under way until the first half of the 17th century. In the Red Register most of the documented properties had shops, and these survived in many instances to the end of the 16th century. In 1609 at least nine houses in the Tuesday Market had shops to let in the Lynn Mart, the annual February fair.[29] Thomas Sandell, who died in 1614, was one of the richest merchants of his time, in whose house Sir Walter Raleigh was entertained when he visited the town in 1589.[30] He had a shop in his house in St. Nicholas Street, as did his neighbour Thomas Clayborne the elder who had built up an equally prosperous trading business. Thomas Revett, the Town Clerk, who had a house on the north-west corner of the Tuesday Market had three shops when he died in 1633. Unfortunately, it is not always clear whether these shops were actually run by the occupants of the houses or whether they were leased to others.

Presumably if shops were no longer required by the greater merchants, newly-built houses would dispense with them at the outset and such documentary evidence as there is on new building after 1560 seems to indicate that this was, in fact, the case. Only one house, built by John Grebby in King Street on two tenements on the west side leased from the Council in 1569, is recorded as having a shop. This house was later occupied by Michael Revett,[31] and John Grebby built a further house for his own use but without a shop on the west side of the Tuesday Market to the north of Water Lane. Similarly the new house of William Hall which was being built on the east side of the Tuesday Market in 1540 and William Killingtree's new house in the north-east corner of the Tuesday Market built in 1570 were without shops.[32] It seems from such evidence as is available that shops, in the larger trading businesses at least, were ceasing to be required after about 1570.

At the beginning of the 16th century most of the greater merchants had sufficient buildings and equipment to victual their own ships, and, like many towns householders of all occupations, to make for themselves such basic household requirements as candles. Several merchants had bakehouses and brewhouses, and some like Michael Revett (d.1636) seem to have gradually begun to specialise in this aspect of their business, although few large bakers and brewers had abandoned other trading interests entirely in this period.

Several descriptions of merchant property have survived in wills dating from the early 17th century. Michael Revett, when he died in 1636 was described as a merchant,[33] and had been registered as a merchant when he was enfranchised in 1598. Nevertheless, his interests included two inns, the *Maids Head* in the Tuesday Market and the *Red Lyon* in Boston, and his brewing activities were clearly extensive. Even so, his property was in many ways typical of a large merchant holding of the 17th century. (Fig.9.) Revett lived in a house, then recently rebuilt, in King Street, on the site now occupied by the Girls' High

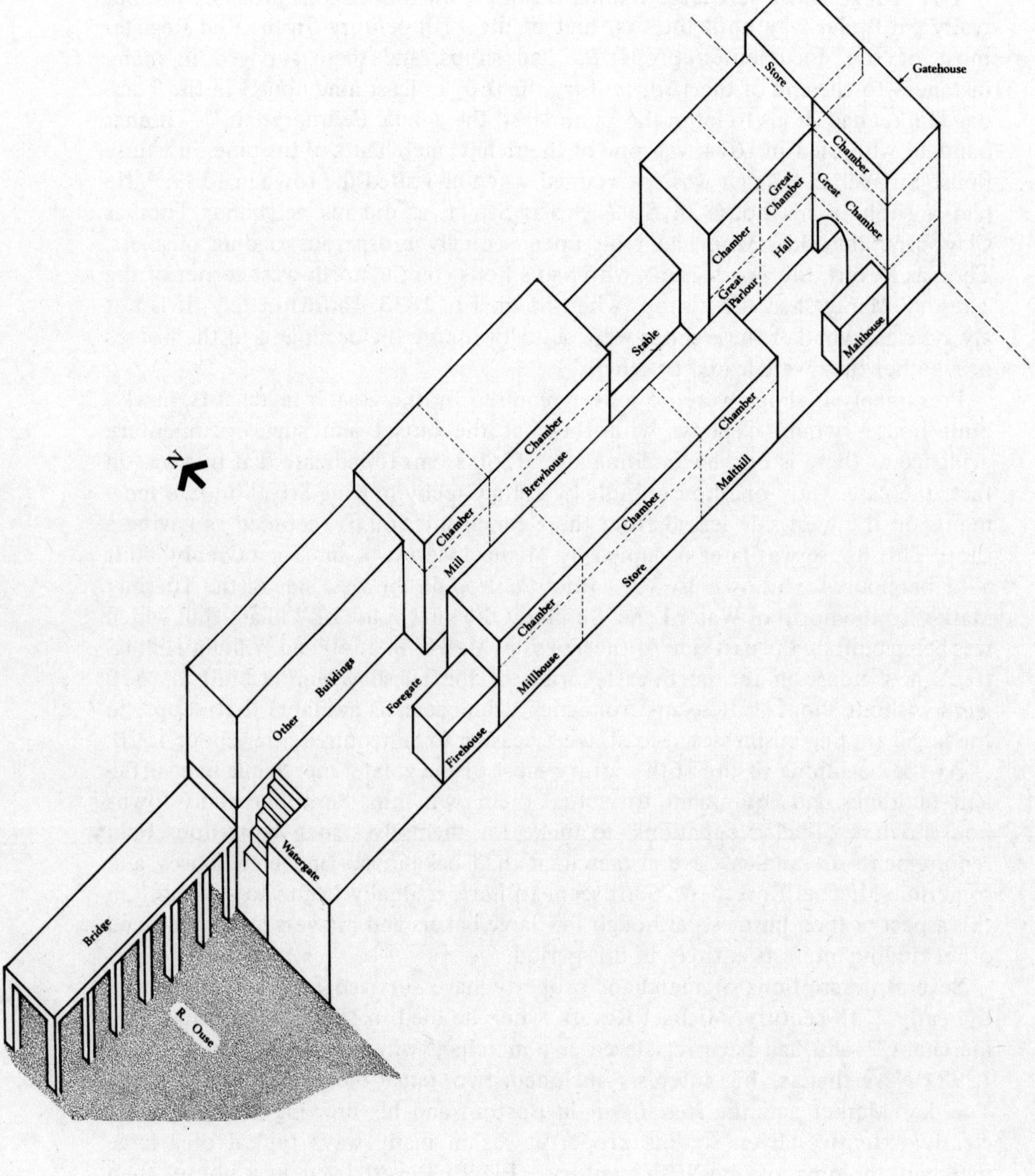

Fig 9 *Layout of a merchant's tenement in King Street, 1636*

School. His house and shop fronted the street, while a gatehouse to one side gave access to an entry passage running down the land behind to the river. This land was divided into an upper and a lower yard. On the south side of the upper yard was a malt house and 'malt hill', both two storeys high, and a millhouse; on the north side was a brewhouse, another mill, and a stable. A 'foregate' closed this part of the premises off from the lower yard where there was a 'fyer house' and coalyard, a garden and 'other building'. At the lower end of the tenement was a watergate and 'bridge'.

John Grebby had clearly built up much less of a business in brewing. When he died in 1587 he lived in a house on the north side of Water Lane, fronting the Tuesday Market.[34] The yard behind the house had a garden on the north side and the buildings beyond down to the quay were described in 1655 as warehouses, a coalyard, an oil house, candlehouse, yards, orchards and gardens, with the entry running down the centre and a kitchen, detached from the house on the south side. The building plot to the north was occupied by William Gurlin (d.1630) and also contained typical merchants buildings.[35] It had a house, where he lived, with orchards and gardens. There was a brewhouse, warehouses two storeys high, the first floors being corn chambers, and 'the newe chamber over the great cross chamber, and the coalyard, and the gallerye next adjoining to the newe dove-cote abutting toward Linn haven on the west'. It is interesting to note that the merchants, although many of them owned country estates not too distant from Lynn, were still living on their business premises and not building themselves country houses. This pattern was to be retained until well after 1700.

One architectural feature of merchant establishments, of which, unfortunately, there is very little known, was the tower. One survives at Clifton House (Plate 23B); there is documentary evidence of another attached to the property of Robert Gervis at No. 1 King Street in 1557;[36] and the 18th century engraving of the west prospect of Lynn shows several along the waterfront. (Plate 3A.) They seem to have been built with both practicality and prestige in mind. They were useful as look-out places for ships entering the Ouse estuary so that berths could be prepared for landings; there was room for extra accommodation either as living or storage space; and they were also a clear sign of wealth and grandeur among rival merchant families in Lynn.

Holdings away from the waterfront were generally occupied by the less wealthy citiznes of Lynn. In consequence the old properties in, for instance, High Street or Norfolk Street, are neither well-documented nor particularly well preserved. It is in these areas especially that the greatest amount of rebuilding has taken place during the last century and a half. In consequence we know very much less about the holdings of men of moderate wealth and almost nothing at all of how the poor lived.

The holding of a townsman of only moderate wealth was naturally smaller than the waterfront properties of the greater merchants. Even allowing for later subdivisions, holdings in High Street were about a quarter of the area of holdings in King Street. Even so, much of the plot was left as open ground. Few are mentioned without yards and gardens, and it was not until the 19th century that these were built over with cottages and warehouses. This open ground played an important part in the domestic economy of such households. It provided space for burying refuse, and a place for keeping a few animals, a cow or pigs or ducks – the subjects of repeated council ordinances in vain attempts to get them off the streets.[37] It was also used for growing fruit, herbs and vegetables, and for outdoor storage space for wood and coal.

In the parts of the town adjacent to the market places or the navigable fleets, most holdings were built over, partially at least, by the 16th century and probably earlier. In the Red Register some brief descriptions are given of properties away from the waterfront which almost always include a shop or shops which might be for either industrial or commercial use. One holding of Adam of Walsoken in Briggate accommodated no fewer than 11 shops,[38] and in 1321, a shop is described in the will of John Whitlocke as 2½ rods long, 3¼ rods wide at the west end, and 3¾ at the east.[39] This particular one stood in Cooks Row, the northern end of High Street. Shops were also recorded in the Red Register in Briggate, Gressmarket, Damgate and Pillory Lane. A good many of these holdings must have been laid out with a single range of buildings running parallel to the street, with shops or workrooms on the ground floor and solars above. When, occasionally, a hall is mentioned, this lay at right angles to the street behind the shops. A narrow passageway was left down one side of the plot onto which the hall window faced and from which it was entered. Shops with halls, or living rooms, behind were not necessarily built both at the same time. A first stage may have been to build a timber-framed front range of shops, either one or two storeys high, such as still survive on the south side of St. James's Street, (Plate 9A) and to add halls with stone side walls later. A good example of this latter development is Lattice House in Chapel Street where two stone halls were added to a long timber range, one room deep, fronting the street. (Fig.13.)

Occasionally, warehouse accommodation was built. William Erle in 1349, left a shop in Briggate with a solar and two warehouses.[40] There are no warehouses left in the town as old as this, however. When in the 17th century, a warehouse was built on – as at No. 2A Norfolk Street – it was built across the plot, at right angles to the hall, with a passageway through to the garden beyond. A further alternative was to build a continuation of the hall range, as at No. 13 Norfolk Street.

From the end of the 16th century, the built-up area of Lynn ceased either to expand or contract appreciably until the middle of the 19th century. Although no maps exist of 16th and 17th century Lynn, the chamberlains' written surveys of the town in 1557, 1568-9 and 1579, are quite detailed about property boundaries and for some areas contain a house-by-house investigation of the boundaries of

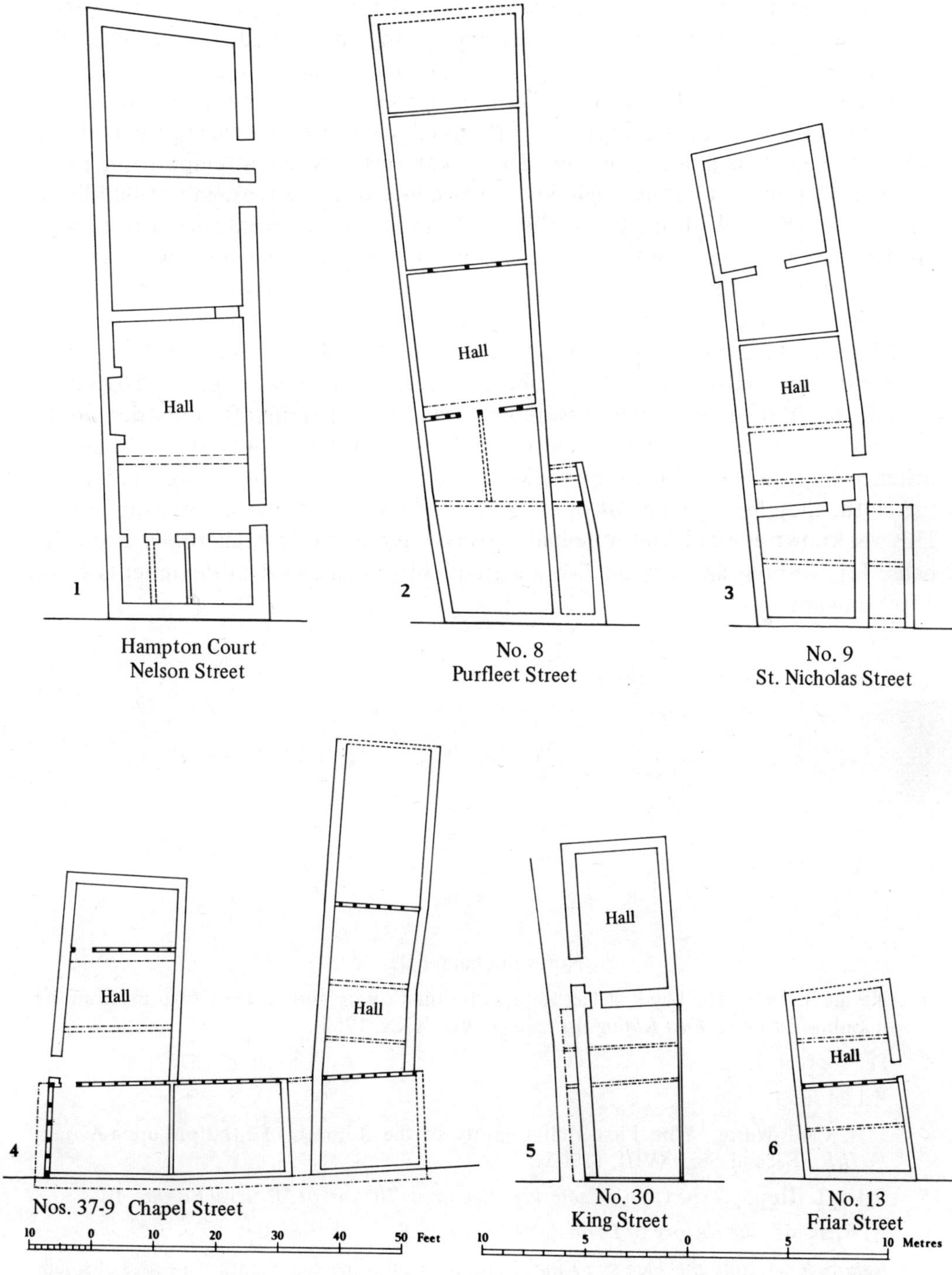

Fig 10 *Medieval houses in Lynn: comparative plans*

every tenement.[41] When compared with the first town map printed at the beginning of the 18th century, they show that hardly any change had taken place in the general layout of the town, and neither Raistrick's map of 1725, (Plate 2) nor even the Plan of Kings Lynn of 1830,[42] shows in fact any very substantial addition to the built-up area. Probably not much change took place in the built-up areas of individual holdings either. There was certainly no attempt to increase accommodation by building high, and no evidence of an increase in out-buildings. By the end of the 17th century, when wills and probate inventories survive with greater frequency, few out-buildings are mentioned in connection with smaller Lynn properties. Exceptions are the expected ones. A fellmonger, for instance, who died in 1692, had, in addition to his house, an alum house, a tan yard, a warehouse, a backhouse and a shop.[43] Brewhouses and inns, too, must have had more extensive outbuildings. But Robert Stonar, a cooper, who died in 1613 had, in addition to his house, only a warehouse, and most handicraft industries would require little space, or special buildings.[44] Where open land was required, as for instance by ropemakers for rope walks, or by clothworkers for drying and bleaching cloth, they held a piece of open land on the outskirts of the built-up area.[45] This was known as a ball, and rope-balls, for laying out and twisting ropes, and fish-balls, for washing and drying fish are frequently mentioned in documents from 1500 onwards.

Notes to Chapter II

1 Neville Bartlett, 'The Lay Poll Tax Returns for the City of York in 1381' offprint from the unpublished *Trans. East Riding Antiq. Soc.* Vol. XXX, 1953.

2 See above p. 5, 7.

3 K.L.M./Bc 1

4 E.M. Carus-Wilson, 'The First Half Century of the Borough of Stratford-upon-Avon', *Ec.H.R.*, Second Ser. XVIII, (1965), 57.

5 Sylvia L. Thrupp, 'The Gilds', *Cambridge Economic History of Medieval Europe*, III.

6 W. Richards, *The History of Lynn*, (1812), I, 416; P.R.O./E178/7046.

7 *Report Respecting the Fleets in Kings Lynn 1841* cites the complaints of owners of small boats 1693; K.L.M./Bc.

8 K.L.M./Bc 7, part 1. There are numerous references to the leasing of these lands for sheep-runs in the 16th and 17th century Hall Books, and a dairy herd is mentioned in the will of Henry Blesby, PCC, F3 Noodes.

9 G.C.F. Forster 'York in the 17th Century', *V.C.H. City of York,* 161. Bartlett, 'Lay Subsidy', *op.cit.* p.52.

10 Gerald L. Burke, *The Making of Dutch Towns,* (1956), 34-41.

11 K.L.M./H.B.VI/367.

12 *Red Register,* I, 207.

13 Ibid, I, 159.

14 P.C.C. 86 Wood.

15 *Red Register,* I, 182.

16 Helen Parker, 'Medieval Wharf', op.cit.

17 For example, a tenement in Lath Street was sold in 1625 as a house in the east side of the street and a quay or wharf 'over against' the same on the river bank. This was at the south end of Lath Street, and the quay was probably to the south of Oxley House: KLM/H.B. VIII/237.

18 *Red Register,* I, 38, 144, 196.

19 The ownership of some tenements in Lynn in the 16th and 17th centuries can be established by an examination of the surviving rentals K.L.M./Bc 7, Parts 1,9,10,11;Bc 8;Bc 9;Bc 11.

20 Town rentals; see also Appendix II. Inventory of Robert Ladyman.

21 K.L.M./H.B.IV/91, 92; Parker, *Thoresby College – Hampton Court,* 17.

22 Most merchant wills dating from the 16th and 17th centuries illustrate this point but see particularly the will of Thomas Grave, P.C.C. 44 Leicester (1589), John Dynsdale P.C.C. 3 Arundell (1579) and of Michael Revett, see below p.45-7.

23 P.C.C. 2. Jankyn.

24 Appendix II Lease schedule.

25 K.L.M./H.B.V/198.

26 K.L.M./Bc 7/Chamberlains A/c, Part 4, p.7.

27 P.C.C. 98 Pile.

28 See below p.164.

29 K.L.M./Dd (1609).

30 K.L.M./H.B.V/392d.

31 K.L.M./H.B.VI/57d mentions the 'new dwelling house' of Michael Revett.

32 P.C.C. 27 Alenger; K.L.M./H.B.V/12d; Dd (1609).

33 P.C.C. 98 Pile.

34 P.C.C. 73 Spencer; K.L.M./A.5/1655.

35 P.C.C. 47 Harte.

36 K.L.M./Bc 8/22d (1589).

37 See below p.160.

38 *Red Register* I, 177.

39 *Ibid,* 51.

40 *Red Register* I, 175.

41 K.L.M./Bc 7/Survey 2 (1586), Survey 3 (1576), see Fig. 7.

42 Maker not known. Copy in Borough Surveyors Office, Clifton House, Queen Street, Kings Lynn.

43 Nor. Rec. Office, Archdeaconry Court Wills. 1692.

44 Appendix II (1).

45 See below p.131.

III

Medieval Houses

IN WHAT ARE NOW the main shopping streets of the town, particularly in High Street and Norfolk Street, most properties have been entirely rebuilt in the 19th and 20th centuries, although there are other parts of Lynn where medieval buildings were only rarely razed to the ground to make way for later work. Along the Ouse bank, for example, or around St. Nicholas and in South Lynn, the building of classical facades and rebuilding work of various periods often confuses, but does not entirely obliterate, the remains of medieval work. A great deal of evidence of medieval domestic building is fragmentary, as might be expected, although there were fortunately, until recently, several complete medieval houses still standing. These, supplemented by corroborative evidence from other less well preserved examples, give a fairly complete picture of late medieval domestic plan-types. It is unfortunate that most of the better examples appear to date from the late 14th and 15th centuries and thus do not cover a wide enough time span for any chronological development of plan-types to be deduced. Nevertheless, such houses as survive represent quite a wide cross section of medieval town's housing. There are three good examples of what most probably prosperous merchants' houses, Hampton Court in Nelson Street, No. 8 Purfleet Street and No. 3 King Street. Smaller houses presumably occupied by lesser merchants or prosperous retailers are represented by No. 9 St. Nicholas Street, and Nos. 37-9 in Chapel Street; at the lower end of the scale, houses in Pilot Street and No. 13 Friar Street are probably typical of the houses of craftsmen, people who were not particularly wealthy, but who clearly lived well above subsistence level. How the poor lived is, at the moment, a matter of complete conjecture.

In analysing the surviving examples of medieval building, the greatest problem has arisen over the matter of dating. Medieval vernacular building is notoriously difficult to date accurately and documentary evidence is often lacking or incomplete. Archaeological investigation without known dated examples to work from can, in many cases, only be the basis for rough calculations. Nevertheless, in ascribing examples of medieval domestic building in Kings Lynn to a particular period reliance has to be placed almost entirely on archaeological evidence, although documentary sources are available to date a limited number of examples as, for instance, the greater number of public buildings, the Hanseatic Warehouse in St. Margaret's Lane (1474) and Thoresby College in Queen Street (1510). These are all useful as sources of comparative details.

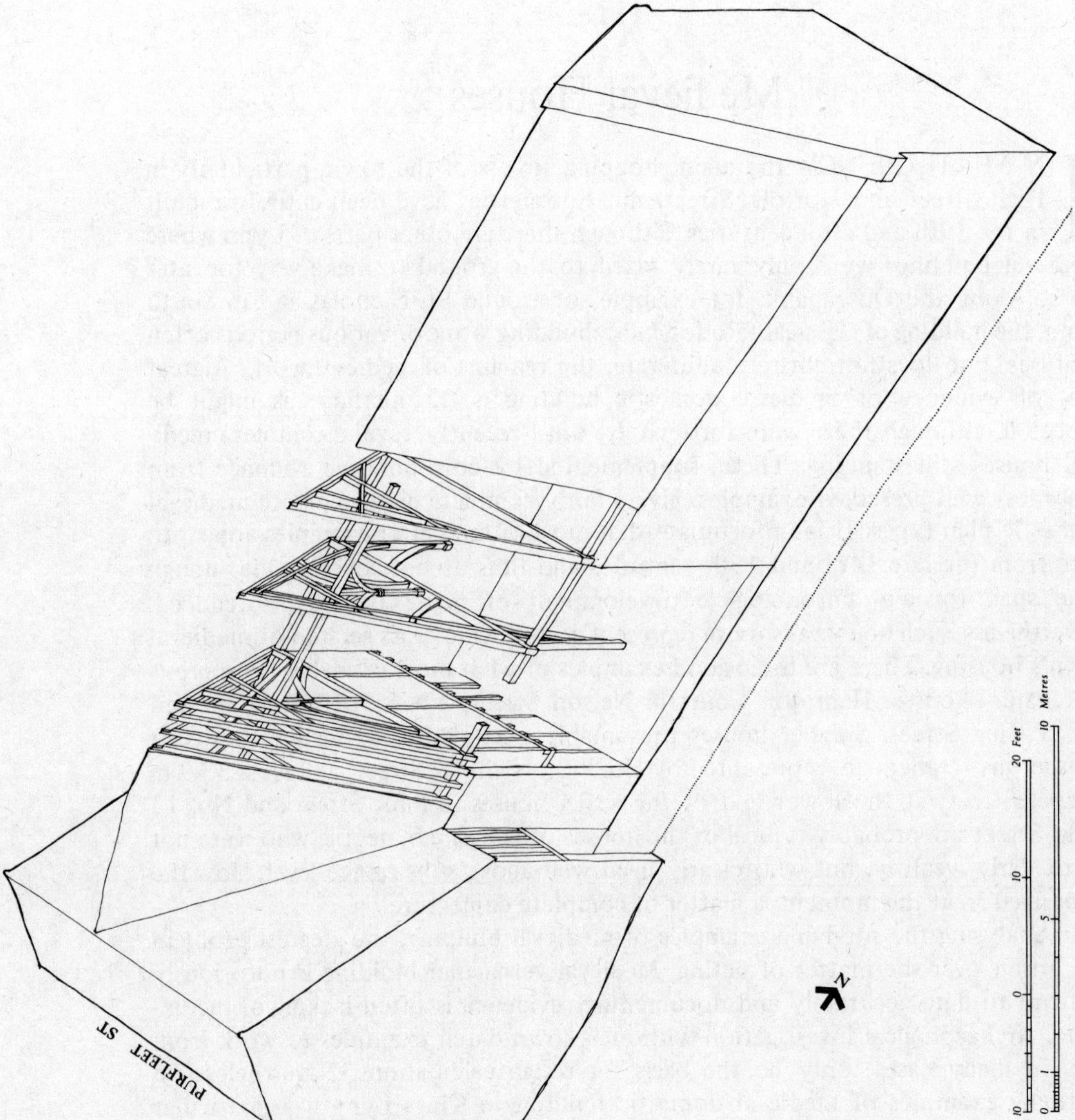

Fig 11 *No. 8 Purfleet Street: reconstruction of the medieval house*

The most useful archaeological evidence for dating purposes is of two kinds: architectural and decorative details in stone or wood which can be used for comparison with similar work in dated public buildings like churches and gildhalls; and details of construction which can be expected to show a progressive refinement of technique. The former category is of little use in Kings Lynn because the survival of details of this kind is of a very limited nature. Some medieval window and door-openings survive in the stone side walls of the hall ranges but these, as at No. 30 King Street (Plate 11A), are often simply carved with a flat chamfer and cannot be confidently ascribed to any particualr period. Timber decoration similarly has almost entirely disappeared, and where it does survive is often roughly executed.

The most hopeful line of investigation for dating purposes is of the technique of timber framing and particularly of roof construction. Whereas many timber walls have now disappeared, the roofs of medieval houses often remain virtaully untouched. The probable evolution of roofing techniques, based on Lynn examples is shown in Figure 17. From this it appears that after the general introduction of brick chimney stacks during the 16th century, the roof, ceiled off for the first time from the rooms below, degenerated into a rough and ready kind of construction such as that found in No. 29 Queen Street. (Fig.40.) Thus the highest refinement of the splendid medieval tradition of timber roof building must have been reached by the mid-16th century at the latest, and is represented in Lynn by the roof of Thoresby College hall, built around 1510 with principal rafters and side purlins. (Plate 16.) Two stages in the evolution of roof construction had clearly preceded this, the earliest being the construction of a scissor braced roof without a purlin or ridge piece and thus without any lengthwise support; the second stage was marked by the introduction of the collar purlin. The exact date of these changes (to be discussed in further detail on p.71) is, of course, more difficult to establish, but such evidence enables buildings to be related to each other in rough chronological sequence.

In general the evolution of medieval house-types in Lynn begins, as was the case in most medieval English towns, from an attempt to adapt the rural hall-house to an urban environment.[1] Thus they preserve, as the basic unit, the ground floor hall, very occasionally raised on an undercroft, open to the roof generally through two storeys. Town houses in England seem to fall broadly into two groups. First there are those in which the hall is placed parallel to the street, either actually on the street, as at the Jews House, Lincoln, separated from the street by a row of shops, as at Tackleys Inn, Oxford, or built on the side of a courtyard opposite the street entry, as at Strangers Hall, Norwich.[2] In the second main group the hall lies at right angles to the street, either entered from a courtyard or entry passage to one side, or through a passage from an opening in the gable end. There is some evidence in Lynn both for halls lying parallel to and on the street, and set back with a courtyard in front. By far the most common arrangement in Lynn, however, for houses of all sizes, was to build the hall at right angles to the street, entered from a side passage or courtyard.

Two examples only, both of them fragmentary, were found to suggest that some medieval halls in Lynn may have been built parallel to the street. Nos. 6-8 St. Ann's Street is now two two-storey cottages, one room deep, divided by a chimney stack. Both front and back walls are rubble built and 13th century scissor-braced roof still survives over the northernmost cottage, No. 6, although the southern section now has a 15th century crown post roof. In the back wall of No. 6 is a double, pointed arch doorway of very fine workmanship, suggesting a hall entry, and to the south a pointed arched opening at a lower level which may have once entered an excavated undercroft. Although there are traces of window openings surviving in both front and back walls, indicating a room open the full height of the building, no traces remain in the interior of the original plan. Since all the buildings at the rear of the plot have now disappeared, it is impossible to tell finally whether or not the surviving range did actually contain the main hall of the house. The quality of the workmanship, and the fact that it was stone-built suggests, though, that it did.

The second example of a hall parallel to the street was found behind the premises of Messrs. Baxters shop in High Street. Here the hall lay some 100 feet from the present line of the street, and would presumably have been entered through a courtyard. Only a part of the brick side walls remained, but the north gable end showed traces of a floor about six feet above ground which may have raised the hall on an unexcavated undercroft. The undercroft door opening, with bull-nosed brick jambs has survived. Again evidence for the medieval use of this building is very inconclusive, but the possibility that it was the hall of a house is suggested by the height of the room on the undercroft which rose, undivided, through two storeys. No roof timbers, however, remained, and the use of brick suggests a date not earlier than the 15th century.

All of the other evidence of medieval house types in Lynn indicates that the standard plan form was 'L' shaped, with a long range at right angles to the street, containing the hall, and a short cross range on the street which probably once contained shops and solars. The front range bridged an entry passage which usually ran the whole length of the tenement, giving access not only to the house, but to the warehouses and outbuildings beyond. (Fig.10.) No evidence has been found of a 'narrow plan' house type where the hall range occupied the full width of the tenement.[3] No old gable ends face the street in Lynn – all are masked by the parallel ridge of the front range, and this appears to have been so from earliest times. It should be noted, however, that the Gildhall of St. George was built as a 'narrow plan' block at the beginning of the 15th century.[4] It has a first floor hall and an entry passage running through to the back down one side of the undercroft. Difficulties of lighting the 'narrow plan' house, unless adjacent to a lane or alley, created in Exeter and other towns in the south west, the need for internal courtyards to act as light wells. Thus typical medieval Exeter houses, like No. 36 North Street,[5] or Museum House, Totnes, have a series of such open spaces, the communication between rooms at first floor level being by means of galleries along one side of the yard. There is no archaeological evidence of this kind of layout in Lynn either, although there are documentary references in the 16th century to galleries linking different parts of a house.[6] In general, however, as at No. 8 Purfleet Street, the whole tenement seems to have been built with a range of uniform width, changing almost imperceptibly from house to warehouse. Indeed, it was a feature of housing developments in Lynn that the house was extended into the warehouse simply by partitioning, making new door openings, and improving the style of the windows. This happened not only at No. 8 Purfleet Street, but at Clifton House, Queen Street, the Steelyard in St. Margarets Place where part of the south range of warehouses has been incorporated in the house, and at No. 1 St. Margarets Place where a small 16th century panelled room lay within the warehouse range. There is no suggestion that these extensions represent courtyard infil between house and warehouse. Indeed, courtyards would surely be unnecessary when adequate light and access could be obtained from the passage.

By the 15th century the width of building plots had been reduced to around 30 feet, leaving room for only a narrow alley to act as an entry. The 'Newland Survey', however, seems to indicate that in the north part of the town there were places where building plots could have been up to 50 feet wide, (Fig.5) and along Nelson Street wide plots have survived today. On such plots the house could be flanked by a courtyard and in fact the oldest surviving house in Lynn is laid out in this manner. Hampton Court in Nelson Street, taking its name from a baker, John Hampton, who occupied the property in the 17th century, is a large complex of buildings laid out, to the west of the street, round an open court.[7] (Figs.8 & 30.) The medieval house, extensive remains of which were uncovered during restoration work in 1958-9, lay on the south side of the court. (Plate 5A.) Built throughout in stone, probably in the early 14th century, it lies a short distance back from the present line of the road, with its gable end towards the street, and was entered from the north side. A hall in the centre was flanked at either end by two-storeyed sections, one on the east containing service rooms on the ground floor with a chamber over, and to the west a larger section with two ground-floor rooms, and a single large chamber over both.

All the internal partitions, with the exception of the west side of the screens passage, were built in stone pierced by pointed arched dressed-stone door openings. The door from the north entered the hall at the east end probably originally through a screens passage of which the timber western side has disappeared. On the east side of the passage three pointed arch openings have survived leading probably into two small ground floor service rooms and then either onto a stair, or perhaps a passageway on the south side. The one room above the service rooms on the first floor communicated with the hall by means of an internal window

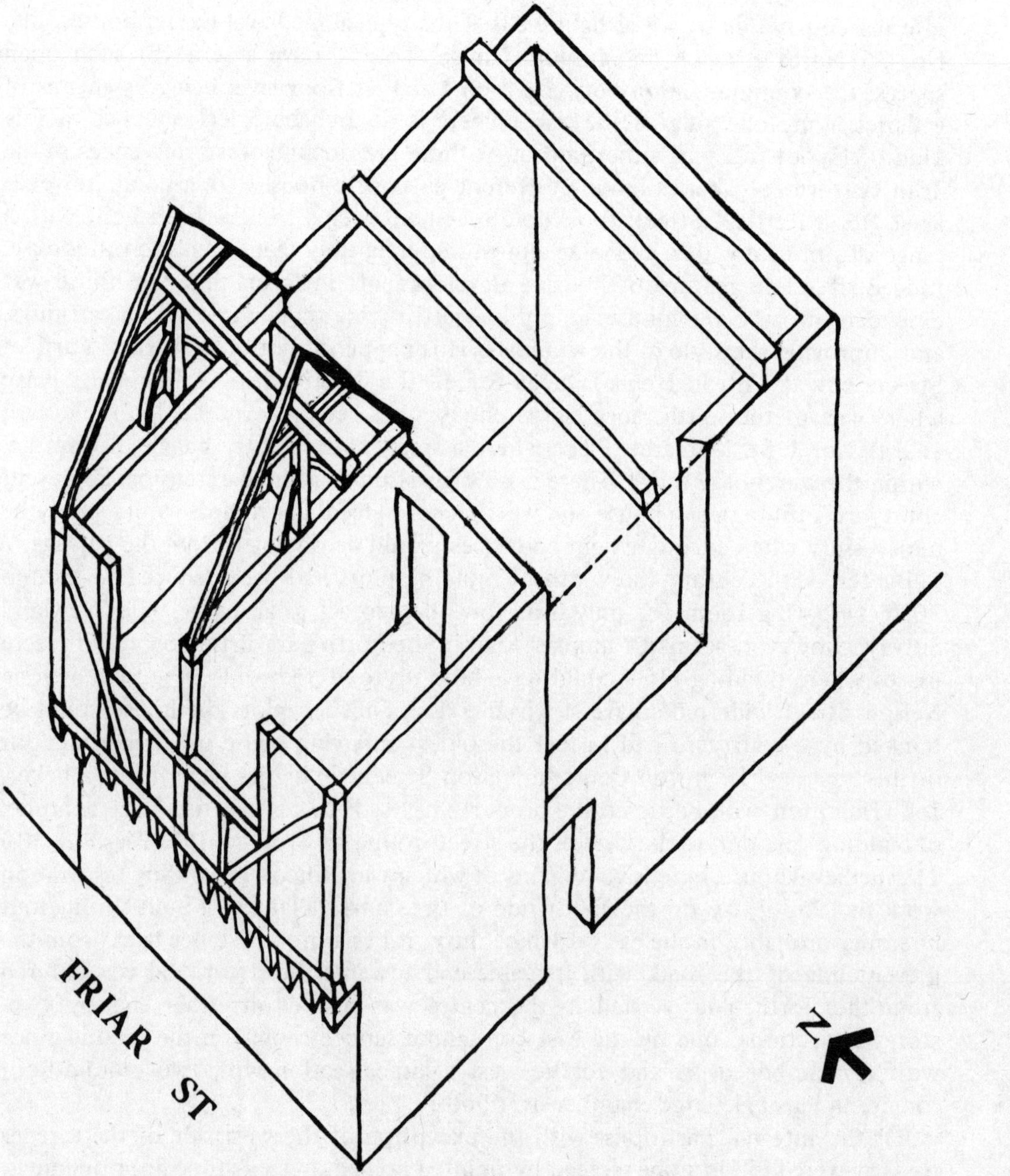

Fig 12 *No. 13 Friar Street: reconstruction of the medieval house*

slit. The hall itself was two storeys high, and, in spite of its stone chimney stack, was open to the roof, where the main truss in the centre was ornamented and the tie beam carried on long, curved arch braces to corbels about one third the way up the side walls. At the west end of the hall a pointed arched opening led to a further room which could also be entered from outside. This was probably a parlour. Beyond it, but accessible only by menas of an outside door, was another ground floor room, presumably an office or counting house adjacent to the warehouse and quay. Over both these rooms was a large solar, open to the roof, access to which was probably by means of steps along the north parlour wall. Only one room, the hall, appears to have been heated and thus was the main living room of the house. In a house of this size, however, there was likely to have been an additional fire for preparing food, housed in a separate building, although no trace of such a building survives at Hampton Court today.

Externally the elevation of the north wall was almost completely uncovered during building work in 1958 and all the remains of the medieval window and door openings were exposed. (Fig.30.) On the ground floor were three pointed, arch door openings with carved stone surrounds. These led respectively into the hall, the parlour to the west and the office or counting house beyond. The hall was lit by two tall pointed arch windows divided into four lights by mullions and transoms, running through what is now the line of the first floor. To the east were two smaller openings one above the other, and at the west end of the hall, ground and first-floor windows lighted the parlour and the solar over it. All these windows were large by medieval standards and must have been filled either with glass or a substitute to keep out the weather. Window openings appear also on the south side of the house. The two hall windows discovered on the north were matched by a pair flanking the chimney stack, and the solar was lit by a circular cusped opening. Thus there must have been at least a passageway down the south side of the building when it was new.

About a century after the house was built, it was 'modernised' by being re-roofed and given larger, flat-headed window openings. Outbuildings were added, extending the property northwards as far as St. Margaret's Lane, and enclosing the large square courtyard. A warehouse lies at right angles to the house at the west end, parallel to the river, and at the east end of the house, along the street, lies a further 15th century range which once included shops.[8] The building now closing the courtyard along St. Margaret's Lane was built in the 17th century.

As far as the plan of the dwelling house alone goes, there is no substantial difference between it and a contemporary building in the countryside. Apart from being oriented so that the narrow gable end fronts onto the street, it makes no other concession to the fact that it is a town house whose occupants are preoccupied not with agriculture, but with trade. We do not, of course, know what, if any, building lay originally between it and the present line of the road, but the east gable end is built up in stone and shows no sign of having been opened with

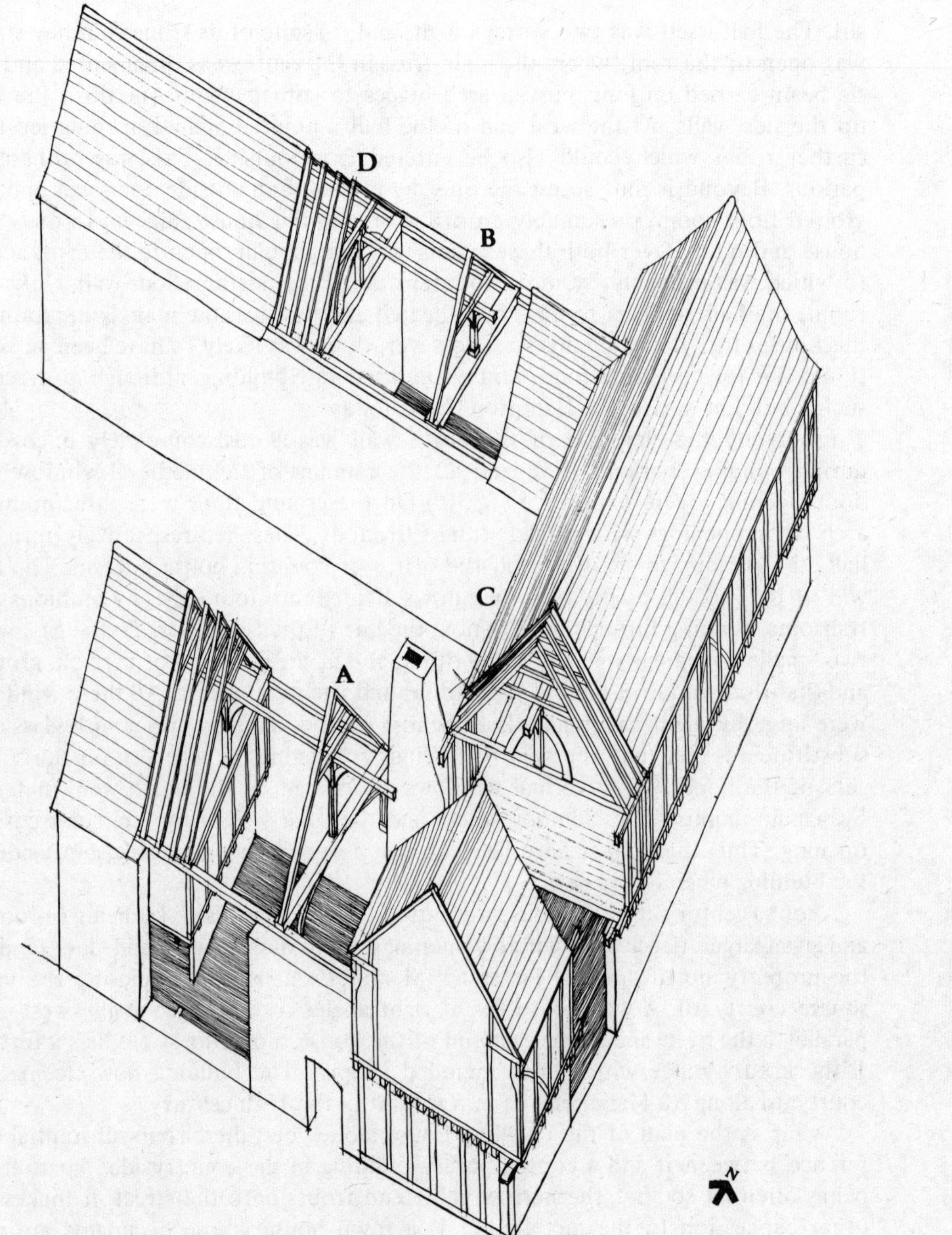

Fig 13 *Nos. 37-39 Chapel Street: reconstruction of the medieval building*

windows or doors to the street. Thus the valuable street frontage, with all its opportunities for trading, was apparently ignored.

The rest of the houses to be discussed in this section are all variants of one basic plan-type, for which the earliest known example is No. 8 Purfleet Street. They retain some of the features of Hampton Court, for instance the two-storey hall at right angles to the street, entered from the side, but they make greater use of the street frontage by building across the width of the plot on the street front, making the building L-shaped. There are both two and three cell varieties of this house-type. Some like No. 9 St. Nicholas Street and Nos. 37-9, Chapel Street, had the hall abutting directly onto the shop with a storeyed section at the lower end. Others, like Hampton Court and No. 8 Purfleet Street had, in addition, a room between hall and shop, or hall and street. At Hampton Court, it has already been noted that this contained the service rooms, as it did at Bridewell, Norwich.[9] This, however, does not appear to have been a normal arrangement. In 'right-angle' type houses elsewhere, the services and kitchen were generally located at the lower end of the hall, as for example at Fox Inn, Low Petergate, York.[10] In Lynn, the upper end of the hall in three cell houses seems more usually to have been a parlour, although surviving evidence for the use of this room is rather ambiguous. The entrance to the house generally seems to have been placed at the upper end of the hall. No. 30 King Street has a medieval door opening in this position, (Fig.27) and the fragment of the east wall of a hall behind Messrs. Scott and Sons' premises in Purfleet Street, in which the medieval stone door opening still stands, entered the end of the hall nearest the street, with a fireplace on the same wall a few feet down. This might suggest the location of service rooms at the street end of the hall, but it should also be noted that except at Hampton Court no evidence of a screens passage survives in any of the houses investigated. Moreover, the door is placed at the upper end of the hall even in the two cell variety of houses, where it cannot possibly have given onto a screens passage entrance to service rooms. Thus a definitive statement as to the use of the room at the upper end of the hall must await archaeological investigation. By the 16th century it was usual to find this room used as a parlour, with services at the lower end of the hall.[11]

No. 8 Purfleet Street (demolished 1966) (Figs.11 and 31; Plate 6) was planned with the intention of using the street frontage for trade. It was a building roughly contemporary with, or perhaps a little later than, Hampton Court, occupying a narrow site on the north side of Purfleet Street. A south-facing range of the house, of which the front wall had been rebuilt in brick in the 19th century, lay parallel to the street. It was two, and possibly at one time three, storeys high and the upper floors bridged an entry passageway which led in from the street on the east. The ground floor of this section had recently been gutted, although the old first floor level had not been changed, and the great height of the ground storey, similar to that in other old houses in Lynn, suggest its use as a shop or workroom or warehouse with direct access to the street. (No. 30 King Street, for instance, has a high ground storey, once protected by a pentice roof, completely open to the street; Fig.27). The upper storeys were timber built and almost certainly jetteyed out at the front, making one, and possibly two, spacious rooms over the shop. Unfortunately, the old roof had not been preserved, but the floor joists, running across the width of the building on large timber beams, were original.

The hall range was of the three cell variety, running at right angles to the street down the western boundary of the plot, leaving a narrow passageway on the east from which the building was entered. The hall itself, rising the whole height of the building, was separated from the street range by a two-storeyed section, the upper room of which was jetteyed into the hall. In the partition beneath the jetty, which was timber-framed, were two door openings, side by side, with pointed arch heads. These were the only evidence of original internal door-ways left in this building. Perhaps, as at Hampton Court, they opened into two service rooms but, more likely in view of the size of the room into a parlour or even a study or office. The hall was two roof bays long with a fine late 14th century carved crown post truss over the centre. (Fig.31; Plate 6B.) The wall posts, into which the straight braces of the tie beam were joined, came down well below the present first-floor level, so the existing first floor, as well as the roof ceiling, had been inserted. The hall ended on the north with an original timber partition. Beyond that the building had continued at least another 40 feet, but had been very much altered internally, so that it is not possible to know how far beyond the hall the living accommodation originally extended. By the 17th century the whole range had been taken into the dwelling house as the detailing of the window frames showed; but when first built, most of this section was most likely to have been used as a warehouse.

Surprisingly, all traces of medieval window and door openings had disappeared from the outside walls; these were of stone, rebuilt in patches in brick. The only detailing that it was possible to use for dating was in the roof, where the main truss over the hall was carved. There was no sign of a medieval chimney, the two axial stacks being late insertions, and no sign of smoke blackening either against the stone walls of the hall, or in the roof. A detached kitchen may have been used for the preparation of the household's food, the house being heated by braziers.

Hampton Court and No. 8 Purfleet Street are the only surviving complete examples of the three cell hall house, although documentary evidence in the 16th century indicates that this was a not uncommon type in the earlier period. All the remaining examples of medieval houses in Lynn had the hall abutting directly onto the street range, but probably with a room or rooms beyond the hall, although these do not always survive. There is a number of medieval examples of this type of house. One, No. 9 St. Nicholas Street, was a merchant's house; others in Chapel Street were probably occupied by industrial craftsmen; and there are several smaller versions of the same plan-type in Friar Street in South Lynn and Pilot Street near St. Nicholas Church.

No. 9 St. Nicholas Street (now demolished) (Figs.32-3; Plate 7) was an L-shaped building on the north side of the street with the front range lying across the width of the plot bridging an entry passage on the east side. The hall range lay at right angles to this down the western boundary of the plot, and was entered from the passage. At one time the river flowed close to the back boundary of the St. Nicholas Street properties and the warehouse, built onto the back of the hall range, had its gable end directly on the waterfront. (Plate 7B.) The street range, the front wall of which had been rebuilt in brick in the 19th century, was two storeys high and one room deep. On the ground floor there was, beside the entry passage, one room and a staircase dating from the 19th century, which rose to a landing between two rooms on the first floor. All the interior details of this front range were contemporary with the staircase, and although the medieval roof was still in place, (Plate 7C) none of the medieval partitions appear to have remained in the house below. The ground floor was almost certainly used as a shop. In the 16th century many houses in St. Nicholas Street, known then as Woolmarket, contained shops which were used by the overflow from the Tuesday Market during the time of the February fair.[12]

The hall abutted directly onto the front range, rose through two storeys, and was open to the roof where the crown post truss was decorated with carving probably dating from about the mid-15th century. (Fig.33; Plate 7D.) Beyond the hall the crown post roof continued for a further three bays, but, as at No. 8 Purfleet Street, it was no longer possible to tell how this end section had been used and whether it had originally been house or warehouse. Cellars had been excavated below the whole of the back range, but they had brick barrel-vaulted ceilings and were probably not contemporary with the original building. There was no sign of the medieval fireplace, the four chimneys along the west wall of the hall range being later insertions; nor was it clear where the original door and window openings had been. A later door leading into the hall at its south end probably marked the position of the medieval door, and a blocked opening further to the north was perhaps a door into the warehouse.

No. 13 Friar Street (Figs.12 and 34) is the most complete example of the smaller version of this house-type. It lies on the east side of the street and has a two-storey range parallel to the street with an entry passage under the south side. A hall, at right angles to the street range, was open from ground to roof as the large medieval window frame looking into the entry passage indicates. It was entered by a door in the angle between the ranges. The front wall of the house has now been rebuilt in brick but was originally timber and the back wall of the front range was timber-framed throughout and has survived. The hall walls also appear to be in their original state and are brick. Over both sections attic ceilings have obscured the medieval roofs and necessitated the removal of the old collars. Only one crown post survives in the north gable end of the street range but the mortices in the tops of the tie beams show where others stood and the rafters show where the old collars were halved and pegged onto them. Thus it is clear that both front and back portions of the house are of similar date. Houses which are exactly the same in plan but have retained their original timber front walls are still standing in Pilot Street. Such houses probably had only the three small rooms in medieval times, a shop on the ground floor fronting the street, a room over it called a solar and used either for storage or sleeping or both, and a two-storey hall open to the roof at the rear. Only the hall with its stone or brick side walls was heated.

Lattice House, Nos. 37-9 Chapel Street, is one of the last of Kings Lynn's complete 15th century buildings to remain standing. (Figs.13-16 and 36; Plates 8, 12, 13A.) The street range, which is two storeys high, and timber framed, extends for about 100 feet along Chapel Street, and there is reason to suppose it once was even longer. At right angles to this there exist now two short cross ranges roughly contemporary with the front, and a third lying between them, which is a 19th century insertion. Both the original back ranges were entered from the side, the one on the south (No. 37 Chapel Street) from Market Lane, and other from a passageway leading under the Chapel Street front. At the present time the property is divided into three. Two dwelling houses occupy the two original back ranges and part of the street front and a third property lies between them, consisting of one room on both floors in the two storey street range and the 19th century extension at the back.

Both of the houses had the same basic plan type as No. 9 St. Nicholas Street and No. 13 Friar Street, but have definite evidence of storeyed sections beyond the hall. No. 37 Chapel Street, on the south, has one ground floor room and two first floor rooms in the part fronting on to the street, divided on the first floor by original timber partitions. The hall, now floored in, and containing the modern stairs, abutted at right angles directly on to the front range. It rose through two storeys into the roof, with a decorated crown post truss over the centre. (Fig.14.) The storeyed section beyond the hall was jetteyed into the hall space on the first floor and although the building now ends one bay beyond the hall, it originally extended further west. The present door, opening from the south into the east end of the hall space, probably marks the position of the medieval door. A chimney in the middle of the north wall of the hall could be original; there is no sign of another position for a medieval fireplace.

No. 39 Chapel Street, the other house in the complex, has a plan exactly similar to No. 37, except that in this case the entry passage from the street halves the size of the ground floor front room. The first floor is divided by original timber partitions and the hall behind it at right angles was two storeys high with a carved roof truss. The use of the building beyond the hall is uncertain. Extensive redecoration of the house in the late 18th century has removed traces of the jetty from the back rooms into the hall space, if it existed.

Taken as a whole the group of buildings known as Lattice House poses some interesting questions about the way in which medieval property was developed in

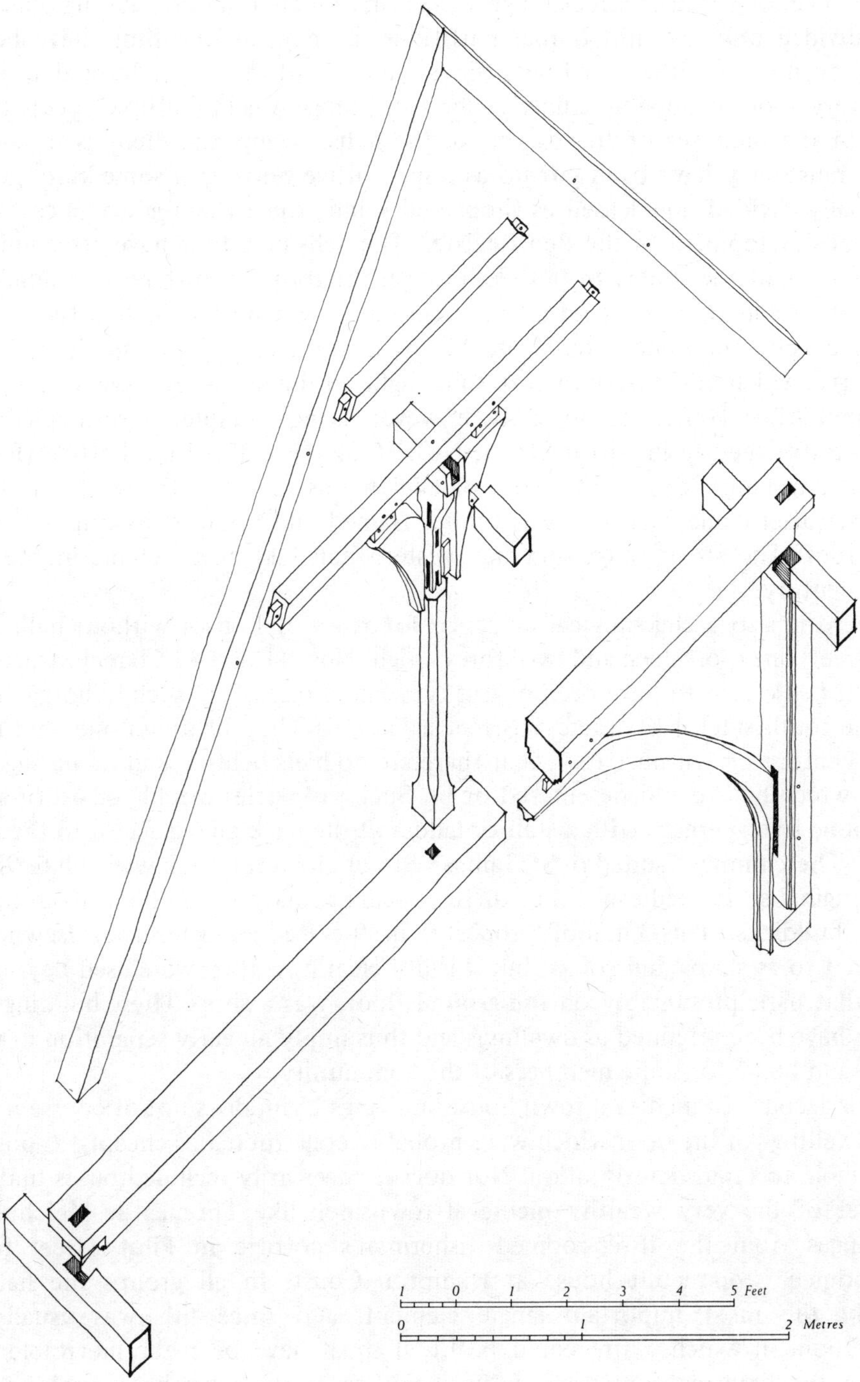

Fig 14 *Nos. 37-39 Chapel Street: roof truss in southern Hall range*

Lynn. The long timber street range was clearly erected in one building operation, and divided only by thin timber partitions. It may, at one time, have been in single occupation either as a house or warehouse, but the two halls behind suggest that very soon, if not immediately, the front range was in multiple occupation as part of the premises of the owners of the halls. It appears, then, as though the front range may have been put up as a specualtive venture of some kind, perhaps originally divided and leased as shops and solars, since there is evidence for this kind of development in the Red Register. The halls may then have been added by the tenants of the shops. In both hall ranges the roofs are different in detail from each other and from the roof in the street range, which suggests that they are not all of exactly the same date. (Plate 15.) It is unfortunate that the deeds of this property, which might have thrown some light on the question, have been lost.

The Lattice House arrangement, however, is not unique. A similar complex stood until recently in Broad Street, Nos. 30-32. (Fig.37.) Like Lattice House it had a long range, one room deep, parallel to the street, with two halls at right angles, eastern one of which was timber framed and retained its original crown-post roof. The street range and the western hall had been rebuilt in the early 17th century.

There is also archaeological evidence for rows of houses without halls lining the streets one room deep and two storeys high. Nos. 41 and 43 Chapel Street (now demolished) seem to have been of this type and a row of six such buildings stands on the south side of St. James's Street. (Plate 9.) They lie under one continuous 15th century crown post roof, and there are no halls behind, and no passageways from which halls could be entered or lit. Such properties would consist of a shop at ground level, perhaps with a stair or ladder at the back giving access to the upper floor. The chimneys added in St. James's Street along the back wall (Plate 9B) are not original so in medieval times there appears to have been no means of heating these buildings. This kind of property, in the Red Register and elsewhere, is referred to as shops and solars, but it is not clear how they were used beyond the fact that part, presumably on the ground floor, was a shop. These buildings may never have been intended as dwellings and thus imply an early separation of work-place and home for some members of the community.

This account of medieval town houses in Kings Lynn does not of course include the dwellings of the poor which were probably constructed as cheaply as possible, and liable to rapid deterioration. Nor does it necessarily include houses that were typical of the very wealthy medieval townsmen like Thomas de Melchbourne. It ranges from the three-roomed fisherman's cottage in Pilot Street to the six-roomed, stone built house at Hampton Court. In all groups the hall was clearly the most important single element, and since this was usually the only room in which a fire could be lit, it must have been the inevitable focus during the daytime for most of the activities of the household, including the preparation and eating of food. Each three-roomed house had a separate room to

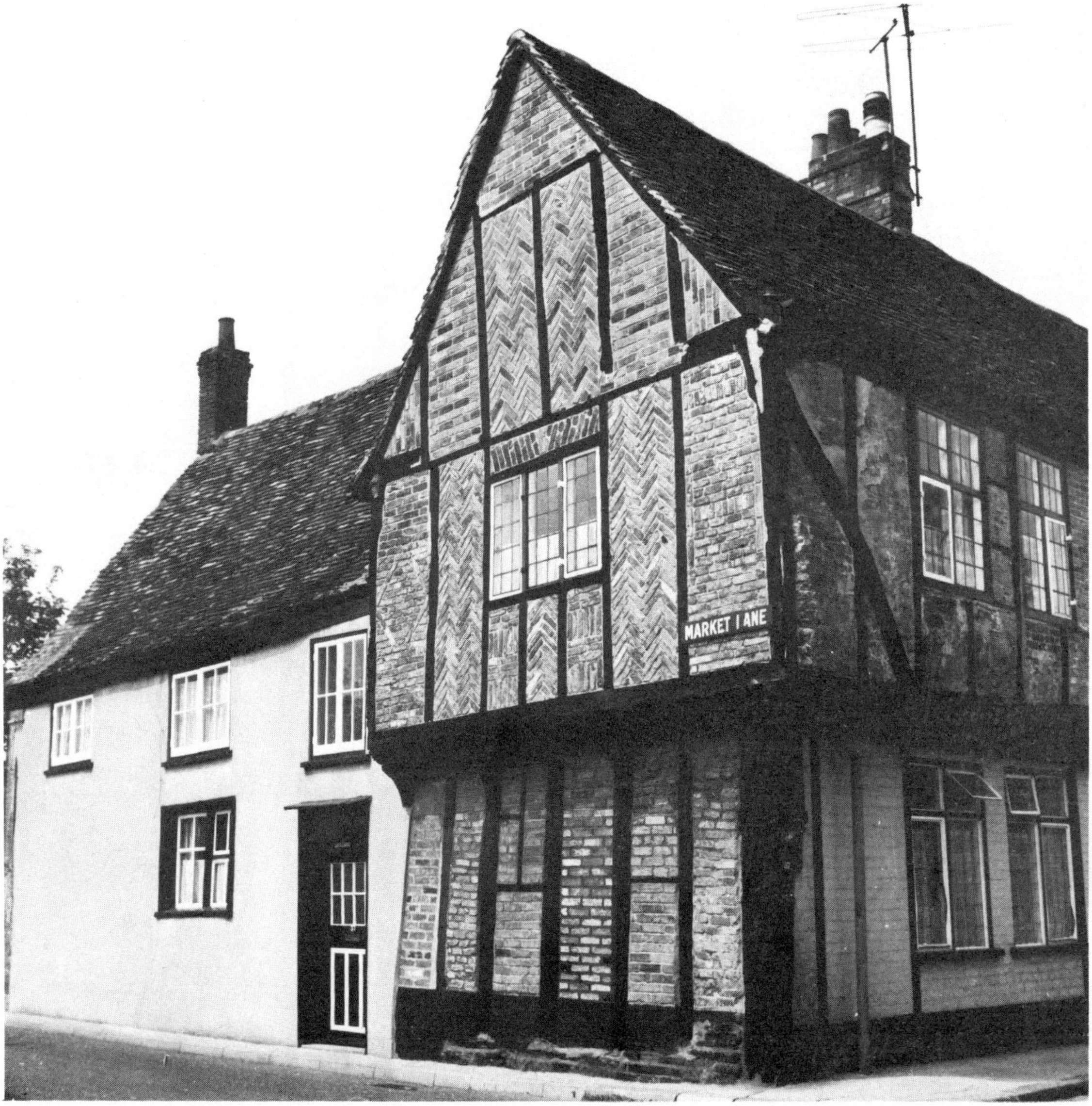

Plate 8 *Nos. 37-39 Chapel Street. No.37 (Lattice House) in foreground*

Plate 9A *Medieval shops in St. James's Street; north elevation*

Plate 9B *Medieval shops in St. James's Street; south elevation*

Plate 10 *No. 30 King Street; west elevation*

Plate 11A *No. 30 King Street; side entry passage*

Plates 11B and 11C *Details of No. 30 King Street showing mortices for pentice over shop*

Plate 12A *No. 39 Chapel Street; detail of timber frame*

Plate 12B *No. 37 Chapel Street; dragon post*

Plate 13A *Nos. 37-39 Chapel Street; timber range*

Plate 13B *Coney's House, Saturday Market*

Plate 14A *Scissor braced roof of No. 6 St. Ann Street*

Plate 14B *Roof of St. George's Gildhall, c.1410*

Plates 15A - C *Crown post details of Nos. 37-39 Chapel Street*

be used as a shop, workshop or store and another which could be used as a private bedroom by the head of the household with some first floor accommodation also used for sleeping. Of the houses surveyed only Hampton Court and No. 8 Purfleet Street go beyond this basic plan type. One important provision made in Hampton Court was the service rooms for the preparation and storage of food and drink; another was the provision of extra accommodation for apprentices or other members of the household in upper room sin the front of the house, and in addition there was a further first floor room at the rear allowing some division of daytime functions of the house, perhaps acting as a withdrawing room for the women of the household. But bearing in mind that there was no separation between house and workplace, accommodation was very limited, even in the larger houses, and privacy and comfort difficult to achieve.

Medieval Building Construction

Neither building stone nor timber is particularly plentiful in the immediate vicinity of Kings Lynn yet both were obtainable at not too great a distance. Oak and elm were purchased in the early 16th century at Snettisham, Middleton and Brandon and such woods are indigenous to the higher sandy soils of west Norfolk if not to the fenland. In addition Lynn merchants dealt in imported timber and could obtain a variety of soft woods in the Baltic. These too were used in medieval house construction for roofs and floors although probably rarely for a timber framed wall. The roof of No. 8 Purfleet Street, for example, was made throughout with fir, and there are references in a number of Chamberlain's Accounts in the 15th century the purchase of fir for building work.[13]

Stone came by river from Northamptonshire. The limestones of the Peterborough region were suitable for dressing and carving and were used for door and window mouldings. Domestic buildings in Lynn were not usually faced completely in ashlar or constructed with limestone. Where stone was used for walling it was usually a rubble mixture using flints and other rounded stones that appear to have been taken from the river bed and may perhaps have arrived in Lynn as ballast. This was then plaster-rendered to keep out the weather.

Brick was not unknown in medieval Lynn but was not widely used until the 15th century. The earliest example so far found in domestic work is the vault of the undercroft at Clifton House in Queen Street built in the 14th century using a large yellowish-pinkish brick, probably imported from Holland. (Plate 21B). Lynn, however, lies on the edge of a region running south-west across the fens within which clays could be dug which were especially suitable for brick making. By the 16th century there were already numerous brick fields in the marshland around Lynn and although the Chamberlains Accounts before 1500 indicate that much of the work repairing the town's tenements was done by carpenters, there are increasing references to the use of bricks and tiles in the second half of the 15th century. By that time most public buildings were using brick in preference

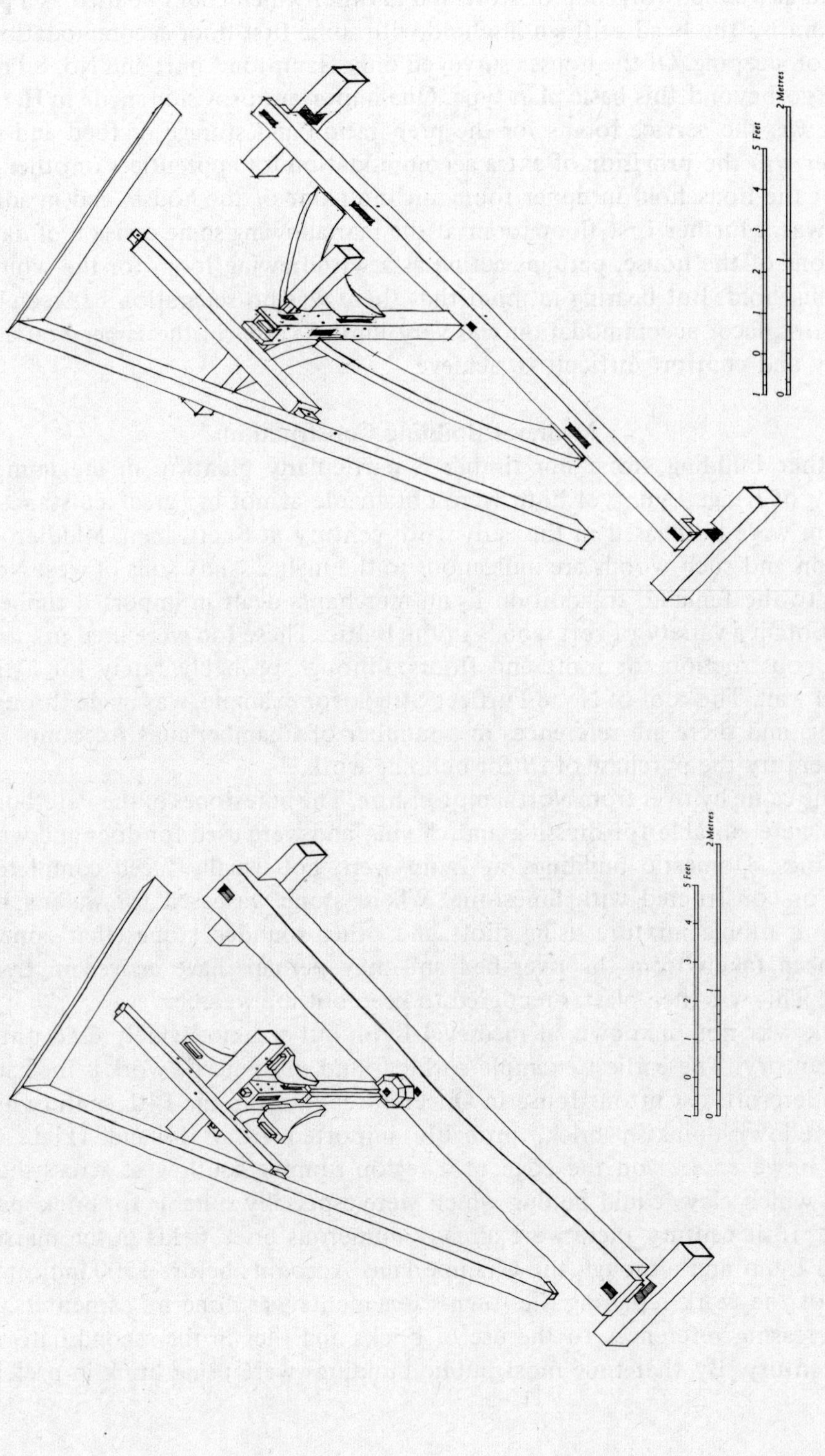

Fig 15 Nos. 37-39 Chapel Street: roof trusses in northern Hall range

to stone. Both the Trinity Gildhall in the Saturday Market and St. George's Gildhall in King Street were built in brick throughout in the first three decades of the 15th century and all the surviving parts of monastic buildings in Lynn are of brick with ashlar details, the only exception being St. Margaret's church. There are also late medieval examples of brick warehouses, the north range of the Hanseatic warehouses, for example, of *c.* 1474 and the Hampton Court warehouse of the late 15th century. It is thus quite possible that brick was seriously competing with timber in domestic work before the 16th century. It is likely that brick replaced timber construction in all towns as soon as it was economically feasible to use it, largely because of the fear of uncontrollable fires in the built-up area. Thus if brick was readily available in 15th century Lynn it was probably used in domestic work.

It is nevertheless unusual in Lynn to find a house constructed throughout in brick or stone before the late 16th century. Hampton Court is the exception. All the main structural parts of the building and all the internal partitions with the exception of the hall screen were built in rubble, with door and window openings picked out in ashlar. It was presumably the cost of such buildings that limited their number, although Hampton Court was not alone. Other stone buildings which may only survive in parts or be built into later structures are mentioned in the Red Register, although the fact that they are singled out for mention suggests they were unusual.

Most Lynn houses were of mixed construction, being built partly of stone and brick rubble and partly timber framed. Timber was generally used in the construction of the street range of the building, and for internal partitions. There are no medieval halls surviving in Lynn built of timber. The hall part of the house, where the main hearth of the household was situated was always walled in rubble or brick. Sometimes, as at No. 30 King Street, the stone side wall of the hall was continued through to the street, at any rate on the ground storey, (Plate 11B) or, as at No. 8 Purfleet Street, it continued the full height of the building on the opposite side to the entry passage making a rigid and fireproof division between two properties.

Probably the oldest timber framed fore range to survive in the town is that of Nos. 30 and 32 King Street (Figs. 27 and 35; Plate 10). This range runs parallel to the street and is now divided into two houses by the insertion of a brick chimney stack on the central axis. Seen from the front, the spacing of the timber studding seems to indicate that the building was always divided across the centre by a thin brick or rubble partition. The street range is two storeys high roofed parallel to the street with the gable ends jetteyed at first floor level across entry passages running down each side. The front wall onto King Street is not jetteyed at first floor level and the vertical studding, each piece of which is of uniform size and thickness, is staggered above and below the first floor sill. On the first floor the vertical studs are placed at 5 feet 6 inch intervals and the main structural uprights held with straight diagonal braces. The ground floor is unusually high and was open at the front between the main uprights on which there are still traces of a flat chamber running also across the underside of the first floor sill. Each vertical stud has the remains of a mortice about two thirds the way up into which brackets were slotted to take some kind of canopy or pentice. (Plate 11B.) This building is unusual in Lynn in that it has no front jetty, the storey heights are very tall, the timbers are of medium scantling but widely spaced and the braces are straight, not curved. The only dating evidence is the pointed arch 13th century hall doorway in the rear of No. 30 (Plate 11A) since the roof has long since been renewed.

The street range of Nos. 37-9 Chapel Street is a good example of 15th century timber framing, since, with the exception of the rebuilt front wall to the ground storey, it survives almost unaltered. (Figs.13 and 16; Plates 12, 13A.) As it stands the building is just over 100 feet long running parallel to the street, although it may have extended further northwards, and two storeys high. The first floor was jetteyed out on the east (Chapel Street) side and on the south into Market Lane, the floor joists being carried out about the usual 18 inches over the ground floor walls. Laid along the upper side of the joist ends was the sill into which the studs of the first floor are joined and the weight of this is transferred at intervals onto the ground floor wall by menas of curved braces beneath the jetteyed timbers. (Plate 12A.) That this ground wall was once timber is shown by the survival of two of its original vertical members flanking the door into the courtyard. The back wall of the range is built in timber throughout and is not jetteyed on the first floor. Instead, a wide sill is used into which both the ground and first floor studs can be jointed vertically above each other and the sill itself is joined at intervals into timbers which run the full height of the building to improve the rigidity of the construction.

On both front and back walls the vertical studs are placed about three feet apart, and no variation in size was made for those which at approximately nine feet intervals, and at first floor level, were framed with the roof trusses to tie the front and rear walls together. These can be identified by the straight diagonal braces which support them in an upright position, and by their jowelled tops cut with tenons to join into a lengthwise wall plate and a tie beam at right angles to it. Where this building was divided internally timber studding was used similar to that on the external walls, joined into roof truss tie beams and the tops of the joists of the floor below. All the panels between the studs, both inside and outside are now filled with brick although originally they were probably filled with wattle and daub. Window openings in the frame were made by joining in horizontal members between the studs, and cutting slots in the window head and near the top end of the jambs into which shaped pieces of wood were fitted to give a four-centred arched head. Probably also a rebate was cut into which a board or a wooden shutter could be fitted.

No timber framed buildings over two storeys high survive in Lynn although the print of Coney's house on the corner of the Saturday Market (Plate 13B) shows a three storey timber building and there may have been others. In 1332, Richard of Brinton purchased a tenement with two solars on the front, one above the other.[14] It would present no particular difficulty to increase the height of timber buildings if a jetty was built at every floor level so that each storey was framed independently of the one below. If, on the other hand, as on the back wall of Lattice House and No. 13 Friar Street, it was intended to build the walls in one vertical plane, large timber uprights would have to be inserted at intervals running the full height of the building to give the structure stability. This would tend to increase the costs of construction considerably.

Roof construction was the same over both the timber and the stone-walled parts of the house. (Fig.17.) The technique of roof building was improved, both from a structural and aesthetic viewpoint during the Middle Ages.[15] Probably the earliest, but at any rate the most primitive, kind of roof construction found in Lynn was a 'scissor-braced' roof in St. Ann's Street. (Plate 14A.) Here all the timbers above the wallplate were the same scantling and each pair of rafters was braced with a collar and diagonal ties crossing just above it. The rafters were halved and pegged at the top and their feet were pegged onto the wallplate. Since this building had stone walls main purpose of the tie beam was probably to provide a holding for the studs of the timber partition walls beneath. Mortice and tenon joints were not used and timbers were halved and pegged together. Beyond the fact that there was a good deal of timber wastage, the main structural defect in the St. Anne's Street roof was the lack of any kind of lengthwise support beyond that provided by the roof covering. The heights of the collars varied to such a degree that a collar purlin could never have been inserted and the tendency of the roof has been to fall sideways.

A similar kind of roof, but a more refined version of it, existed in the front range of No. 9 St. Nicholas Street (now demolished). (Plate 7C.) Here the scantling of the timbers had been considerably reduced and the joints, wherever possible, were mortice and tenon. Finally the Gildhall of St. George and the Holy Trinity Gildhall, both constructed in the first quarter of the 15th century, had scissor braced roofs, but perhaps this form of roof was chosen at this late period for its aesthetic rather than its structural qualities. Unbroken by tie beams and crown posts the roof of the Gildhall of St. George looks like a barrel vault over the main hall. (Plate 14B.) A similar effect in the Trinity Gildhall was reduced by the tie beams, but with the undersides of the rafters now plastered the barrel shape of the ceiling is emphasised.

Lengthwise strengthening of later roof structures was provided by a collar purlin supported at intervals by a crown post standing on a tie beam.[16] The crown post was held upright by two or four braces, initially perhaps springing upwards, but in the Hanseatic warehouse of 1474 the crown post braces spring up to the collar purlin, and those at right angles run down to join into the tie beam.

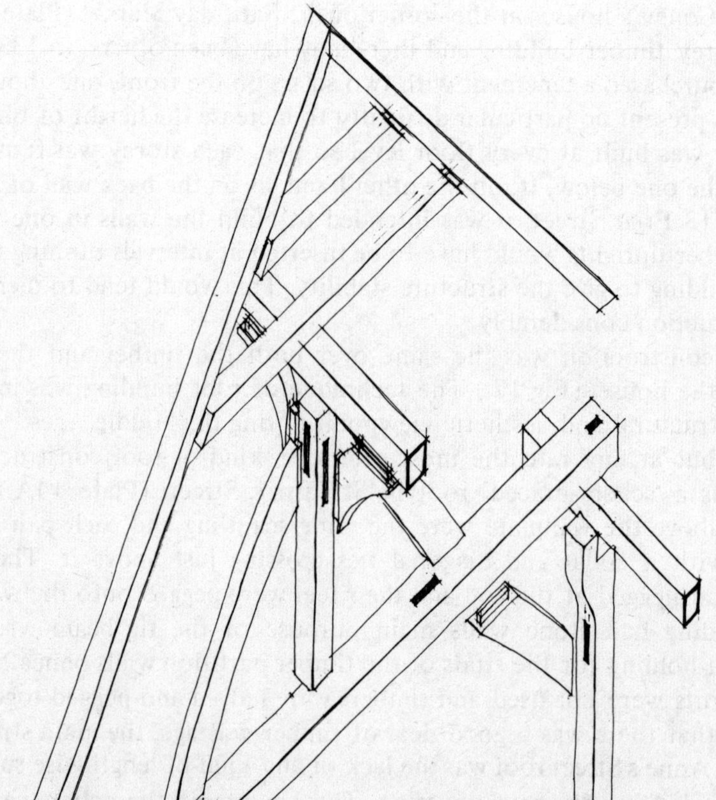

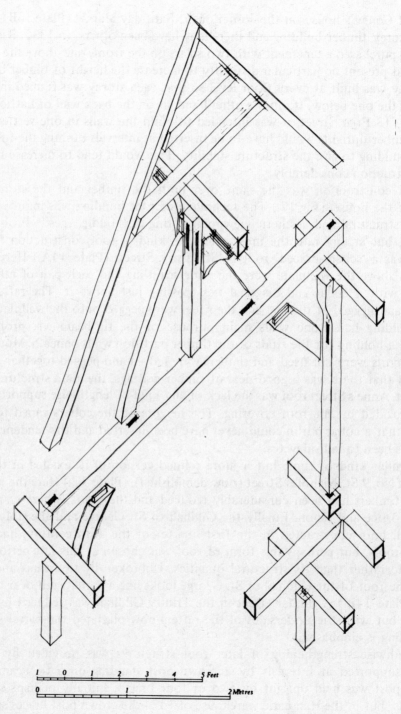

Fig 16 *Nos. 37-39 Chapel Street: roof truss and timber framing in eastern range*

A hole was bored through each collar and collar purlin beneath and a long wooden dowel driven through both to prevent movement. Where the collar purlin had to be jointed, a scarf joint usually fell over one of the crown post braces.

At first the collar purlin was inserted into the scissor-braced roof type without any reduction of the original truss members. Such a roof, with scissor-bracing, collars, collar purlin, and crown post trusses with tie beams, existed over the hall range of No. 8 Purfleet Street (Fig.31; Plate 6B) and the parallel rafters of the crown post truss over the hall was a further variant not found elsewhere in Lynn. By the time Lattice House came to be built, however, the diagonal scissor bracing had disappeared, and the collars to each pair of rafters are pegged onto the collar purlin. Crown post trusses with tie beams onto which the feet of the rafters are pegged occur at regular intervals and the tie beams are arch-braced onto the vertical studs in the wall below. Where a crown post truss occurs in the stone walled section, the arch-brace is attached at the foot into a timber wall post, joined at the top into the tie beam. (Fig.14.) The only further refinement to this kind of roof was to use iron nails instead of wooden dowels and this was attempted in No. 3 King Street where one crown post truss, the one over the hall, was nailed together. (Fig.17; Plate 20B.) This, of course, would be possible only where fir, not oak, had been used in the construction of the roof.

A late medieval roof-type in Kings Lynn is a trussed roof with side purlins, arch braced collars and wind bracing. (Fig.17.) The best surviving example of this kind of roof is found in all four ranges of Thoresby College, dating from around 1510, (Plates 16-17) but what was clearly an open hall roof in No. 9 King Street was constructed in this way, (Plate 18); as was the roof over the street range of Nos. 21-23 Broad Street (Fig.37), now demolished. Typical of these roofs are the occurrence of principal rafters at intervals joined at the top without a ridge piece and, where intended to be exposed from below, they are not tied at the foot but only pegged on to the wallplate. One side purlin, and occasionally two, on each side are either morticed and tenoned into the principal rafters or else are halved into the front of the principals and clasped by the collar. (Plate 17.) Only the Thoresby College roof has windbraces, and collars arch braced onto the principals. The common rafters lie on the backs of the side purlins, are morticed and tenoned into each other at the top and pegged onto the wallplate at the foot. Where intended to be exposed this kind of roof was ornamented with runs of moulding on the edge of the principal members. (Plate 9.)

As far as we know medieval houses were planned, and their structures devised, for practical rather than aesthetic reasons. Nevertheless, certain parts of the structure were treated decoratively if exposed to view, and a good deal of scope was offered by the custom of enriching the roof space by decorating the timbers over the hall. This section of the roof, in the absence of a chimney, would be left open for smoke from an open hearth to escape. In medieval Lynn a crown post truss was usually needed to break the span of the collar purlin across the hall.

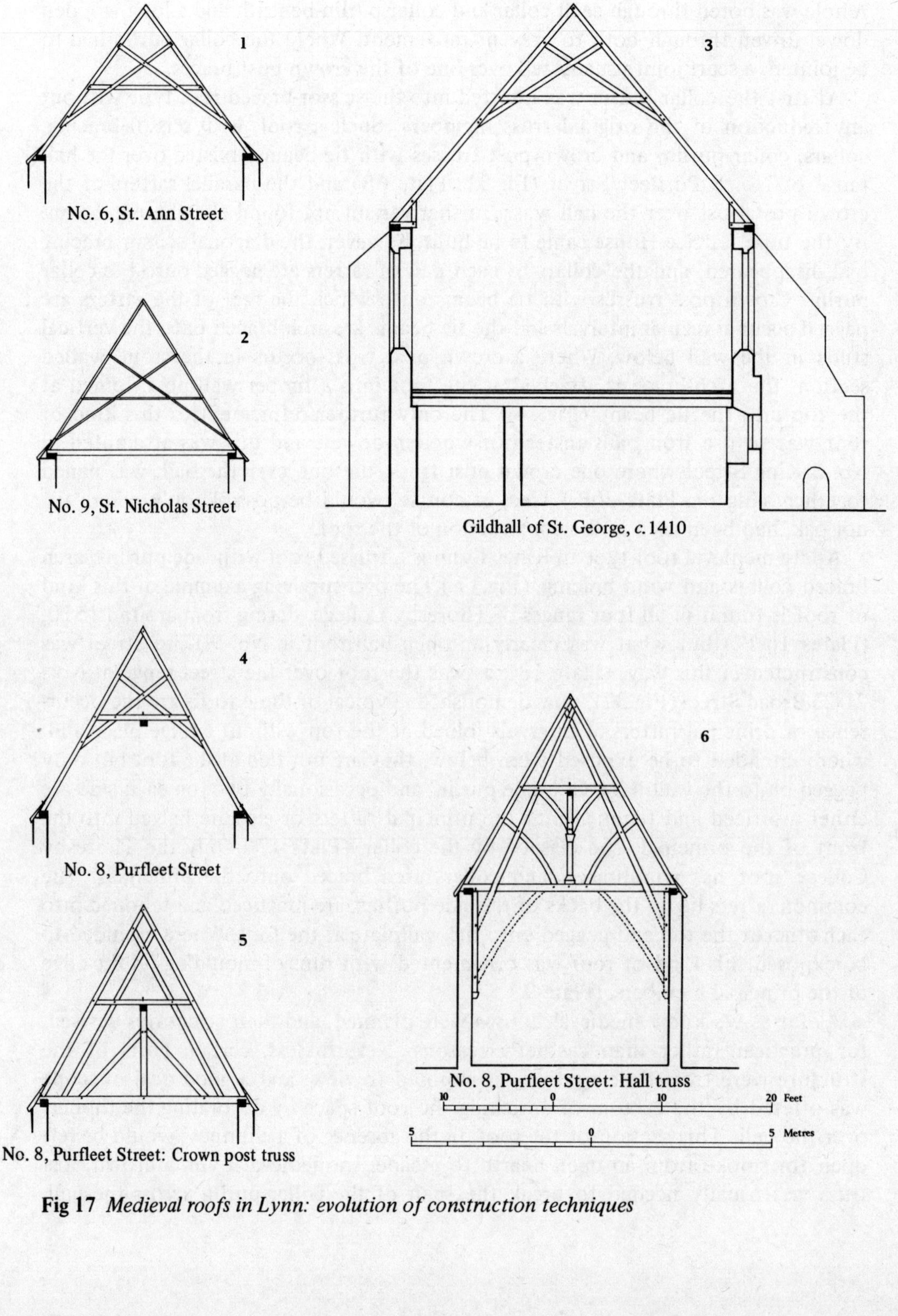

Fig 17 *Medieval roofs in Lynn: evolution of construction techniques*

7

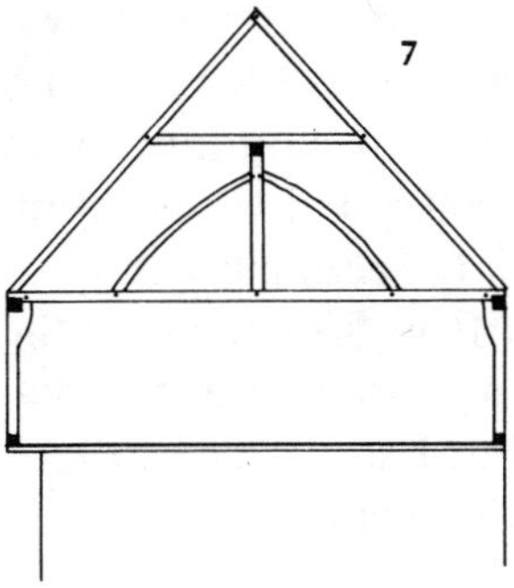

Hanseatic steel yard, South warehouse range, *c.*1474

8

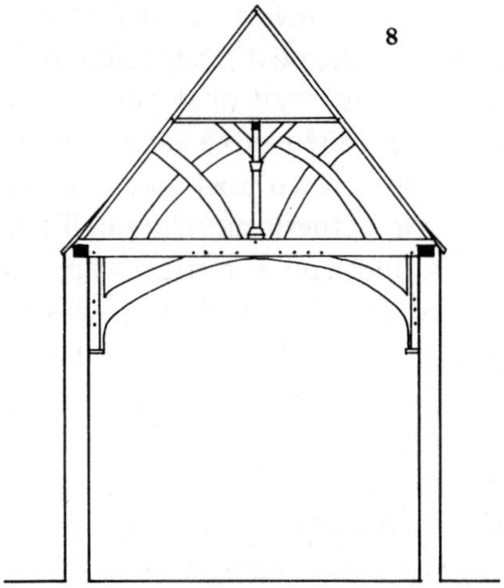

No. 3, King Street: Hall truss

9

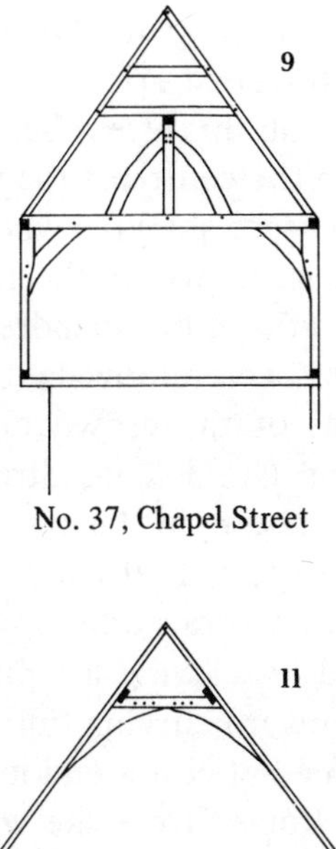

No. 37, Chapel Street

10

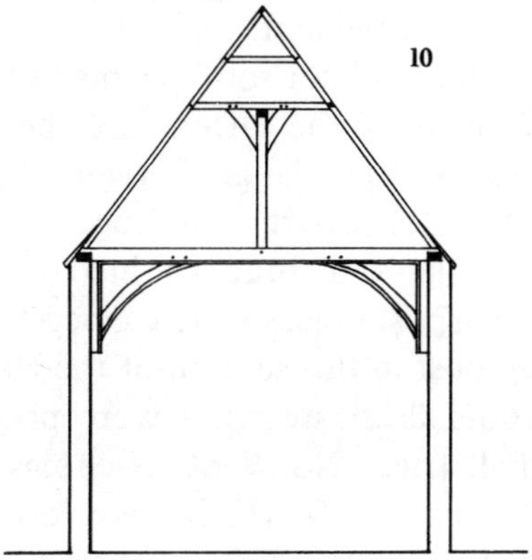

No. 37, Chapel Street

11

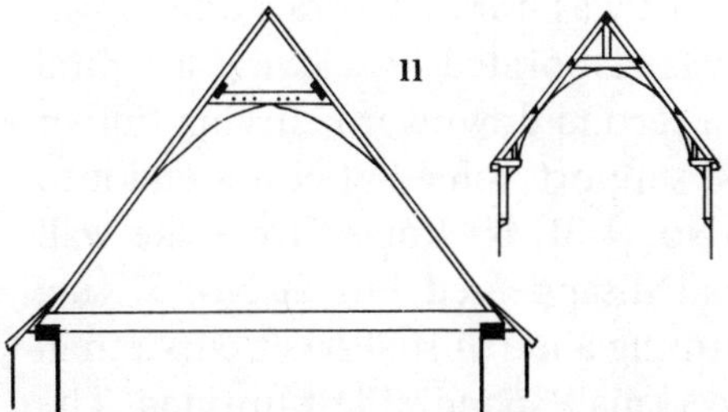

Thoresby College, *c.*1510

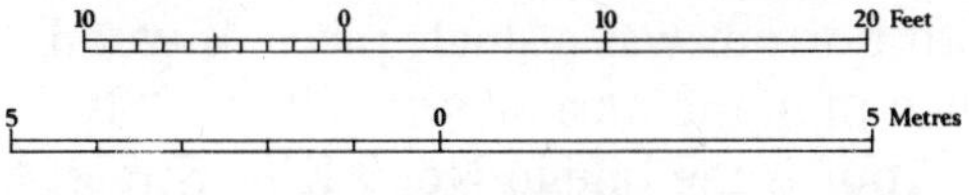

12

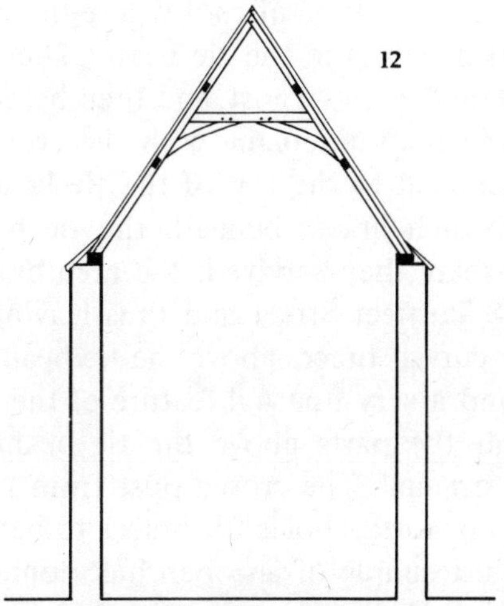

No. 9, King Street: Hall truss

This was almost always treated decoratively; the cap and the base of the crown post were carved, the post itself made polygonal, the underside of the tie beam and the arch braces and wall post beneath the tie were given runs of moulding, or at least a flat chamfered edge; and the space between the collar and tie beam on either side of the crown post was filled with curved or flat intersecting braces.

Probably the earliest surviving hall truss was in No. 8 Purfleet Street, where the crown posts and collar purlin were used in conjunction with scissor-bracing. (Fig.31; Plate 6B.) The hall truss was not scissor-braced but had parallel rafters, the inner pair of which were halved into the side of the tie beam, continuing to join with the wall post below. A straight brace on each side joined the outer rafters below the collar to the top of the tie beam. The crown post was octagonal with moulded capital and base and the braces holding it in place sprang upwards above the capital to the collar and collar purlin. The underneath edges of the tie beam had been given a flat chamfer but otherwise the wood was left plain.

In Hampton Court a very similar kind of roof may have existed over the hall although only fragments of it now remain. (Fig.30.) The objective in Purfleet Street as well as in later roofs seems to have been to create a traceried effect in the triangle formed by the rafters and the tie beam and to continue this effect below the tie beam in the triangle between braces and wall post. In the centre of the tie beam at Hampton Court mouldings still exist carved on the surface showing where the tops of the arch braces joined in, and slots survive to show where the flat timber crown post braces were carried through the tie beam to fill in the spandrels. The crown post in this section of the Hampton Court roof has been removed.

Two roofs illustrate what were probably the final stages of the crown post type of hall truss. No. 9 St. Nicholas Street (Plate 7D) and No. 3 King Street (Plate 20A) had roofs which were very similar, although the design, in the case of No. 3 King Street, was carried out on a larger scale. Both were inserted into a collar and collar purlin type of roof where the crown post was normally braced by down curving timbers onto the tie beam. The truss was elaborated by carving a capital and foot on the crown post, and then by adding a second downward curving timber to cross in the same plane with the crown post support, joined at either end into the rafters and to the top of the tie beam. In No. 9 St. Nicholas Street the wall post and arch braces beneath the tie beam had disappeared but at No. 3 King Street, where they survived, the arch braces forming a much shallower curve than at No. 8 Purfleet Street and thus leaving only a small spandrel left unfilled. The crossing curved braces above the tie beam were very smoothly cut, as though with a saw, and a very unusual feature of the truss in No. 3 King Street was the way in which all the parts above the tie beams had been joined with nails. This was entirely original. The crown post from top to bottom was a single piece of wood and had no mortice holes for braces to be joined in in the normal way. (Plate 20B.)

A final example of an open hall domestic roof is the one in No. 9 King Street. (Plate 18.) The roof was a trussed one with principal rafters and side purlins,

(Fig.17), although it may have been built without tie beams as was the case in the front range of Nos. 22 and 23 Broad Street. The three bays of the roof that were open had runs of bead moulding along the edges of the principals and the side purlins, and the undersides of the collars were chamfered. This is the only domestic hall roof of its kind remaining in Lynn and it probably dates from the end of the 15th century.

Door and window openings in stone or brick walls were usually of dressed stone and ornamented with a runs of moulding. Probably the shapes of door and window heads followed architectural fashion by changing from pointed to four-centred in the 15th century. A very good example of a stone pointed arch window with a cusped head still survives in No. 9 King Street. (Plate 19A.) Stone pointed arch doorways are found in several places in Lynn, usually marking the hall entrance in the rear range of the house (Plate 11B), although there must also in places have been doorways closing off the entry passage down the side of the house. Nearly all of these have disappeared in later rebuildings of the front of the house, but two of the old timber doors have survived, both elaborately carved, in St. Nicholas Street and Nelson Street. (Plate 19B.) Stone windows with four-centred arch heads seem usually to have been made in groups of two or three divided by mullions, and occasionally, as in a recently demolished building in Chapel Street, with cusped heads.

Doorways and windows in timber buildings may, in many cases, have been left the simple rectangular shape which would have emerged naturally from the vertical and horizontal members of the timber frame. In No. 8 Purfleet Street, however, the doors in the screens passage were given pointed heads by cutting slots in the head and jambs of the doorway and joining in shaped wooden spandrels, (Fig.31) and a window in No. 11 St. Nicholas Street was given an arched window head in the same way. The windows that survive in the timber framed upper storey of Lattice House, however, were left rectangular with a rebated inner edge to take a shutter.

Doorways, window openings and hall roofs were the principal elements in the house to be treated decoratively. Internally there may have been either painted plaster walls or painted cloths or tapestries to give the interior colour and protection from draught. Floors also, although normally of packed earth, may in the larger houses have been laid out with tiles. A very fine medieval tiled floor has been partially uncovered in Clifton House. It was laid with locally-made brown tiles patterned with cream slip infil and probably dates from the first half of the 14th century. (Plate 21A.) Such tiles were made at Bawsey until 1340. The furnishing of medieval houses can only be a matter of conjecture, but it seems certain that all the rooms in the house were used for a variety of daytime functions as well as bedrooms. Thus one would expect to find miscellaneous collections of furniture indication the hall as the main living room with long tables, stools and cooking implements, and the other room furnished with beds as well as stools and tables for daytime use.[17]

Notes to Chapter III

1 W.A. Pantin, 'Medieval English Town House Plans', *Med. Arch.* VI-VII, (1962-3), 202-239, *passim.*

2 Margaret Wood, *The English Medieval House* (1965) Pantin, 'Medieval Town Houses', p.217-19, *Guide to Strangers Hall Museum,* (Norwich Museums Committee 1956)*passim*

3 Pantin, 'Medieval Town Houses', 228-33.

4 See below p.145-6.

5 D. Portman, *Exeter Houses 1400-1700,* p.85, Fig. XII

6 e.g. Appendix II, Inventory of Thomas Revett.

7 Pantin, 'Medieval Town House', 233-35.

8 The arms of the Amfles are carved in the spandrel of the entry arch. William Amfles, baker, and others conveyed the property to Richard Amfles in 1482. K.L.M./Charters, 290.

9 Pantin, 'Medieval Town Houses', 236-7.

10 Ibid, p.230.

11 See below p.85-8.

12 References to rents collected from these occur in the Mart Accounts, K.L.M/Dd, 1609-1690.

13 e.g. 13 fir spars purchased to make a pentice 1457. K.L.M. Ea53.

14 *Red Register* I, 88.

15 J.T. Smith, 'Medieval Roofs: a Classification', *Archaeological Jnl.,* CXV (1958) *passim.*

16 J.M. Fletcher and P.S. Spokes, 'The Origin and Development of Crown Post Roofs', *Med. Arch.,* VIII, (1964) 152-83.

17 Lynn houses were probably furnished in a similar way to Colchester ones, for which inventories exist in the late 13th century. G.H. Martin, *The Story of Colchester,* (1959), 27.

IV

Dwelling Houses, 1500-1700

IN THE COURSE of the 16th century living standards in certain parts of England began to rise markedly, particularly among the middle orders of society, merchants, gentry and yeoman farmers. These were the people who had benefitted both from the rising tide of economic prosperity in the country as a whole, and in particular from the redistribution of wealth following the mid-century inflation. The visible signs of their increasing affluence were widely noted by contemporaries like Leland and William Harrison who saw the countryside sprinkled with newly-built or newly-modernised houses, stoutly built in brick or stone in place of the older less convenient medieval dwelling.[1] Archaeological evidence for this 'housing revolution' has been found in farmhouses and villages throughout the country; but the towns too, particularly the east coast ports, whose merchants participated in the expanding trade with the Low Countries and the Baltic, were also largely rebuilt in the late 16th and early 17th centuries.[2] Norwich, Hull and Yarmouth, for example, are all ports where evidence of this rebuilding has been found.

In Kings Lynn a major rebuilding of medieval town houses was taking place from around 1560. This coincided with the expansion of the town's trade both overseas and along the coast. Lynn merchants, after a serious set-back in the late 15th century as first wool and then cloth exports found other routes to continental markets, were, by 1550, beginning to find new methods of exploiting their strategic position at the mouth of one of the most extensive systems of inland waterways in the country. In 1722 Defoe could still write of the Ouse and its tributaries that it 'supplies about six counties wholly and three counties in part with their goods, especially wine and coals'[3] and an unknown author quoted in Badeslade noted that Kings Lynn stands 'at the gate thereof as though it were the Turnkey of it'.[4]

From the mid 16th century, much of the new wealth earned by trade, was invested in building both public and private, domestic and commercial. The evidence for this is mainly archaeological, although there are also two major documentary sources – the town Council minutes which record the growing interest of the governing body in the improvement of the town's buildings; and the increasing volume of Probate Records particularly wills and inventories. These documents have been used extensively to supplement archaeological material in the following analysis.

Modernisation or rebuilding of dwelling houses in this period was carried out by many people in Lynn, from merchants, whose building activities were often fairly extensive, to small shopkeepers and craftsmen whose improvements were mostly limited to the insertion of a brick chimney and window glass. Behind all the rebuilding programmes was the desire for greater comfort and greater privacy. The provision of more numerous separate rooms, and warmth throughout the house – not just in the hall – were the major improvements of this time and both were made possible by the installation of brick chimney-stacks. Such chimneys had two effects: first, they enabled the hall, and any other rooms formerly heated by open hearths, to be floored in and the roof space ceiled, thus making room for extra accommodation on the upper floors. Secondly, it became possible to heat rooms in all parts of the house, and not just on the ground floor, giving rise to a multiplication of rooms with special functions. When, as had often been the case, only one room, the hall, was heated, it had to combine the function of kitchen, dining room, living room, bedroom and even counting house or business office. When it became possible to heat more of the house satisfactorily other rooms came into use as living rooms. There was thus an increase in the number of special purpose rooms like kitchens, dining rooms, and studies, as well as a multiplication of general living rooms like parlours.

It is clear, though, from those buildings that remain, that in a great many cases in this period improved living accommodation was obtained, not by complete rebuilding, or by the introduction of entirely new features into the design of houses, but by the alteration and adaptation of already existing buildings by the use of elements, like chimneys and window glass, already in use in the better medieval dwellings. Many 16th and 17th century house plans in Lynn are clearly derived from medieval plan-types, and cannot be understood without reference to the medieval houses around whose walls, floors and partitions the alterations took place. A few of the surviving new houses of the period were strongly influenced by medieval precedent in the disposition of their main rooms. The mid-17th century builders of No. 29 Queen Street, for example, still employed an L-shaped plan with a hall, rising through two storeys, situated in a back range at right angles to the street, as at Hampton Court. (Figs.22 and 40.)

There were a few 17th century buildings in Lynn in which a new approach was made to the planning of large town houses. Perhaps because Lynn in the 16th and 17th centuries inherited so many fine medieval houses, or perhaps because there was after all not sufficient wealth to rebuild them completely, the practice, by then fairly common in other towns, of placing all the living accommodation in ranges running parallel to the street across the width of the plot was adopted slowly, and there are only a few examples of this plan-type in Lynn. However, both single-pile (one range) and double-pile (two ranges parallel under one roof) houses were built in the 17th century, for example at Greenland Fishery House in Bridge Street (1605), (Figs.23 and 41) St. Nicholas House in St. Nicholas Street (1645). (Figs.38-9.)

A further new house-type to emerge during the 17th century was the two-storey, two-roomed cottage. These were built for labourers and the growing numbers who, in this period, were finding employment away from their homes. No comparable plan-type exists for the medieval period, and the 17th century examples suggest a rising standard of life for this class at this time. There are good examples at Nos. 30-32 Bridge Street. (Fig.24; Plate 26A.)

There were, then, three main house-types developing in Lynn from 1560-1700. First, there were those houses which were rebuilt and incorporated an earlier medieval dwelling. The sizes of houses in this group, which were invariably L-shaped in plan, varied from those with two small ground floor rooms, to those like No. 29 Queen Street where the rooms were not only more numerous but of a much greater size. They form by far the largest group of houses for which documentary and archaeological evidence survives. A second, smaller, group comprised those new houses in which the range at right-angles to the street had disappeared and living accommodation had been compressed onto the street frontage of the plot. A third group, the cottages, reflects a similar tendency among the smallest dwellings to abandon the old arrangement of the house at right-angles to the street and to build across the plot's width. Thus, in both these latter groups is to be found a new approach to the design of town houses; they are the immediate forerunners of the 18th century double-pile terrace house.

Houses Incorporating Medieval Work
The L-Shaped House 1560-1700

The medieval house in Lynn was usually L-shaped in plan. One range lay across the width of the plot and was roofed parallel to the street; a second range lay behind, at right angles; and in order to secure access to the back part of the house from the street a passageway was left running under the front range and down one side of the plot. In the back range of the building was the hall and other rooms in domestic use; in the front range there was usually a shop.[5] This basic plan-type was shared by both the wealthy and the less wealthy during the Middle Ages; the difference between the house of a great overseas merchant and a fisherman's cottage was one of scale rather than a fundamental difference in planning. Surviving remains of medieval houses in Lynn indicate that L-shaped houses almost invariably incorporated shops. There may well have been other plan-types, built by those who had no need for such accommodation, where the hall range was left on its own, either in its usual position at right-angles to the street, or even turned and had across the width of the plot. Halls in this latter position have been found elsewhere, in towns, for example, as far apart as Burford in Oxfordshire and Totnes in Devon.[6]

Since by far the largest number of medieval houses were L-shaped in plan and had halls at right angles to the street most of the later, rebuilt houses retain this form. The simplest house of this type had two ground floor rooms, hall and shop.

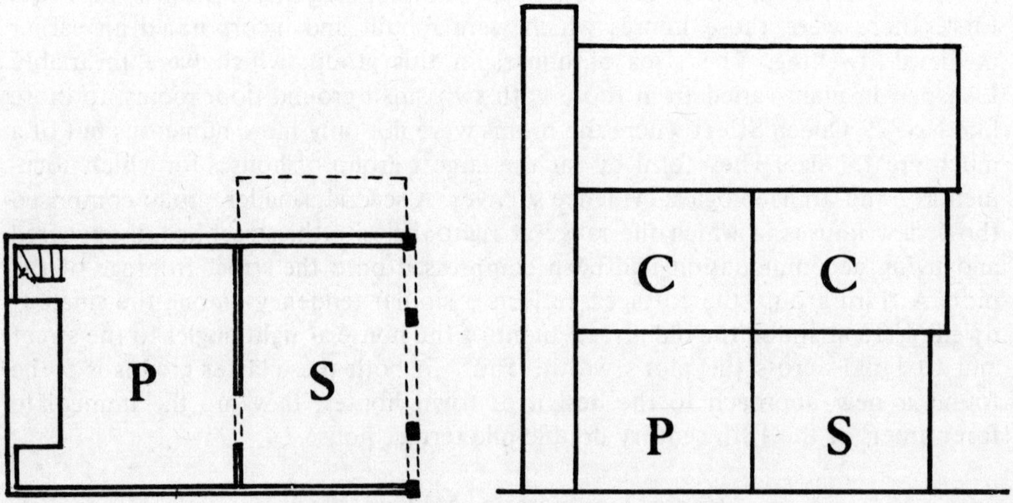

Fig 18 *Robert Stonar's house, 1613: reconstructed from a Probate Inventory*

No surviving examples of such houses have been discovered, but an inventory of 1613 probably described such a house after its 'modernisation' by the introduction of a chimney. This was a house occupied by Robert Stonar, cooper. His Probate Inventory[7] lists a parlour next to the shop, a buttery, a chamber over the parlour, a chamber over the shop and the shop. Thus his main living room, behind the shop on the ground floor, was called a parlour, but was in fact furnished, as the hall usually was, with tables, stools and benches as well as a bed, and had a buttery within it, possibly partitioned off. The two upstairs rooms, the chamber over the parlour and the chamber over the shop, were both furnished with bedding although the room over the shop stored among other oddments 300 hoops belonging to his business. Since only the parlour was heated and not the shop, the stack was probably not placed between them (which would have given each a fireplace) but in the gable end of the parlour. The stairs for the upstairs rooms were probably built into the width of the chimney stack. (Fig.18.)

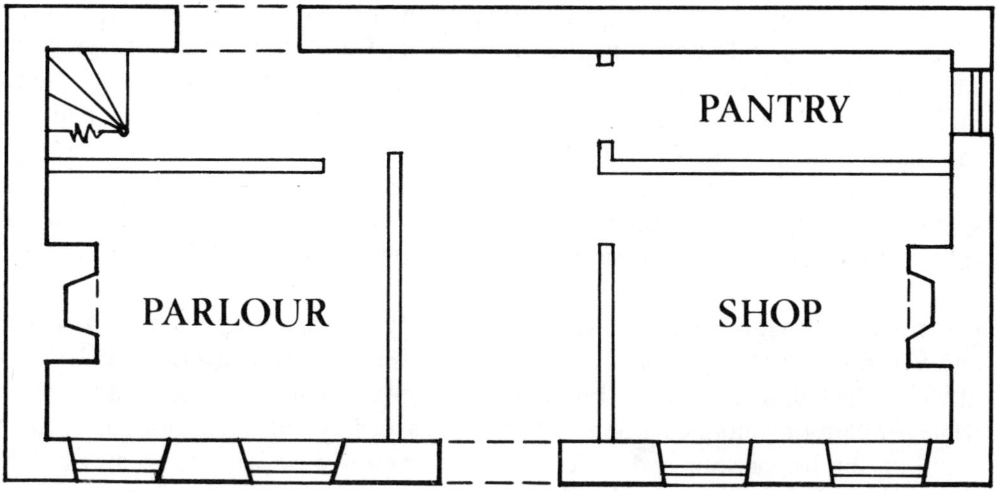

Fig 19 *Plan of a cottage on the west side of the Tuesday Market, built c.1620*

Although it has been assumed that modernised versions of the shop and parlour type house would lie at right angles to the street, new small houses built in the 1620's on the west side of the Tuesday Market, had the same accommodation as William Stonars laid out parallel to the street. Non of these houses now survive, but a plan (Fig.19) is preserved[8] and a drawing of their elevations (Plate 41). The plan shows a central entry passage with parlour on one side and shop on the other, both heated by stacks in the gable ends of the building. At the rear, a narrow space had been partitioned off making a small pantry behind the shop, with a staircase and a short corridor to it, from which a door led outside the building behind the parlour. This interesting little house may well be the forerunner of the two storey cottages with gable end stacks in Bridge Street, (see below p.100). It also suggests that in some parts of the town, at least, the practice of building living accommodation on the street frontage was not uncommon. It is unfortunate that no archaeological evidence has yet been uncovered to make possible a firm assessment of the importance of 'parallel' house-types in Lynn.

L-shaped houses were usually extended not by building upwards but by adding more ground-floor rooms to the hall range. In a rear range with two ground-floor rooms it was usual, in medieval houses, to find the hall abutting directly onto the street range with a room beyond, as at No. 37 Chapel Street. When the chimney was later inserted into this type of house it was placed axially between hall and lower room, thus heating both. The hall then continued to be used as the main living room of the house; food was prepared there as it had been in the medieval hall and it became the living kitchen of the 17th century house.

A typical example of an L-shaped house with the hall directly behind the ground-floor front room is described in the inventory of Robert Ladyman, a shipmaster, who died in 1589 in his house on the west side of Lath Street (now Nelson Street).[9] In his case, the hall was not yet floored in, although both his hall and the room at the lower end called the parlour, were heated, probably from a stack axially placed between them. Since a shipmaster had no need for retail or work space the 'foreparlour' probably replaced the medieval shop. The assessors of the inventory entered the house by the hall, next to which was the great parlour, and two small rooms, a small parlour and a buttery, either in outshots off it, or partitioned off within it. Upstairs there was only one chamber, over the parlour, and returning to the ground floor, they surveyed the foreparlour and lastly a kitchen. The hall contained the big family dining table with its forms and benches, while the parlour contained a posted bedstead as well as stools, cushions and chairs and, like the foreparlour and little parlour, was clearly a bedroom, whatever day-time use it may have had as well. The chamber, on the other hand, did not contain a bed, or indeed any furniture of note, but was used for storing the household linen; it may simply have been the ceiled-off roof space, with access by a ladder through a trap door, or by a stair in the thickness of the chimney stack. The kitchen is mentioned last, after the foreparlour, and may well have been a detached one. (Fig.20.)

The archaeological evidence for this kind of house in Kings Lynn has unfortunately, in many cases, been obscured by later rebuilding. A good example, however, where the old hall is still used as a kitchen, is No. 9 King Street. (Fig.20.) This is a two-storey, L-shaped building on the west side of King Street. The street range has one large room at ground level and two rooms on the first floor, but the whole range has been redecorated and the panelling and plasterwork is all post-1700. It does, however, retain part of the old 15th century crown post roof so the main structural walls of this section are clearly original. At right angles lies the hall range walled in stone. The original entrance to the house was in the angle between the two ranges on the south and gave directly into the hall. The present wall closing off a passageway to the north and east of the kitchen is clearly an insertion. West of the hall was the parlour, now decorated with 18th century panelling, and the main chimney stack lay between these two rooms with a fire-place on either side. In the late 15th century, the hall was open to the roof and the carved roof members were exposed to view. When the hall (and parlour) were floored in, a staircase was built as a separate compartment, in line with the wide chimney stack, but projecting into a yard on the north side of the house. This is the only example of a staircase compartment in this position. The cramped spiral stairs in the thickness of the chimneystack, which was the normal arrangement, clearly became inconvenient and when the hall remained in use as at No. 9 King Street, a staircase in the hall itself would have caused too much obstruction; so here at least a separate compartment was built. The possibility of doing this, however, would depend on there being open ground on one or other side of the hall range, and a stair in this position would normally have blocked the side passageway through to the rear of the property.

A description of the same type of house in the early 18th century is given in the inventory of John Butler, a woollen draper who died in 1708, and in his case it is clear that his hall had become known as a kitchen.[10] His house had three rooms on the ground floor, shop, kitchen and parlour, with first floor chambers and attics above the latter and a chamber over the shop. It seems clear from the order in which the rooms were surveyed that his kitchen chamber and shop chamber were adjacent, and the stair, this time not in the thickness of the stack because the staircase was large enough to contain a bed, probably descended along one of the kitchen walls. There were no beds in the ground floor rooms, but on the first floor there were two bedrooms, and also the room over the shop which was used to store silk and fine cloths. (Fig.20.) In layout of rooms this was almost exactly similar both to No. 9 King Street and to No. 13 Friar Street. The latter was a basically medieval building of two, and possibly later, three ground floor rooms, L-shaped with a shop at the front, and had the remains of a crown post roof over front and rear sections. Sometime during the early 17th century a chimney had been inserted at the parlour end of what was once an open hall and a new floor put in. Two new windows were made, one in each floor, in the north wall of the hall, and replaced the large medieval window running through two storeys in the south. A stair was built in the hall, against the timber back wall of the shop. Until recently a room to the east of the old hall was used as a kitchen, and the front room, once the shop, as a sitting-room. (Fig.34.)

There was also in Lynn a number of houses in which there were three rather than two ground-floor rooms in the rear range with the hall in the centre. Hampton Court south wing was of this type with service rooms at the upper end and a parlour at the lower end of the hall. This plan could vary, and other houses like No. 8 Purfleet Street, may have reversed the order of the rooms so that the parlour was at the upper end of the hall next to the shop. When chimneys were inserted two were usually placed in this kind of building, one between the shop and the room at the head of the hall, and one at the lower end of the hall, so that all the ground floor rooms could be heated.

One such house was occupied by Valentine Thacker, a butcher, who died in 1668.[11] In the Probate Inventory made after his death, two ground floor rooms are mentioned, hall and kitchen, and those were probably open to the roof. In

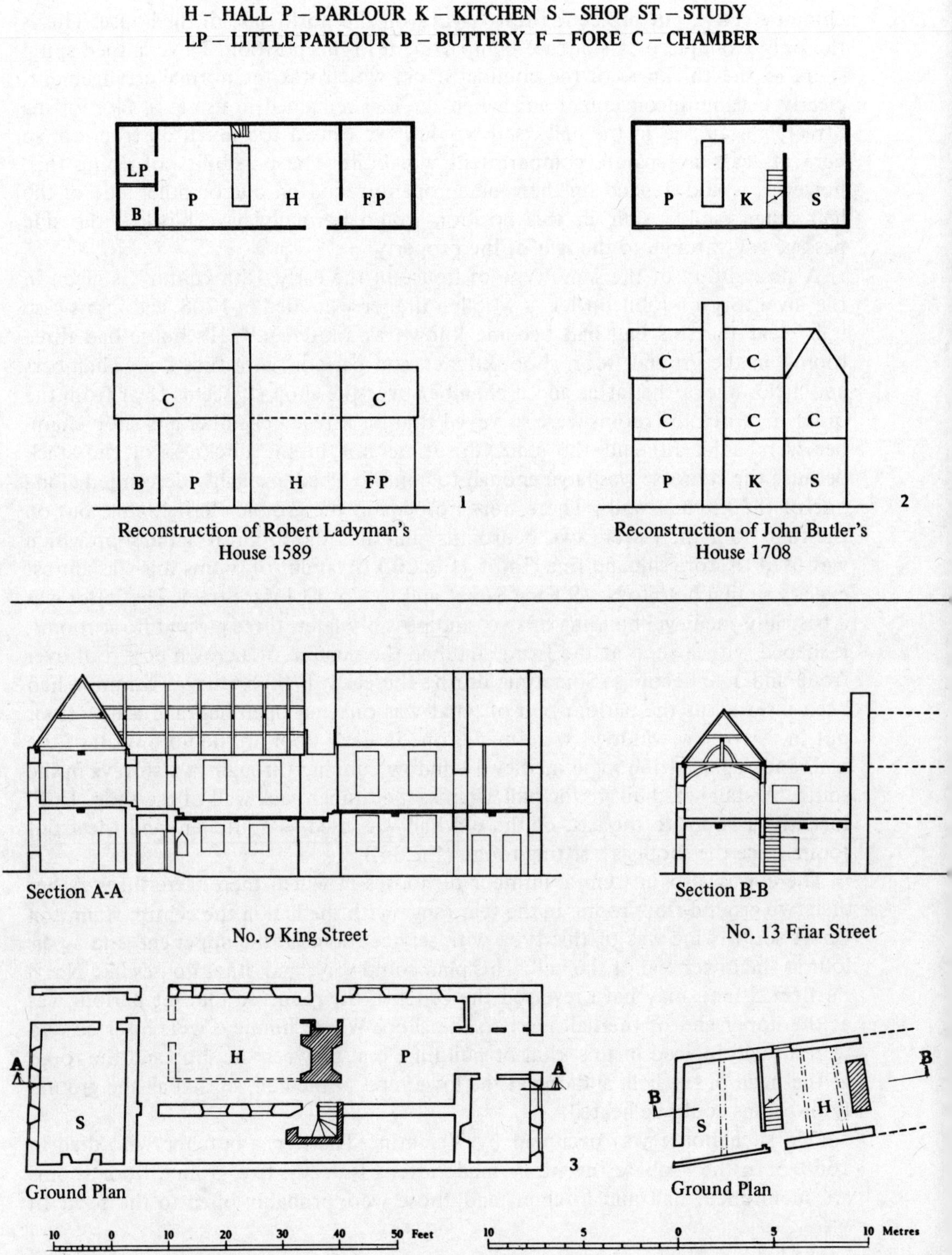

Fig 20 *Post-medieval houses with two rooms in rear range*

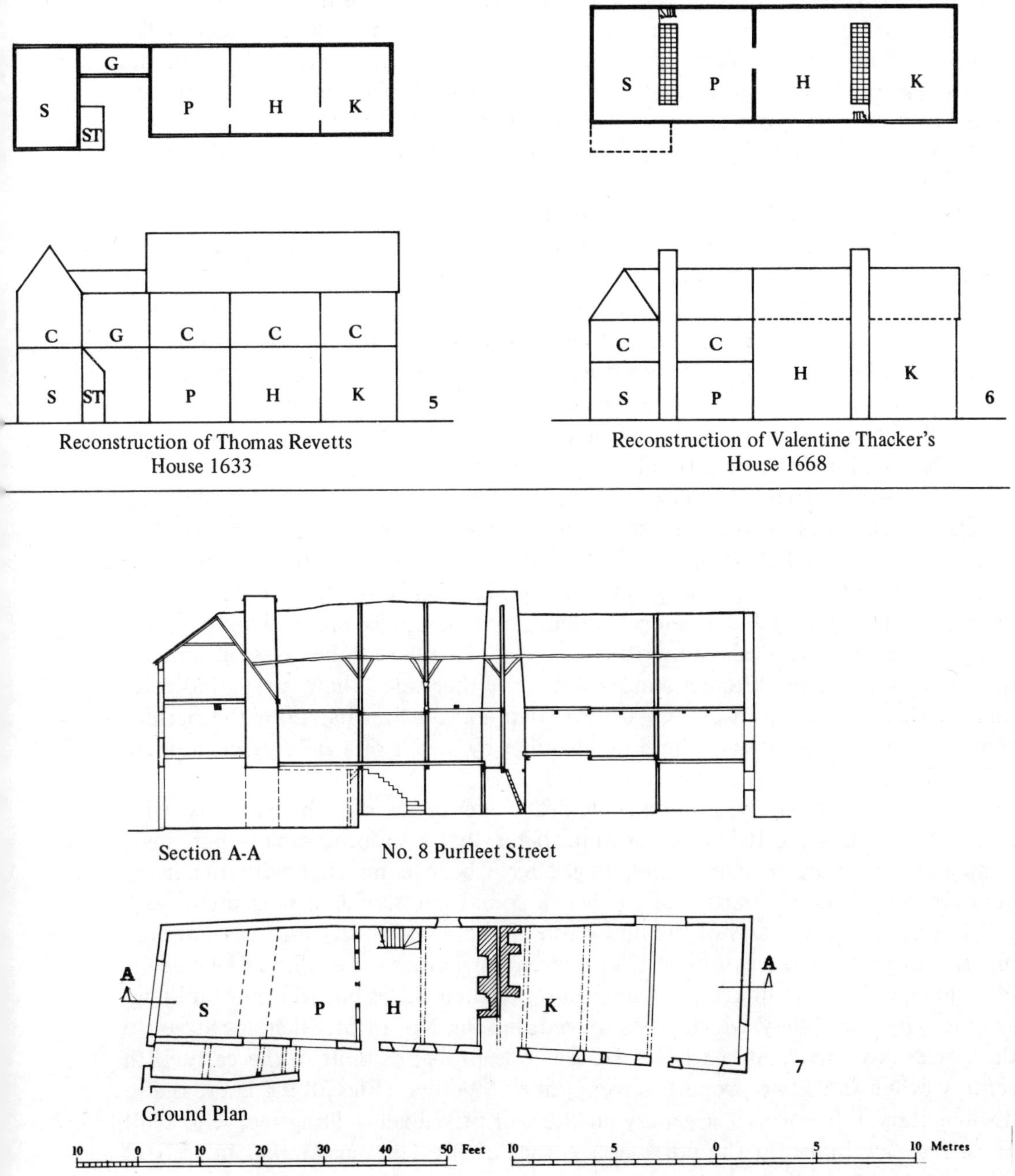

Fig 21 *Post-medieval houses with three rooms in rear range*

addition there were two chambers, a shop chamber and a parlour chamber, which interconnected, presumably at the front or street end of the house. Thus on the ground floor he had a shop, and a hall range consisting of a parlour nearest the street, hall and kitchen. Both hall and kitchen were heated, probably from the same stack; the parlour and chamber and shop chamber also contained fireplaces, probably from a stack placed between them. (Fig.18.)

No. 8 Purfleet Street was a house which, when altered in the late 16th century, must have been almost exactly similar to Valentine Thacker's. (Fig.21 and 31.) There was a large medieval room at the upper end of the hall into which a chimney was inserted at the top end between parlour and shop. At the lower end of the hall was a further brick chimney with a large cut brick fire opening in the room beyond the hall. This was probably the kitchen hearth. The hall and kitchen in this case were both floored in, as well as the parlour and the shop, so this house, unlike Valentine Thacker's was two-storeyed throughout. In addition, in the course of the 17th century, the dwelling house was considerably extended to include about 90 feet of former warehouse building at the back. It then became a very large house with at least six ground floor rooms in the hall range.

An interesting variant on this plan type is the house, once occupied by Thomas Revett, which stood on the west side of the Tuesday Market at the corner of Page Stair Lane. Thomas Revett died in 1635 and his inventory describes a house with a three-roomed hall range, not immediately abutting onto the shop range but linked to it by a gallery.[12] The shop fronted the market place and had an adjoining study furnished with a desk and writing materials. At the rear the assessors entered the hall first, then the kitchen and parlour on either side. Their survey indicates that all this rear section was two storeys high and on the first floor the parlour chamber was connected with the shop chamber by means of a gallery, where linen and household implements were stored. (Fig.21.)

There is, unfortunately, no archaeological evidence for an L-shaped house with a layout of this kind. It seems not improbable that a shop, originally perhaps a temporary structure of some kind, might have been connected with the living quarters by a gallery, particularly since a somewhat similar arrangement with galleries used to link parts of the house round a series of courtyards was common practice in parts of the south-west, in Exeter and Totnes for example.[13] Galleries in Lynn may also have linked not only houses to their shops but to other buildings as well. The one gallery which has survived, linking No. 11 St. Nicholas Street to the house next door, St. Nicholas House, was probably built in the early 17th century when these two properties were joined together. (Figs.38-9.) There is also documentary reference to a gallery in the will of William Killingtree, who built himself a new house in the north-east corner of the Tuesday Market in 1570.[14] When he died in 1586, he left his son the bulk of his property including his house. His wife, however, was to have 'her dwelling in the new kitchen chamber with the little chamber over it and the gallery adjoining.' These must have been rooms over the new kitchen at the rear of the plot linked to the main house by a gallery. In Exeter (No. 47 High Street), there are examples of such kitchens being built across the width of the plot at the rear, but this was an unusual arrangement in Lynn because of the need for easy access from the house to a rear range of warehouses. No archaeological evidence for such a layout survives.

One final example of a medieval house, rebuilt during the 16th and 17th centuries, is Clifton House in Queen Street. (Figs.42-44.) This was altered from a medieval building with not one, but two hall ranges, at right angles to the street, and a cross range on the Queen Street frontage. Clifton House lies on the west side of the street, bounded on the north by King Staithe Lane and on the west by the river. Between the house and the river lie the inevitable ranges of brick warehouses (see p.120).

The plan of the medieval house, or houses, on the site has still not been fully unravelled in spite of extensive excavations in the south range. Under the northern range is a semi-excavated brick rib vaulted undercroft, three bays long, once entered by steps from Queen Street. The mouldings on the central piers carrying the vault, date this part to around 1350. In its south wall, however, is evidence of an earlier 13th century doorway, which appears to have led into a house in what is now the south range. Here excavation has uncovered a very fine tile floor, (Plate 21A) and two hearths, one made of brick in the centre of a room, and a second against the 'crypt' wall, some 20 feet to the west. This seems to indicate a hall in its customary position in the range at right angles to the street, and a parlour beyond. It has not yet been finally ascertained whether a service area lay at the upper end of the hall.

These remains suggest an early house on the site of the southern range, entered from the King Staithe Lane side. A subsequent division of the property may have meant that in the 14th century a hall on a vaulted undercroft was built parallel to the old range, blocking the original entry passage. A new entry to the older house was then made in its present position to the south of the block. Unfortunately, however, the level of the tiled floor and the supposed level of the early door opening in the south crypt wall do not coincide in an entirely satisfactory way. Nevertheless, it seems almost certain that Clifton House was once two medieval tenements, thrown together at some later date.

This putting together of the two tenements had almost certainly taken place by the late 16th century when a tower was added at the west end of the entry passage, (Plate 23B) and a double range of warehouses at the rear, interconnecting at all floors. Alterations were probably made to the house too in this period, although it is not entirely clear what form they took. To the west of the present staircase both ground and first floor rooms over the crypt retain original early 17th century panelling, and the southernmost room over the tiled floor area was similarly panelled with a highly ornate carved wooden Jacobean chimneypiece. This was removed to America in 1889.[15]

The last major alteration to the house was made in the early 18th century, and was probably complete by 1708. A rainwater head bearing this date, and the initials S. T. was erected in the Queen Street front, the initials standing for Samuel Taylor, a gentleman-merchant and Member of Parliament. It has been suggested that the work was carried out by Henry Bell, the architect of the Customs House, and the *Dukes Head.* This, however, is based on stylistic evidence alone and is not documented.

After early 18th century alterations, the house was approached from Queen Street by a porch which then projected some distance into the street. This had a segmental headed wooden canopy carried on twisted columns, a not uncommon Baroque detail, although found rarely in this country. (Plate 23A.) The porch led to a passage through the street range, and the house itself was entered in the angle of the rear and front ranges. A narrow stone flagged hall, and two rooms to the south, comprised this part of the dwelling, the southernmost of which was the kitchen. From the hall a flight of steps rose over the crypt to a staircase hall lit by two long sash windows in its north wall. This was decorated with plaster swags and floral garlands, in a manner very similar to the Norwich Music Room, while the stairs themselves had turned balusters, moulded tread ends and carved brackets. The rooms in the street range, both at ground and first floor level were all wood panelled in the 18th century manner, and had wood modillion cornices and moulded chimney pieces. The rooms to the south of the stair were left with their earlier wood panelling.

Externally the building was given new flush-framed sash windows, but only the inner south wall facing the entry seems to have been entirely rebuilt. This was constructed in a fine red brick, with rubbed brick flat arches to the windows. The foundations indicate that this was rebuilt on the site of an older medieval stone wall.

Beyond the fact that it comprised two, not one, ranges at right angles to the street, Clifton House was altered in a not dissimilar manner to other merchant houses in Lynn. The old hall entry from the side passage was preserved, and the staircase built into the northern hall over the undercroft. The room below the hall became the kitchen as in No. 8 Purfleet Street, and the rooms along the street front were clearly parlours not shops. The unusual feature was the tower, four storeys high with one small room on each floor and a spiral staircase on the south. This, however, although a unique survival in Lynn, was once one of several along the waterfront. (Plate 3A.)

The increasing use of the first floor as living accommodation during the 16th and 17th centuries made it necessary to devise some kind of satisfactory means of access to the upper storey. While only part of the house was floored, ladders may well have been sufficient, particularly if the upper rooms were used only for lumber or for rough sleeping for children or servants. However, as soon as first floor rooms came into general daytime use, as it is clear they did, not only from the evidence of inventories but from the panelling and other decorative work found in them, some more permanent form of access had to be made. Initially stairs seem to have been placed in the thickness of chimney stacks, and good examples of this survive in the south gable end of Greenland Fishery House, (Fig.41) and alongside the central chimney stack in No. 11 St. Nicholas Street. (Fig.38.) These, however, were small and cramped. An early attempt to make a more spacious stair has already been noted at No. 9 King Street, and with the growing fashion for lavishly carved grand staircases in gentlemen's houses during the 17th century, Lynn merchants began making larger staircases still into what had originally been the hall of the medieval house. The choice of the hall as a site for the new stair was the outcome not of chance but of a combination of factors which made this the most satisfactory place. The main entrance to the house, even after modernisation, seems still to have been from a side entrance into the hall, and this remained the case as long as the front part of the building was used as a shop. The hall itself had undergone changes. In many cases it had been ceiled at first-floor level and because it no longer contained the only hearth, it had lost much of medieval function as the focus for the life of the household. Except when it became the later kitchen it was no longer necessary to keep this space free of encroachments. In addition a staircase, particularly a carved one, in the hall, would be a major decorative feature in the main entrance of the house. Only one early 17th century staircase survives in its original position in the hall, at No. 29 Queen Street. But in many houses in King Street (Nos. 3, 5, 11, 13, 15, 23, 25, 33) and in Clifton House in Queen Street the staircase still occupies a position within the site of the medieval hall. These stairs, in fact, date mainly from the 18th century when the interiors of many large houses were redecorated; but the fact that they are found in this position, which bears no relation to normal Renaissance town house planning practice, suggests that they were remodelled in the position in which they were found at the end of the 17th century.

No garderobes or latrines are mentioned in inventories of houses, or in any other documents relating to building, nor has any archaeological evidence of internal closets in the buildings themselves come to light. The most likely places for closets would be in the thickness of chimney stacks since these, whether axially placed or not, could often be given drains leading outside the walls of the house. But few houses had, in fact, room beside the stack, where one side or the other was often taken up either with the staircase, or the door opening to the next room. It seems possible that there were no internal closets, but that latrines were placed in the yards, or over nearby fleets, and that closet stools were used indoors.

By the end of the 17th century it seems unlikely that many medieval houses would remain without inserted floors and chimneys. Craftsmen and shopkeepers, as in the Middle Ages, were living in houses not very different in plan to those occupied by more wealthy merchants, but differing in scale, in the size of rooms and in quality and quantity of furnishings and fittings. This can be seen by com-

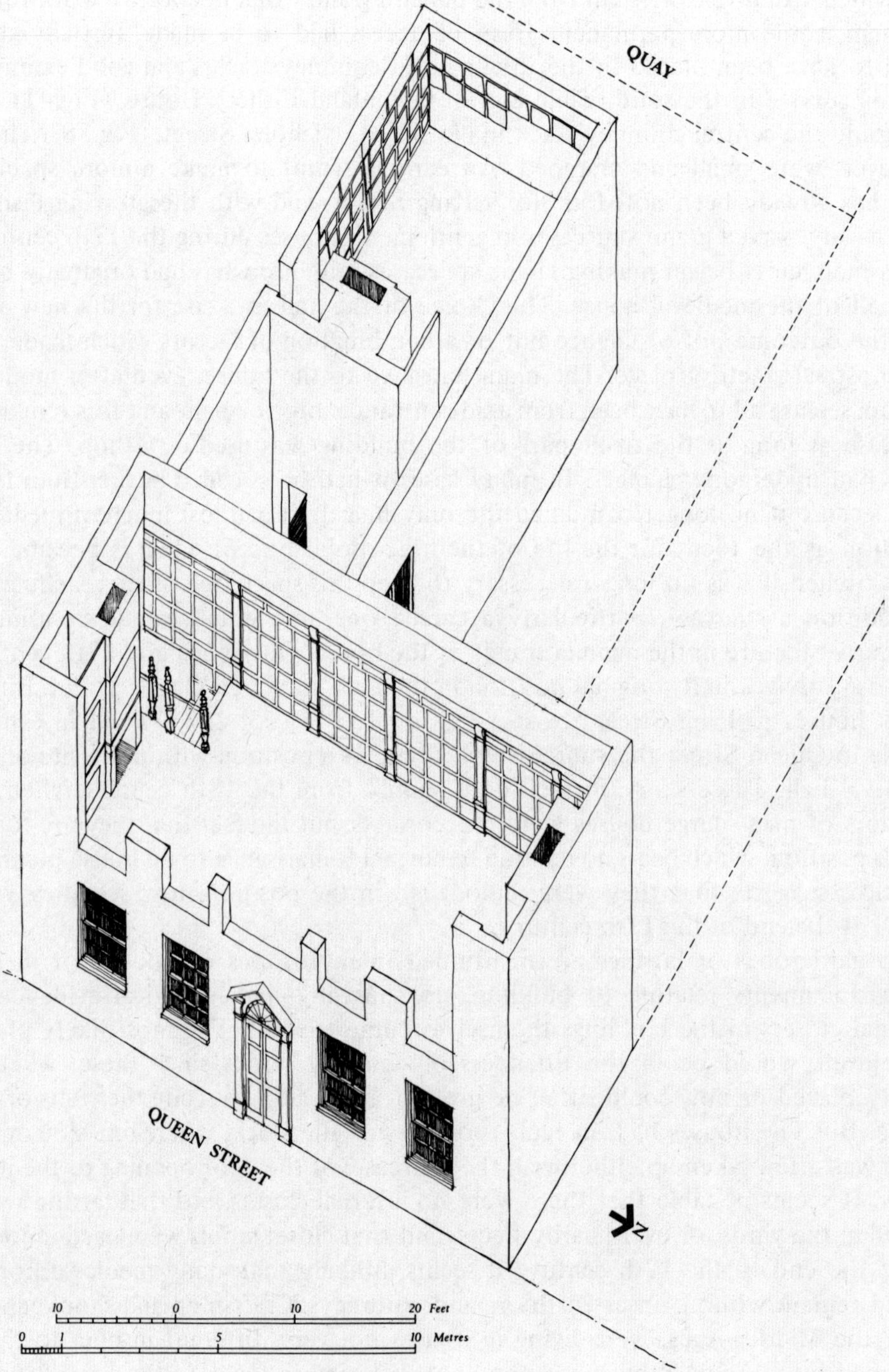

Fig 22 *No. 29 Queen Street: reconstruction*

paring No. 9 King Street and No. 13 Friar Street, houses which in plan are identical but which in size show considerable disparity. (Fig.20.) But it was also probably true by this time that the more wealthy the household, the greater the number of rooms to their houses. Margaret Miller for instance, the widow of Thomas Miller, lived until her death, in 1552, in a house in King Street which had seven ground floor rooms, including a chapel and a 'mortuary', and chambers above.[16] Even then beds were apparently needed in the warehouses, presumably for apprentices or servants. Except for the chapel and mortuary, relics perhaps of the ancient Corpus Christi Gildhall on the site of which her house stood, no special functions are designated to the various rooms and this was probably true of most Lynn houses of this period. With a few exceptions, furnishings indicate that most rooms, on the ground floor at least, were used both during the day and as bedrooms at night. Until the end of the 17th century it was usual to find beds in the parlour and even in the hall, although, in fact, Margaret Miller, along with others of her class, normally slept on the first floor.

A New House With An L-Shaped Plan

No. 29 Queen Street was newly built throughout in the first half of the 17th century. (Figs.22 and 40; Plate 22.) It stands on the west side of the street to the north of Thoresby College, and was probably occupied in this period by a gentleman-merchant, William Hoo. The layout comprises not only the house but extensive warehouses running down to the Ouse bank so trade was clearly still being conducted in the vicinity of the house. The building plot, lying between the street and the river Ouse, was broad enough to enable two ranges of buildings to be laid out at right angles to the street range separated from each other by a narrow courtyard. This courtyard was entered from the street by a passage through the street range, and the yard was closed at the western end by a range of warehouses. It was thus a somewhat elongated courtyard layout similar to Hampton Court.

The dwelling house occupied the full width of the street front and the range at right angles on the south side of the plot. This latter contained the hall, in its customary position abutting on the street range, and a two storeyed section beyond the hall, the first floor room of which was a panelled parlour or solar, while the kitchen lay beneath, the kitchen hearth being in the back of the hall chimney stack. The hall itself was two storeys high, lit by a large eight-light mullioned and transomed window in the north wall. (Plate 22B.) Two staircases descended into the hall space, both contemporary, with rectangular section carved baluster shafts, one leading from the first floor parlour at the west end of the hall, the other from the first floor room which ran the whole length of the street range. This long gallery kind of arrangement must have been impressive, since the room was pannelled with small, square shaped panels in moulded styles and muntins, punctuated along the west wall by carved pilasters. At either end were fireplaces, the one on the north still retaining its carved Jacobean ornament. The two ground floor rooms on the north side of the entrance passage were also panelled and entered through door openings from the court decorated with a flat chamfer and carved stops. Clearly neither was intended for use as a shop and had no means of access to the street. The house thus comprised hall, kitchen and two 'fore-parlours' on the ground floor, and two great chambers on the first floor, with attics above in the front range which were ceiled and had fireplaces. Not a large amount of accommodation was provided, even by 18th century standards, and since all the rooms were heated and all panelled there was probably no distinction between those used in the daytime and those used at night. Even here one would expect to find beds and dining tables occupying the same room.

Double Pile House 1560-1700

Typical merchants' houses in Lynn between 1560 and 1700 were L-shaped as their medieval predecessors houses had been, and had the principal living rooms in the back range. This on the face of it would seem a good arrangement. It not only kept the merchant at all times of the day in close proximity to his business, and his cargoes and workmen under constant surveillance, but it also meant the noise, dirt and bustle of the busy street was excluded by the range of shops which lay across the width of the plot on the roadside. Nevertheless by 1700 new houses in Lynn (like the splendid No. 29 King Street said to have been designed by Henry Bell) were being built with all the principal living rooms along the front of the house. In order to do this the shop and the side entry to the house had to disappear and the houses were planned to occupy two ranges laid parallel to each other across the width of the plot.

This change in the planning of houses began to take place in the 17th century for two reasons. First a positive incentive towards re-styling dwelling houses came from the growing use of the double-pile terrace house in London, particularly after the Great Fire. The Renaissance town house, either double fronted or of three bays with the entrance to one side, planned both internally and externally in accordance with the rules of Classical symmetry and proportion, became the prototype for the houses of fashionable provincial society.

Secondly, the practical difficulties of designing living accommodation on the front of the plot were being overcome. Chimneys made it possible to heat upper rooms and thus one of the difficulties of building several storeys high was removed; wider roof spans were being used; but above all it was the disappearance of the shop as a normal part of a merchant's business that permitted a more flexible approach to the planning of the street range. The ground floor front rooms could be used as living rooms, and the entrance to the house placed on the front instead of at the side. There was thus no reason why the house should not be planned in the Renaissance manner when the fashion for doing so caught on, especially since the streets were beginning to be better kept and cleaned.[17]

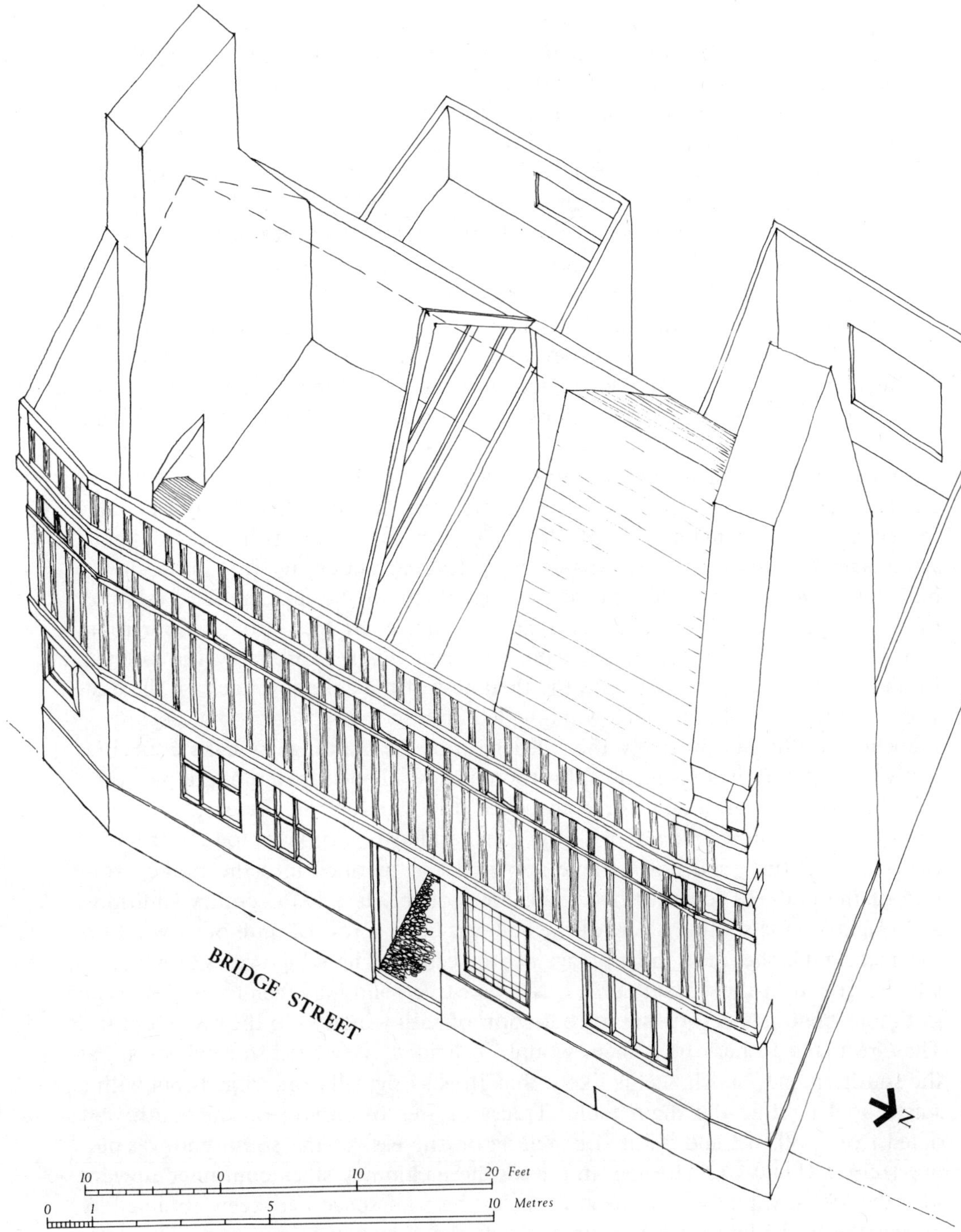

Fig 23 *Greenland Fishery, Bridge Street: reconstruction*

The merchants' house was brought forward to the street by slow stages. It has unfortunately been impossible to uncover every step in the change from the L-shaped to the double-pile house but the process had clearly begun at Greenland Fishery House in 1605 and was almost complete by 1645 when St. Nicholas House was built. The intermediate stages have unfortunately not survived.

Greenland Fishery House in Bridge Street was built by John Atkin, a merchant who immigrated to Lynn from Wells in Norfolk. He purchased his Freedom of the Borough in 1584 and was twice mayor of Lynn before his death in 1617. His new house was built on the west side of the old road from Lady Bridge over the Mill-fleet to the south gates and a stone, carved with his initials and the date of its erection, was placed in the north gable end. It is unlikely that this was a virgin site but all traces of a previous medieval building have disappeared above ground.

Greenland Fishery is a timber-framed building, one room deep and two and a half storeys high, built on brick cellars running parallel to the street. (Figs.23 and 41; Plate 24.) Although the main living rooms were all in the street range, a rear range did exist, running down the north side of the plot and may have contained either an extension of the living quarters or a warehouse – it is now not possible to tell which. The main part of the house on the street front was designed symmetrically about a central passageway leading under the first floor of the building to the yard behind, and had two great chimney stacks in each gable end. From the passage there was an entrance on the south to a ground floor room containing a large fireplace in the gable wall, and this was probably the kitchen. From it a flight of steps built into the thickness of the chimney stack on the east, still lit by its original mullioned window, led up into a first floor room, occupying the whole width and probably the full length of the building, to make a spacious hall with a fireplace at each end. This room is now divided by a modern partition, and the two parts are lit by three corbelled oriel windows in the east wall. Only one of these windows, however, – the northernmost – appears to date from the early 17th century, and has a frame mortised and tenoned into the timber front wall of the house. The other two oriels are probably late 17th century additions, and originally the southern part of the hall was lit by a row of mullioned windows two feet eight inches deep, high up against the ceiling. These high rows of windows are also found in the *Valiant Sailor,* Nelson Street, and may well have been usual in timber buildings before the introduction of sash windows in the 18th century. The Greenland Fishery hall, then, would, if divided, have been somewhat dark at the southern end, and it seems likely that it was originally one large room with a single oriel lighting the main table. Traces of frescos survive on the south wall dated from 1605-12 and painted panelling on the east at the south end was put in *c.* 1654.[18] (Plate 25.) The stair in the southern chimney stack continued upward into the attics, where greater head-room in the roof space had been obtained by raising the wall plate on a low timber wall above an attic floor jetty. This attic space has an original timber partition, leaving a two bay room at the southern end decorated with frescos. This was probably the solar, and principal bed chamber.

On the north side of the entry passage was a door, now blocked, into a ground floor room probably used as a shop with a cut brick fire opening. No access to the upper floors seems to have been possible from the room, the present stair along the back timber wall being a later insertion. There was, however, probably always a separate entrance from the street, and the cut brick surround to a large window opening can still be seen, with part of the original mullioned and transomed wood window frame *in situ*.

Although Greenland Fishery is an unusually wide building, extending to 30 feet instead of the more usual 18 to 20, it was not divided lengthwise to provide extra accommodation. It was, however, a relatively large house with five or six living rooms, which was probably rather more than a converted medieval house had. Apart from the brick chimneys in the gable ends it was built in the traditional way using timber construction with a jetteyed front wall and a rear wall built all in one plane. The front of the building was given moulded coverings to the joist ends but otherwise it was left unadorned.

There seem to have been no further attempts to design a house at the front of the plot until the 1640's when St. Nicholas House in St. Nicholas Street was built. (Figs.38-9.) The site was an awkwardly shaped triangular one and at the time of its rebuilding the house seems to have been linked to No. 11 St. Nicholas Street. The combination of these factors makes the intention of the 17th century builder difficult to unravel. At present St. Nicholas House is a double-pile building with two parallel ranges running alongside St. Nicholas Street.

The northern range has at its eastern end a curvilinear Dutch gable dated 1645, while the southern one is a 19th century rebuilding, although it seems likely that a similar building once occupied the latter site since entry by the 'gallery' from No. 11 St. Nicholas Street was through its west gable end. The main entrance is now in the centre of the inner (northern) range and was approached by a lane that once ran from St. Nicholas Church to the waterfront. This inner range was built brick, two storeys high, and was planned internally to be symmetrical with one room on either side of the entrance hall and staircase. The first floor of the front range is now laid out with a series of small rooms entered by a corridor from the head of the stairs. Unfortunately, documentary evidence for the rather complicated history of this awkwardly placed corner plot is lacking, although from 1587 it appeared to have belonged to the Clark family (Richard and his son Matthew were both merchants and local landowners), until Matthew's death in 1623 when it passed to Thomas Snelling, his son-in-law. For a time during this period part of the property, which seems to have included 11 Nicholas Street, was used as a brewhouse.

Cottages

In Lynn, as in other towns in the 16th and 17th centuries, there was a large number of wage earners in employment of all kinds. It has been calculated that

Coventry, for example, with a population of about 5,000, had about one third including the poor belonging to this group,[19] and this proportion may have been even higher in Lynn where the busy port offered employment to even larger numbers of labourers, porters, boatmen and others employed in handling and stowing cargo. These were all people whose home and workplace were separate and who had thus no need of a workroom attached to the dwelling.

The medieval houses of such people have all disappeared, although some remains may yet be uncovered by excavation. At the end of the 16th century, though, the Common Staithe Accounts indicate that in Common Staithe Lane and Pudding Lane, now Water Lane, the porters, boatmen and others doing various jobs on the waterfront, were leasing from the town buildings described in the Accounts as cottages.[20] These must, in most cases, have consisted of a single room with or without a chimney, and similar dwellings must have existed elsewhere in the town.

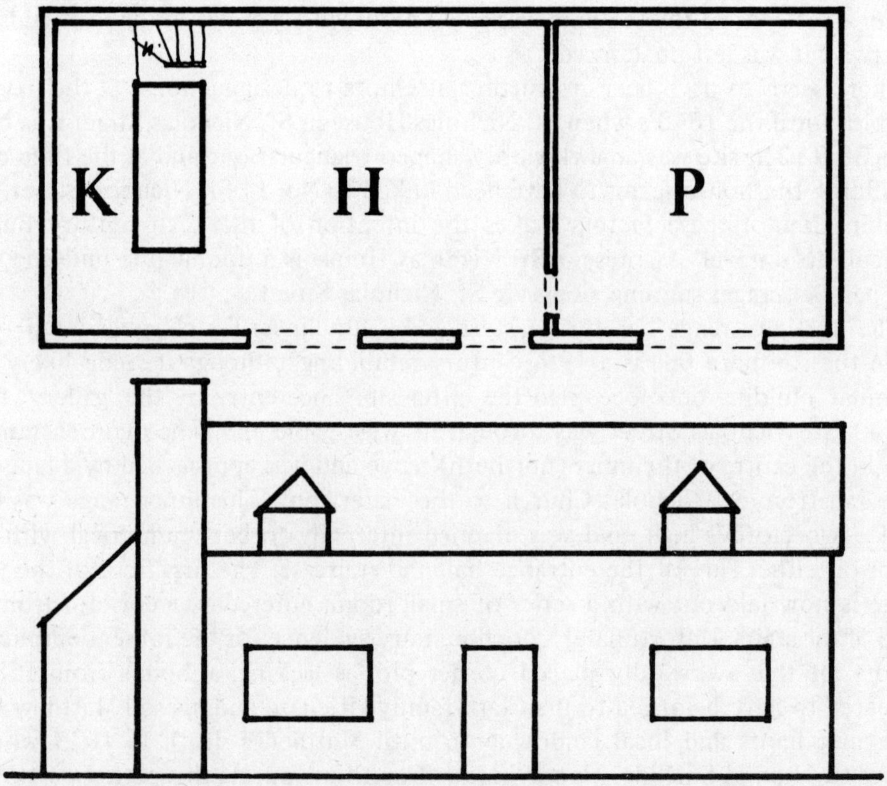

Fig 24 *Thomas Purdy's house in 1591: reconstructed from a Probate Inventory*

Some among the wage-earning class, however, were comparatively wealthy, people like master builders and shipmasters. These were often sufficiently well off to erect more substantial dwellings and to bequeath household goods in their wills.

Plate 16 *Roof truss of Hall of Thoresby College*

Plate 17 *Thoresby College, roof detail from south range*

Plate 18 *No. 9 King Street; detail of Hall roof*

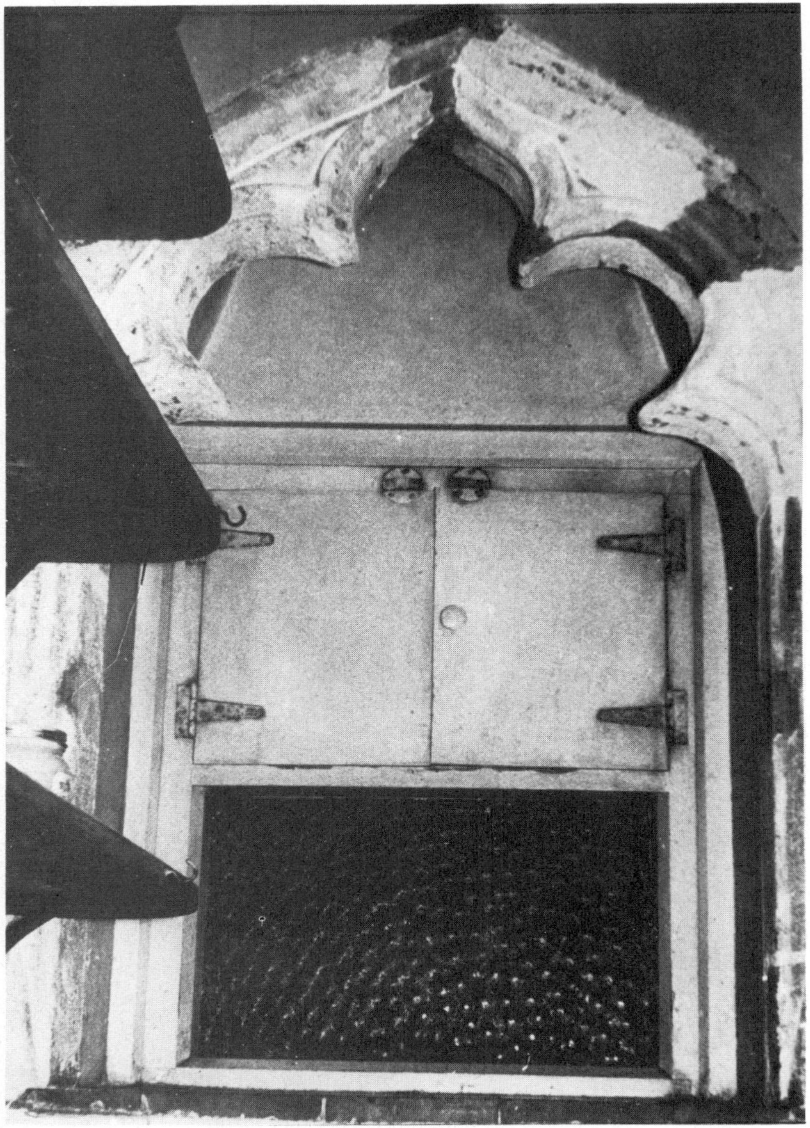

Plate 19A *Medieval window of Hall; No. 9 King Street*

Plate 19B *Medieval door in Nelson Street*

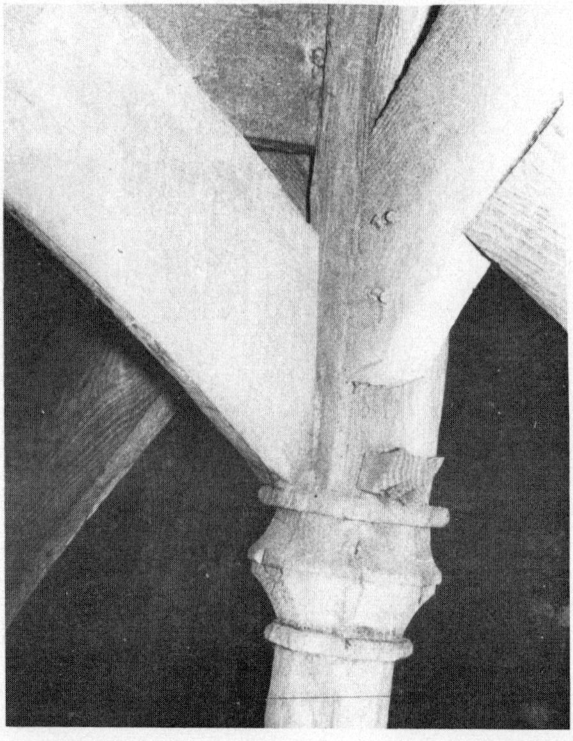

Plates 20A and B *No. 3 King Street; details of hall crown post truss*

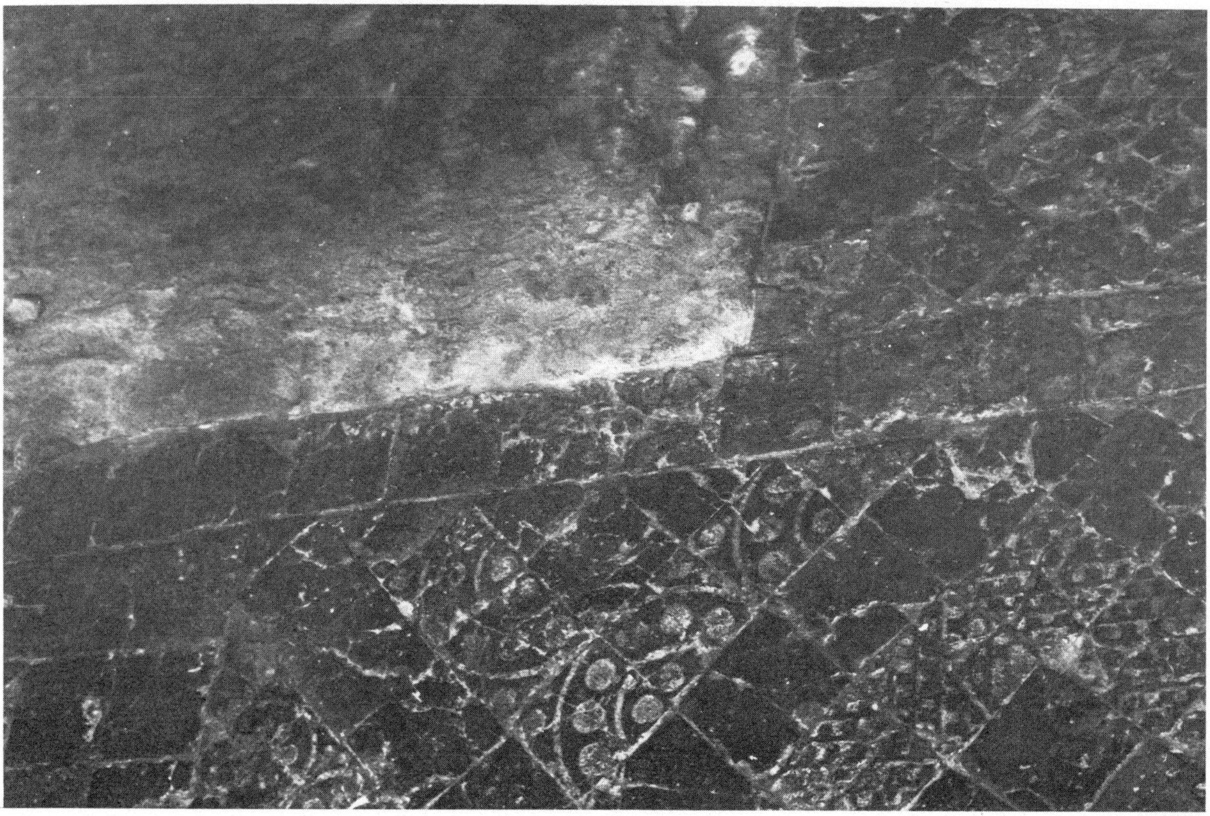

Plate 21A *Clifton House; part of hall pavement and edge of hearth*

Plate 21B *Clifton House; medieval undercroft*

Plate 22A *No. 29 Queen Street; street elevation*

Plate 22B *No. 29 Queen Street; courtyard and hall window*

Plate 23A *Clifton House; street door*

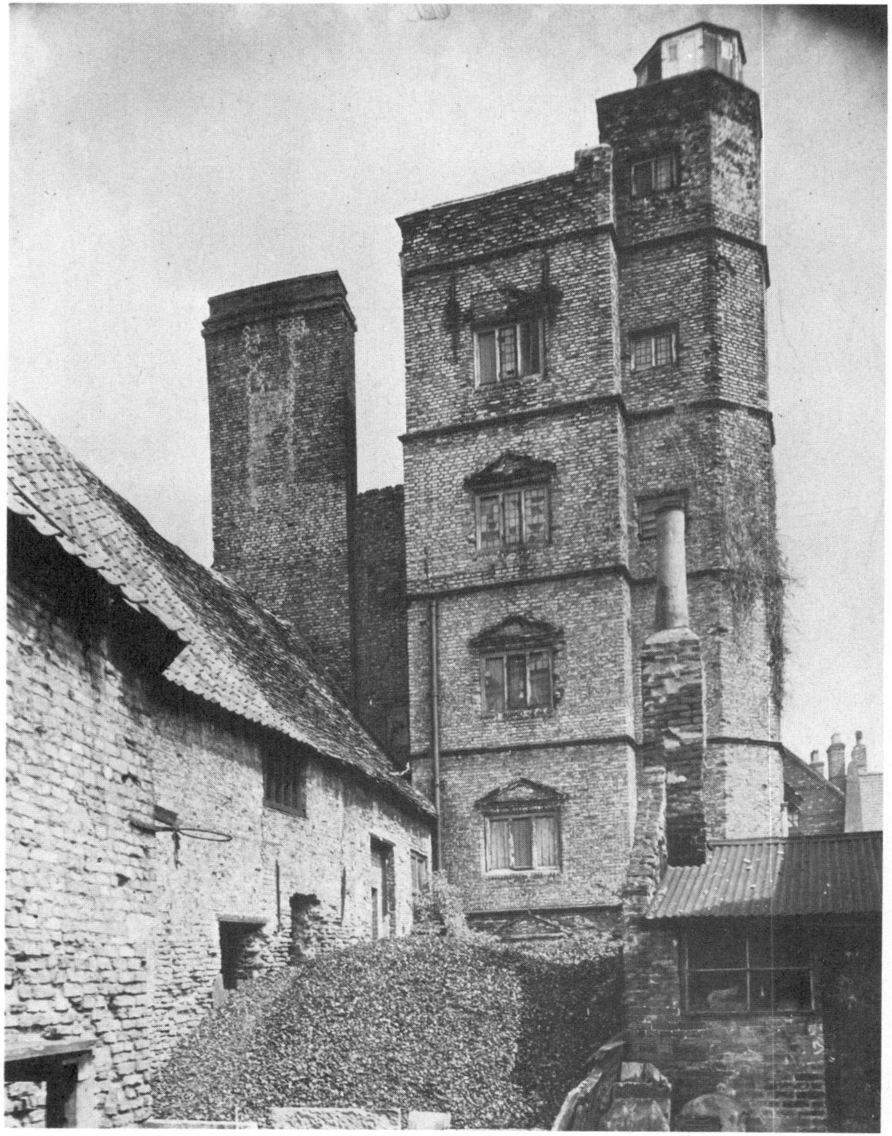

Plate 23B *Clifton House; tower*

Plate 24 *Greenland Fishery; street front*

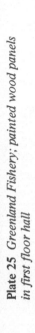

Plate 25 *Greenland Fishery; painted wood panels in first floor hall*

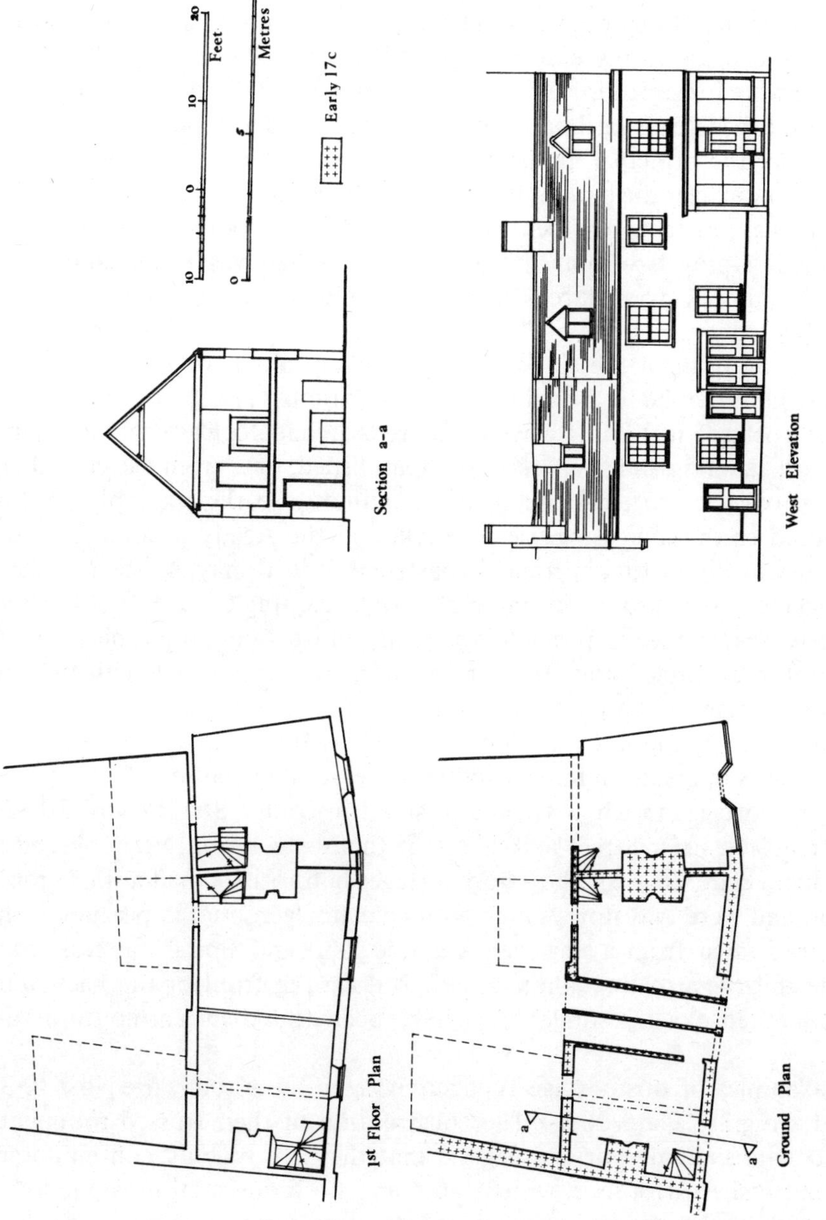

Fig 25 *Nos. 30-32 Birdge Street: plans, section and elevation*

Unfortunately no medieval houses survive known to have belonged to this group, but there are documentary references to such buildings in the 16th century from which some attempt can be made at reconstruction. A typical example might be the house of Thomas Purdy, a glazier, who died in 1591, and whose Probate Inventory records that he had household possessions worth £60 12s. 10d.[21] His house had two ground floor rooms, a hall and parlour, both of which were ceiled and a kitchen in a single-storey extension, possibly a lean-to or an outshot. Both hall and parlour were furnished for day and night-time use with large framed dining tables and posted bedsteads, although the pewter platters and pots were kept in the hall, probably the principal dining room. The room over the hall was used for lumber, and the room over the parlour had only a bed and a long plank table. These upstairs rooms may, in fact, represent the ceiling-in of the roof space in what was originally a single storey two-room dwelling. Only the hall was heated so it seems likely that the chimney was placed in the hall gable, an easy place to install it, without involving any rebuilding of the roof, and the kitchen may have been built to make use of the back of the stack. The most likely place for the stairs to the upper rooms would then be in the thickness of the chimney. (Fig.24.)

The earliest cottages in Lynn for which there is archaeological evidence, some of which are still standing and some recently demolished, date from the early 17th century. The survival of cottages of this date, and not of earlier examples, can be partly attributed to the increasing use of brick, and the steady decline from the late 16th century of flimsy timber framed construction.[22] It may also be the result of a substantial increase in prosperity among the wage-earning class. Although there is unfortunately no evidence to prove this assumption for Lynn, it has been shown for Antwerp, for example, how the service industries connected with the port prospered as the trade of the city expanded in the first half of the 16th century.[23] In Yarmouth, too, economic expansion in the mid-16th century resulted in the building of cottages in greater numbers and in more durable materials.[24]

17th century cottages in Kings Lynn still stand in Bridge Street (Nos. 30-32), All Saints Street and Friar Street and a row of them was recently demolished in Sedgeford Lane. (Plate 26.) All the Lynn cottages before 1700 had a single room on each floor, and were two storeys high with an attic; were roofed parallel to the street and were heated from a single stack in one gable end. Spiral staircases were built into the thickness of the chimney, either along the front or the back wall. Cottages built to an exactly similar plan have been found in Yarmouth in the Rows.

The best examples of this cottage type surviving in Lynn today are Nos. 30-32 Bridge Street. (Fig.25; Plate 26A.) The construction of their trussed roofs with arch-braced collars and side purlins suggests that they are roughly contemporary with Greenland Fishery House in which the same roof construction is employed and which is dated 1608. All had originally one ground-floor room with a through passage down one side giving access to the yard at the rear. The chimney stack was in each case placed on the party walls between the houses and the stacks of Nos. 30 and 31 are back to back thus economising on walling material. The staircase in each cottage was built into the thickness of the chimney stack, Nos. 30 and 31 having their at the rear of the stack and No. 32 at the front, and they mount in each case to the attic made in the roof space by ceiling underneath the collars of the roof trusses. The accommodation of these houses, two living rooms, both heated, and an attic, was the same as that of Thomas Purdy's house, but the important change from his basically medieval plan-type was that accommodation was acquired not by extending the ground floor horizontally, but by utilising the chimney stack to heat an upstairs as well as a downstairs room, thus making a compact block one room deep on the roadside.

The reason for suggesting the Bridge Street cottages as house-types in their own right rather than as whittled down versions of the medieval dwelling is that the disappearance of the shop on the ground floor made possible a quite new subsequent development of the basic cottage plans. When the shop occupied the ground floor front room there was no reason to invest in the installation of a chimney stack in the gable end of this street range. As a result it was the rear part of the house, where there were chimneys, that was important from the point of view of improving the living quarters, and the presence of one or perhaps two stacks placed axially in a range at right angles to the street prevented an easy solution to the problem of extending the living capactiy of the part of the house built across the width of the plot. With a stack in the gable end of the street range, however, accommodation could be increased by widening the span of the roof, at first by means of an outshot at the back giving extra rooms on the ground floor, and later roofing the whole house two rooms deep, the normal practice of 18th century town house builders. Thus the Bridge Street cottages mark the beginning of an important development in town housing.

The absence of dated examples of cottages in Lynn makes it difficult to trade the chronology of the later stages of the development of cottage plans towards the 18th century terrace house. Probably the first room to be placed in an out-shutt at the back was a scullery or larder or even a kitchen with its own chimney as in some of the cottages in Sedgeford Lane. A staircase compartment housing a dog-leg stair under a lean-to roof was probably the next to be built out at the back, and finally the whole back section was carried up the full height of the building. There are no traces in Lynn of the two cell cottage, gable end to street with an axial stack, found by W.A. Pantin in Oxford and D. Portman in Exeter.[25] In such houses too, as the stair, once in the thickness of the stack, encroached further into the central space, became the two room deep terrace house with dog-leg stair and two ground floor rooms. Lynn terrace cottages seem to have developed exclusively from a gable-end stack plan-type, an unexpected finding in view of the earlier 'right-angle' type hall layout.

Building Construction 1500-1700

In medieval Lynn most houses were built partly of timber and the use of brick or stone confined to the hall and some party walls. Even in the 15th century, however, the use of brick was becoming increasingly common in non-domestic work, and, in the course of the 16th and 17th centuries, brick was used to a greater extent in house-building too. The change from timber to brick in domestic work was slow, and even at the end of the 16th century it was very unusual to find buildings walled throughout in the one material. In 1562 when an Ordinance was passed by the Council settling the wages of building workmen, the carpenters were still the largest and most important group of building craftsmen and their wages were correspondingly higher. A master carpenter was paid 11d. a day in summer and 9d. in winter, and 'meanor' carpenters 9d. and 7d. respectively. Tilers and masons were grouped together in a lower paid category and their master workmen received the same rates as the journeymen carpenters.[26] Bricklayers are not found at all in the Freemans' register before 1620 and even then are not mentioned frequently until after 1670, although in the early part of the century their numbers were probably increasing much faster than this suggests.

Although the archaeological evidence for the change from timber to brick in domestic building is uncertain owing to the lack of dated examples, it appears that timber was widely used at least until the last two decades of the 16th century. Thoresby College, it is true, was built in brick throughout at the beginning of the century but the *Valiant Sailor* on the corner of Nelson Street and Priory Lane cannot have been built until after the dissolution of St. Margaret's Priory and was a timber building. So was Greenland Fishery House in Bridge Street, although when that was finished in 1605, brick was already being used extensively by the Council for their new warehouses and cottages on the Common Staithe, and this is the latest known timber building in Lynn. No. 29 Queen Street, a new house of the 1630's, and St. Nicholas House, St. Nicholas Street, new in 1645, were both brick, and from decorative details in the brickwork of other rebuilt houses like Clifton House in Queen Street and No. 11 St. Nicholas Street, by the beginning of the 17th century timber had given way to brick both in rebuilding work and in new building.

The adoption of brick in preference to timber in domestic work in Kings Lynn in this period can be accounted for partly by the shortage of timber and the known fire risk where timber buildings were concerned in towns, both of which made the search for a more suitable material inevitable, and by the increasing supply of brick from the second half of the 16th century which made it the natural alternative. The disadvantage of stone as an alternative to timber was its cost. Since there was no large supply of stone in the immediate vicinity of Lynn this had to be brought from Northamptonshire by barge, not a difficult journey but a costly one which may have as much as doubled the price of the load. Brick, on the other hand, was manufactured in the vicinity of Lynn or brought the relatively short distance from Ely and Cambridge. Even this journey, though, increased the price of a load of bricks by a fifth at the beginning of the 17th century.[27]

By the end of the 16th century there were three main sources from which brick could be obtained for building work in Lynn, and incidentally no evidence at all that bricks were imported from the Low Countries. The major source for public works, at least until the beginning of the 17th century, was the used brick from the abandoned conventual buildings of the monastic houses after their suppression in 1539. The land and buildings of the most important houses in Lynn were all acquired by the town Council and it was they who authorised the carrying away of stone and brick as for instance in 1570 when Alderman John Kynne was sold 100 loads of 'ragged' stone from the Greyfriars at 4d. a load. In the main, most of the materials were probably disposed of after the Council had granted leases of the lands to others, retaining only the site of the Austin Friars as their own source of materials for public building projects. Brick from this source is mentioned in the accounts for building the pump at Kettlemills in the 1570's[28] and for the Common Staithe warehouses until 1630.[29]

A second source of supply was the brickworks in or around Lynn. In 1505 there was a 'tile-kiln' in West Lynn,[30] perhaps the one mentioned in the will of Thomas Thoresby in 1510, and the Thoresby's also had a brickworks at that time in West Winch.[31] In 1560 there was a substantial brickworks known as a brick 'clampe' in Tilney belonging to John Repps from the stocks of which he bequeathed 40,000 bricks to complete various projects when he died.[32] None of these sites may have been productive for very long but they indicate the possibilities of brick production in the immediate vicinity of Lynn. The town Chamberlains in the 17th century purchased brick from Gaywood, Wiggenhall St. Germyns, Wigginhall St. Mary Magdalen, Terrington and Stowbridge, and carriage from all these places in the first half of the century was around 2s. 0d. per thousand.[33] They were also presumably made in Lynn itself. In 1620 holes had been dug in the clay at the East Gates, presumably for the purposes of making bricks,[34] and in 1586 the Chamberlains bought ridge tiles from a potter in Damgate.[35]

The third and largest supply of bricks recorded in the Chamberlains accounts came from Ely and Cambridge. These were of better quality than those made in the marshland and were more expensive. The main supplier to the Council in the early 17th century was a man called Tuck in Ely, who sent both bricks and roof tiles up to Lynn by barge from 1600 to about 1649, and the Council seems also to have purchased bricks at Stourbridge fair.[36] In 1613 when 10,000 bricks were brought from Stourbridge they were purchased for £5 and cost £1 to carry by barge to Lynn, but there is no account of the carriage of bricks from Ely and it is not known how their price was inflated by the distance they had to travel.

Bricks and tiles, then, were available in Lynn from a variety of sources. The price depended on a number of factors including both the quality of the bricks and the distance they had to travel. Prices paid by the town Chamberlains were recorded in

Table II

Year	Bricks per Thousand	Tiles per Thousand	Ridge tiles each	K.L.M. Document Reference
1404		4s. 6d.	1d.	Ea 42
1415	5s. 6d.			Ed 1
1447		5s. 0d.	¾d.	Ea 51
1457		5s. 0d.		Ea 53
1462	4s. 0d.	5s. 0d.	1d.	Ea 54
1466		4s. 8d.	½d.	Ea 55
		2s. 4d.		
1474	5s. 0d.			Ea 56
1479	5s. 0d.	5s. 0d.	1d.	Ea 54
		2s. 0d.		
1483		6s. 0d.	1d.	Ea 58
1491		6s. 8d.	1d.	Ea 61
1527		7s. 0d.	1d.	Ea 70
1528		8s. 0d.		Ea 71
1531			1d.	
1557	10s. 0d.	12s. 0d.	3d.	Ed 1
1584	12s. 6d.	13s. 4d.	3d.	Ed 3
	12s. 0d.	13s. 0d.		
1586	14s. 0d.		2d.	Ed 3
	15s. 0d.			
1587		16s. 0d.	2d.	Ed 3
		15s. 0d.		
1595	13s. 4d.	12s. 0d.	2d.	Ed 1
1598	15s. 0d.	16s. 0d.		
1599	14s. 0d.	15s. 0d.	1d.	Ed 4
1602	13s. 4d.	14s. 0d.	1d.	Ed 4
		13s. 4d.		
1604	10s. 6d.	14s. 0d.	1d.	Ed 4
		13s. 4d.		
1607		15s. 0d.	1d.	Ed 4
1609	17s. 0d.	13s. 8d.	1d.	Ed 4
	13s. 4d.	15s. 0d.		
	16s. 0d.			
1610	16s. 0d.	13s. 4d.	2d.	Ed 4
	14s. 0d.	12s. 0d.		
1611	13s. 0d.	12s. 0d.	1½d.	Ed 6
	14s. 0d.	13s. 0d.		
	10s. 0d.			

Year	Bricks per Thousand	Tiles per Thousand	Ridge tiles each	K.L.M. Document Reference
1612	12s. 6d.	12s. 0d.	E	Ed 5
	13s. 4d.	12s. 6d.		Ed 6
		13s. 4d.		
1613	6s. 8d.	12s. 0d.	1d.	Ed 6
	8s. 0d.	13s. 0d.		
	20s. 0d.			
1614	6s. 8d.	12s. 6d.	1d.	Ed 6
	13s. 4d.			
	16s. 0d.			
1616		14s. 0d.		Ed 6
1617	10s. 0d.			Ed 6
1618	9s. 0d.	13s. 4d.		Ed 6
1619	7s. 0d.	12s. 0d.		Ed 6
	10s. 0d.	13s. 0d.		
	13s. 1d.			
	15s. 0d.			
1620	11s. 0d.	26s. 0d.		Ed 6
	20s. 0d.			Ed 7
1621	10s. 6d.			Ed 7
	14s. 6d.			
	15s. 0d.			
1624	10s. 0d.		1¾d.	Ed 7
	13s. 0d.			
1625	10s. 6d.	13s. 0d.		Ed 7
1627	14s. 0d.	12s. 0d.	1¾d.	Ed 7
		14s. 0d.		
1628	10s. 0d.	12s. 0d.		Ed 7
	12s. 0d.			
	14s. 0d.			
1629	10s. 0d.	12s. 0d.		Ed 7
1649	18s. 0d.			Ed 10
1650	13s. 0d.			Ed 10
	15s. 0d.			
	17s. 0d.			
1654	17s. 0d.	15s. 0d.	1s. 2d. per 100	Ed 10
1658	13s. 0d.	19s. 0d.		Ed 10
	19s. 0d.			

their annual accounts,[37] and the surviving references have been listed. (Table II). Unfortunately there are only spasmodic references to the purchase of small quantities of bricks until the mid-16th century, but there does seem to have been a major increase in price between 1479 and 1557. From the 1580's onwards, however, bricks were bought in greater quantities and it is clear that there were stocks of widely differing prices available. In 1613, for example, it was possible to pay as little as 6s. 8d. a thousand, although most of the bricks purchased by the town in that year cost them 20s. a thousand. Wide variations in price were accounted for by the purchase of bricks from different localities. In 1609, for example, Ely bricks cost 16s. 0d. or 17s. 0d. a thousand, while 'red' bricks, probably from Terrington or Stowbridge were only 13s. 4d. In 1620 the latter had dropped further to 11s. 0d. a thousand while Ely bricks in the following year were 14s. 6d., and in 1628 Stowbridge and Wiggenhall St. Mary Magdalen bricks were 10s. 0d. and 12s. 0d. respectively, with those from Ely costing 14s. 0d.

As variation in price would suggest, the bricks used in Lynn before 1700 vary widely in colour and texture and were clearly made from a great variety of clays. At Clifton House, for example, the bricks used in the tower are hard and somewhat yellowy-brown, whereas the north wall of the house and the warehouses in King Staithe Lane are built in a much softer textured brick of deep red-brown. These in turn differ from the paler, pinkish bricks of No. 29 Queen Street and the bright red-brown of St. George's warehouses. The size of bricks also varied although 9½" x 2½" x 3" was a more or less standard size in most buildings. Very few rubbed bricks seem to have been used before the mid-17th century so most openings were either flat-headed using a wooden lintel or four-centred arch where complicated and accurate brick rubbing was avoided. (Plate 31.) Two kinds of cut brick were used for decoration in Lynn in this period, a bull-nosed shape used for door, window and fireplace details and an ovolo moulded brick used for pediments in relief and drip-moulds over window and door openings, as on Clifton House tower. Some of these were probably bought moulded from the brickworks, and others shaped on the site. In 1625, 10s. 0d. was paid for cutting bricks 'for windows, doors, and tables' on the Common Staithe.[38]

Most brick walls were built without a cavity and, in order to make them more weatherproof, they were often rendered with plaster and painted. In 1579 a tiler or bricklayer at work on some repairs to a house in Damgate plastered the walls of the building and required 12 lbs. of red ochre for 'whiting and redding them on the outside'. A green colour was apparently also used for the same purpose and size, spanish white and 'brown of Spain' were used on the new houses on the common staithe.

Very little surface decoration on brick houses survives from the 17th century, although brick bandcourses were used as at Clifton House and No.29 Queen Street, and there were drip moulds and pediments to window and door openings. What we have lost today is the variety and extravagance of the brick gables that formerly decorated the facades of most large houses. Illustrations of the Tuesday and Saturday Markets in the early 18th century show how widespread this form of adornment was, (Plates 40A) in spite of the fact that few Lynn houses actually had a gable fronting the main street in this period, and were thus restricted to elaborating the dormer gables in the roof. An example of what many houses must have looked like can still be seen at Thoresby College where the Queen Street front was rebuilt in the early 17th century with a row of curved gables with alternating segmental and triangular pediments around the dormer windows. (Plate 27A.) There are also two good curvilinear brick gables built in 1635 and 1645 on the south and west of St. Nicholas churchyard, (Plate 28A) and a pair of stepped gables facing the waterfront in Nos. 23 and 25 King Street. (Plate 28B.)

Although brick was used increasingly in Lynn for walling, roofs, floors, and occasionally internal partitions, were made of timber, as well as fittings such as door and window frames, internal panelling and chimneypieces. Timber for these purposes came from a variety of sources and many different woods were used in 17th century buildings. Local woods included oak and elm and the Council was supplied with these from their manors at Snettisham and Brandon Ferry. In 1578 they paid 10s. 0d. for an elm tree and 2s. 0d. for its carriage from Middleton to the Kettlemills, while in 1658, an oak tree from the same source cost 14d. the foot.[39] Oak was the most expensive wood used for building. In 1584 eight to nine foot long oak joists cost 12d. a couple, and small rafters (spars) 12d. each. Deal, on the other hand, imported either direct from Danzig or purchased in the Low Countries, was cheaper, and appears to have been used extensively in the Council's building work, both on new buildings and on repairs to old property. In 1587, small 'fir' spars cost only 6d. a pair, while in 1597 10 foot rafters were 10d. each, and the larger size 17 feet long cost 2s. 2d. a pair. In 1612 a new house in Common Staithe Lane used 225 seasoned deals, 82 feet of firs and a quantity of oak, all of which, including the oak, seems to have been imported.[40]

Softwoods were used for roof and floor construction. In some buildings, probably warehouse, the roofs were ceiled with boarding beneath the rafters and in 1599 six and a half deals and four boards were purchased for 6d. for 'lining of spars'.[41] The roof covering was usually tiles fixed to a layer of laths by means of a wooden peg known as a 'thack pin'. Thatching, because of the danger of fire, was forbidden by an Ordinance of 1572.[42] Timber floors and joists were also made from softwood and on the Common Staithe there was a saw-pit where such timbers were cut. Ground floors were of brick or tile probably laid straight into the earth. John Kercher at the end of the 16th century paved his house with 'Ely Brick', and in 1625, 80 paving tiles were purchased for a house on the Common Staithe at a cost of 6s. 8d.[43]

Window and door frames were made of oak and painted on the outside with 'Spanish white' to keep out the weather. By the end of the 16th century most windows were flat headed and mullioned and transomed and some hall windows were very large, being anything up to six feet square as is the one in No. 29 Queen Street. (Plate 22B.) Such windows were clearly intended to be glazed and indeed window glass was quite common in Lynn by the end of the 16th century, not only in the homes of the wealthy but even in the workshops of the towns craftsmen. In 1579, for instance, when the Council altered a house in Damgate to accommodate a canvas weaver, they put three new windows in the workroom all of which were glazed at a cost of 6d. a foot.[44] At the same time, it was not until 1639 that James Revett had a window in his house 'which usually stood open' glazed and a casement made so it could be opened and closed.[45] Window frames for the new houses on the Common Staithe were purchased ready made, including the casements for those that were to be made to open. The glass was then inserted on the site. Most window glass used in Lynn at the beginning of the 17th century came from Burgundy and was fixed in lead cames in diamond shaped panes about three inches across. Where the glazed portion was not intended to open the lead cames were fixed to thin wooden bars between the mullions.

By the 17th century many houses had probably replaced the coloured cloths that kept out the draught inside with wooden panelling. This was made of oak and there are several good examples surviving in Lynn, the best of which is in No. 1 St. Margaret's Place in a small back room next to the warehouse. The panels are square shaped and fixed in narrow stiles and muntins with shallow bead moulds round the edges. Occasionally, as in No. 32 Bridge Street, there was also a carved wooden cornice and there is a frieze in the upper parlour in No. 29 Queen Street. Usually panelling has the appearance of having been bought by the yard and cut later to fit a particular room.

Notes to Chapter IV

1 W.G. Hoskins, 'The Rebuilding of Rural England', *Past and Present,* IV, (1953) 44-8, 50-51; M.W. Barley, *The English Farmhouse and Cottage* (1961) 57-61.

2 Hoskins, 'Rebuilding', 44.

3 Defoe, *Tour,* 73.

4 Badeslade, *Navigation,* b.

5 See above Ch. IV

6 I am grateful to Mr. J.M.W. Laithwaite for this information.

7 Appendix II, p.177.

8 Norfolk Archives (Bradfer Lawrence Collection), Maps 42.

9 Appendix II, p.180.

10 Appendix II, p.187.

11 Appendix II, p.185.

12 Appendix II, p.184.

13 D. Portman, *Exeter Houses 1400-1700,* (1966), 34.

14 P.C.C. 47 Windsor; K.L.M./H.B.V/12d.

15 It was illustrated in *The Builder,* 1889, II, 117.

16 P.C.C., 6 Ketchyn.

17 See below, p.160.

18 M. Bardswell, 'Kings Lynn: Greenland Fisheries Building', *Norf. Arch.,* Vol. XXX, (1957), 198-9.

19 W.G. Hoskins, 'English Provincial Towns', 18.

20 K.L.M./Db27/1595 et seq. References occur throughout the series in the rental.

21 Appendix II, p.182.

22 See below p.102.

23 H. van de Wee, *The Growth of the Antwerp Market,* (1963), II, 384-7.

24 B.H. St. J. O'Neil, 'Some Seventeenth Century House in Great Yarmouth', *Archaeologia,* XCV, (1953), 141 passim.

25 W.A. Pantin, 'Domestic Architecture in Oxford', *Antiquaries Jnl.* XXVII, (1947), 130-3; D. Portman, *Exeter Houses,* 71, Fig. XX.

26 K.L.M./HO IV, 22 Oct. 1562.

27 K.L.M./Db 27, 1613 and 1618.

28 K.L.M./Bc 7/Part 5.

29 K.L.M./Db27/1595 et seq.

30 Will of John Palmer. P.C.C.3, Adeane.

31 P.C.C. 34 Bennett.

32 P.C.C. 12 Loftes.

33 K.L.M./Ed/4-10.

34 K.L.M./H.B. VII/306.

35 K.L.M./Ea. 1586

36 K.L.M./Db27, esp. 1599, 1613.

37 K.L.M./Ea and Ed *passim.*

38 K.L.M./Db 27.

39 K.L.M./H.B.V., 185d; H.B. VII/1658.

40 K.L.M./Db 27 (1612).

41 *Ibid* (1599).

42 K.L.M./H.B.V/59d.

43 K.L.M./Db 27 (1625).

44 K.L.M./Bc 7

45 K.L.M./Db 27 (1639).

V

Commercial and Industrial Buildings to 1700

A GREAT MANY of the early commercial and industrial buildings of Kings Lynn have now disappeared, party because many of them were not built of durable materials, but mainly because the advanced technology and altered pattern of work of a later period made them obsolete and their sites were redeveloped. Reconstructions of such buildings, whether from documentary sources or from their remains above ground, are always incomplete, and this is the more unfortunate because this type of building could tell us so much about the way in which the people of Lynn have gained their livelihood. More evidence survives about those buildings in which a relatively large capital outlay was involved; thus we know most about commercial buildings such as warehouses, and those industrial buildings whose construction was financed from public funds, like the town corn mill. Practically nothing is recorded about the premises of the small craftsman, and it is particularly unfortunate that the parts of the town centre where they worked were redeveloped in the 19th century. It has often been assumed that most of these people occupied a dual purpose building, combining the dwelling house with the workroom under one roof. For the many who needed only limited space and had no bulky machinery this seems a reasonable assumption and it is borne out by accounts of their equipment in documents like Probate Inventories. Others like tanners or ropemakers needed special accommodation, separate from the house, yet very little survives in Lynn to tell us what it was like.

The commercial and industrial buildings are here treated under four categories; warehouses for storing merchandise; shops where goods were not only sold but often made as well; inns; and buildings erected to accommodate certain special industries.

Warehouses

Warehouses were needed in Lynn for two quite different purposes; first for relatively short periods of time, to house goods in transit; and secondly, to house those goods that were either to be processed by industrial craftsmen or to be marketed in the town retail. The accommodation in either case was probably much the same; the difference lay in siting and layout of the building. The former were built as near as possible to the main routes, particularly where important points of interchange occurred between one system of transport and another; the latter were to be found among the side streets of the town in the areas occupied by craftsmen and shopkeepers. Warehouses survive in Lynn in great numbers and there are very well-preserved examples dating from the 15th century to 1700. Indeed, it must be unique for a town to have preserved so much visual evidence of its past commercial activity. Most of the surviving examples were built to house goods in transit. They stand almost exclusively in one part of the town, along the waterfront where, from the end of the 13th century, was located the most important point of interchange between the sea-going vessels and the barges from the hinterland. Practically all other warehouses have disappeared, including all the early medieval ones in Damgate at the points of interchange there between road and river transport, and all the industrial warehouses in the town centre. Although no complete description of the warehouse accommodation in Kings Lynn can now be given, the surviving examples along the waterfront are nevertheless important evidence of Lynn's later period of commercial expansion.

Merchants built warehouses to protect their wares from theft, and from the weather. The need for warehouses in a town like Kings Lynn was inescapable. It was a port where goods had to be transferred from boats to carts, or from small river craft to sea-going ships, thus demanding that merchandise must at least touch land; their building was also affected by the urban xenophobia of the late Middle Ages. In each trading town only its own merchants should handle any transaction within the town walls. Lynn merchants thus made it impossible for merchants from other towns, or overseas, to by-pass them in any transaction involving the use of their port, and in this way they succeeded in turning the town into a halting place for merchandise of all kinds. Public warehouses were provided for 'foreign' merchants on the Common Staithe, and Lynn merchants themselves had their own warehouse accommodation usually attached to their dwelling houses. From the 15th century, these private warehouses were, like the public ones, sited by the waterside. Indeed, it was they which determined the site of the house rather than the other way about.

The choice of a waterfront site for a warehouse housing goods in transit was an obvious one. For goods being trans-shipped in Lynn harbour it was clearly a waste of effort to move them far from the waterfront and warehouses were laid out accordingly. From this point of view, a warehouse lying parallel to the river bank could operate most efficiently. Goods could be unloaded into it along its whole length and it could be filled in such a way that all wares were equally accessible from the river bank. A number of warehouses in Lynn were, in fact, laid out this way, and a good example survives in Hampton Court. There were difficulties in this kind of layout. One was that, because the average building plot along the waterfront was only between 20 and 30 feet broad, to provide adequate storage space parallel to the river would have meant building high. Furthermore, any warehouse in this position would, in addition, have cut off access to the rest of the plot from the waterfront. Finally, since the waterfront in Lynn was being reclaimed westwards slowly all the time to 1700, a building layout that permitted lengthwise extension was necessary. A warehouse across the width of the plot only made this more difficult, apart from the fact that once the line of the waterfront had receded, a cross-wise warehouse left alongside the earlier line of the quay was of no advantage.

Warehouses were, therefore, most often laid out at right angles to the waterfront but built right up to the edge of the bank so their gable ends were accessible from a boat. Whenever a new length of bank was reclaimed the warehouses were extended to the waterside. This is demonstrated in the long, unbroken lines of such buildings in King Street, where the river once flowed close to the line of the road on its west side, and where about 200 feet were reclaimed by slow stages in the 15th and 16th centuries and built on. Access from the land was by means of a passageway running down one side of the plot. (Fig.9.) Although this is the most common form of warehouse layout, there were variations depending on the size and shape of the plot. In the part of the town to the south of the Purfleet, the river Ouse flowed closer to the line of the waterfront streets than it did in King Street. The plot between street and riverbank in the southern sector, was broader in relation to its width than a plot of equal size in the north end and in many cases two parallel ranges of warehouses could be accommodated. Sometimes they were laid out side by side as at Clifton House in Queen Street (Fig.42) or were separated by the width of a passageway as at No. 29 Queen Street (Figs.22 and 40). Where the plot was very wide, and some of the tenements in Nelson Street were almost square, a courtyard arrangement was the usual result, as at Hampton Court, with one warehouse range lying parallel to the river. (Fig.8.)

Lynn merchants handled a variety of goods, from the bulky wares – grain, timber, wool and coal – to the small but expensive commodities brought from overseas – dyestuffs, spices and household goods of all kinds. None of these commodities, however, was difficult to store. Two more problematical cargoes were wine and fish, wine because the barrels were heavy and awkward to lift, and fish because much of it will have been fresh and wet. There is no archaeological evidence on the warehousing of fish, although the Council leased special fish houses on the Common Staithe and this may indicate that they were specially designed for the purpose. Wine, like millstones, could presumably be housed at ground level, although it was always said that the long tunnel-vaulted chambers beneath the warehouses along the waterfront were designed so that barrels could be rolled into the building without any hoisting from a boat.

Medieval Warehouses

All merchants needed at least a pound in which goods could be made safe from theft and probably the first provision a merchant made for the storage of his wares was a strongly walled enclosure, not necessarily roofed, which could be made safe at night. In the Red Register there are references to courts enclosed by stone walls among the merchant houses, and the practice of building these courts persisted into the 17th century for storage of timber, coal and other goods that could be left out in the open. Most merchants were also dealing in commodities like grain and salt which had to be stored in a place protected from the weather and required a roofed structure for storage. Warehouses must have made an early appearance among the buildings of Lynn and by the time the Red Register was compiled there were already many of them lining the waterfront.

Very few warehouses that can be confidently ascribed to a period before 1500 now survive in Lynn. There are only three examples, all to the south of the Saturday Market, where later rebuilding was less widespread than in the northern part of the town. They are the so-called 'Hanseatic' warehouse on the south quay, the Hampton Court warehouse, and the warehouses of the Hanseatic steelyard in St. Margaret's Lane. Of these, only one, the south range of the Steelyard warehouses, was built in timber, the rest being in brick or stone. Brick or stone was clearly the better material to use, being more durable, and fire-proof, but before the beginning of the 17th century it was also probably more expensive than timber construction. An accident of survival then should not be read as significant. Medieval warehouses were probably timber built but the evidence for this has not survived.

There were good reasons why stone rather than timber should have been chosen for the 'Hanseatic' warehouse on the south quay. (Plate 29.) This building, which uses the same walling material as the Hampton Court house and thus may be as early as *c.*1300, was sited about 150 feet forward of the line of the medieval river bank. Even on a map of 1830, the warehouse can be seen to have occupied what was, in fact, an island in the Ouse estuary.[1] High tide must have surrounded the building; floods washed frequently at its walls. Timber construction may well have been considered too fragile for a building in this position and it was built in a rubble mixture faced in patches, at least on the ground storey, with dressed stone. As it stands now the warehouse is two storeys high; the upper storey and its gable ends are mainly brick and may, in fact, date from a later period of rebuilding, perhaps the 15th century, when a crown post roof was installed. It is a wider building than was customary in Lynn, the roof span being nearly 40 feet. The steep pitch of the medieval roof has been preserved because the recent re-roofing has been carried out without altering the pitch of the gable end walls. It was laid out parallel to the river bank, partly for the convenience of loading goods from the water, and partly perhaps to present the shorter wall faces to the ebb and flow of the tide. The vulnerability of the building to the water may account for the series of arched openings which still survive in the ground floor of the north gable end; they were perhaps put there to reduce the danger of structural damage from floods by allowing the water to be taken through the building in a special channel which has since disappeared.

The main entrance to the warehouse was from the west, in the centre of the long side where boats could be drawn up alongside. From the town to the east it was probably approached down Leadinghall Lane, either on a causeway, or by a wooden jetty such as existed at the end of College Lane in 1557.[2] Windows to light and ventilate the storage space are found in all four elevations, but they vary in size and design and many of them appear to be post-medieval insertions. In the ground storey on the west there are four openings, symmetrically arranged about the central door, which are medieval. Two of these, now made into doors, have segmental heads, the lintol of which is carved from one piece of stone, and are rebated to take a wooden shutter. In the windows on the first floor the span of the flat window head, carried on the top horizontal member of the wooden window frame, is broken by a mullion, a 16th century form of window construction. In the south gable end the windows have segmental arches made with cut bricks and are probably 19th century. Internally, all the evidence of the medieval plan has disappeared. It was presumably without internal partitions, providing large areas of uninterrupted floor space for layout merchandise. There is no sign that this building was heated.

Hampton Court warehouse was also built in brick rather than timber, and perhaps for the same reason. It was laid out in the 15th century, at right angles to the already existing hall in Nelson Street, and lay parallel to the river Ouse which flowed right beside its western wall. (Fig.8; Plate 5B.) Thus although it was not as vulnerable to the action of the tide as the 'Hanseatic' warehouse it was nevertheless sufficiently exposed to render timber construction, at least for the ground storey, unsuitable.

In the course of the 19th century, the whole of Hampton Court, including the warehouse, was converted into a number of separate cottage dwellings and this has obscured most medieval work in the warehouse range except the ground floor arcade in the west wall. (Plate 5B.) All the original door and window openings have gone and all trace of internal planning. The arcade, however, is a most valuable piece of archaeological evidence. It divides the ground floor of the west, or riverside, wall into eight bays by circular brick columns with stone caps, simply moulded, the wall of the upper storey being carried on four-centred arches made with cut bull-nosed bricks. This arcade allowed merchandise to be unloaded into the warehouse along its whole length. There is no evidence that the openings in the arcade could be closed with wooden shutters so the first floor alone must have been used for safe storage. This type of warehouse was not built in 16th century Lynn even where a wide waterfront site was available, perhaps because of the cost of construction or because of the disadvantage of having a ground floor that could not be made secure.

All the warehouses of the Hanseatic Steelyard survive as a part of their complex of buildings on the corner of St. Margaret's Lane and the Saturday Market. (Fig.26; Plate 30.) This was a fairly wide site with room for two parallel rows of warehouses on either side of a narrow courtyard. At its western or river end, this court may originally have been closed off with a short cross range as it is at present; but the existing building is of different construction from the rest and may be later in date. All the Steelyard buildings date from the years after 1474

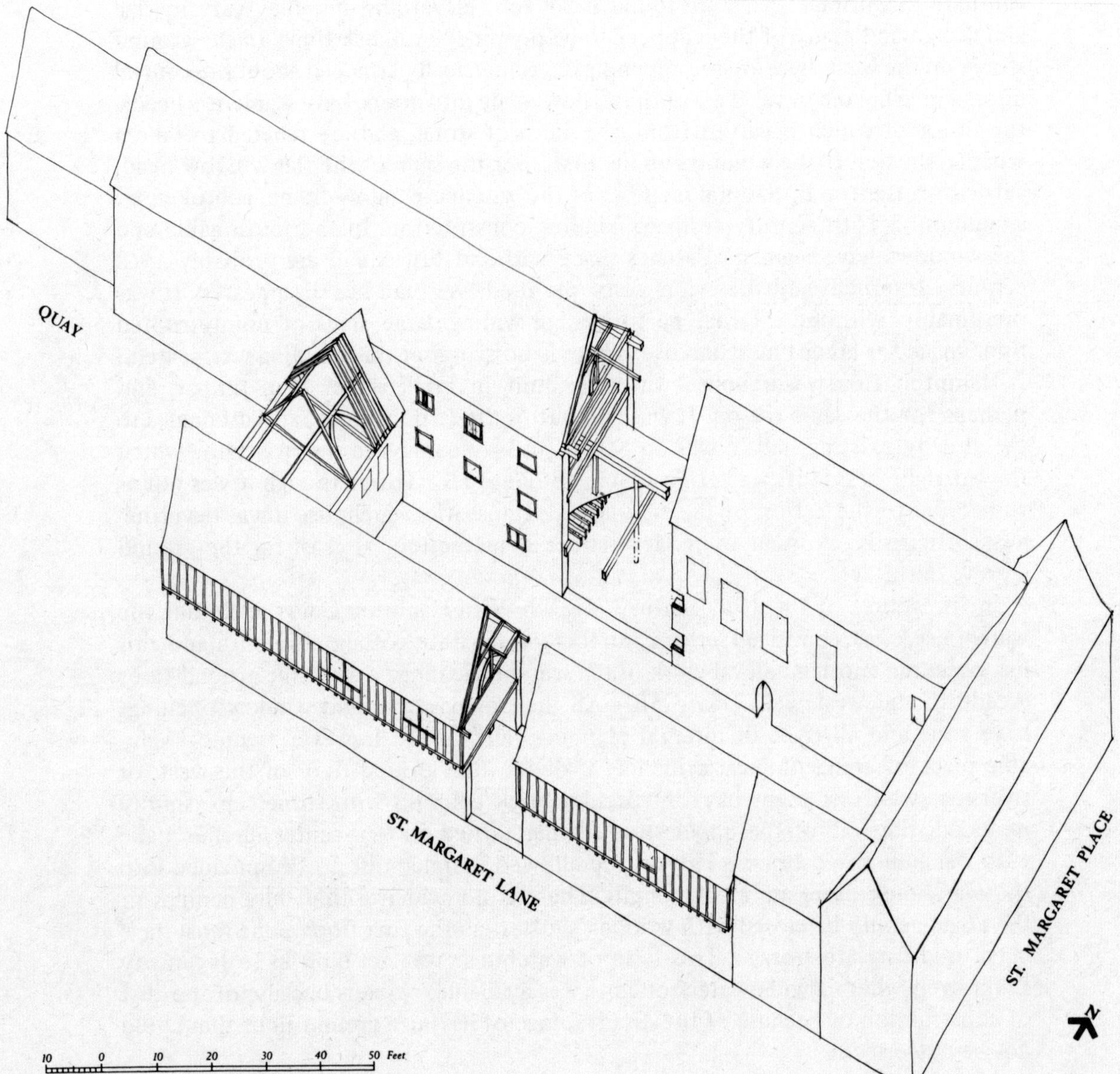

Fig 26 *The Hanseatic Steelyard, St. Margaret's Place: reconstruction*

when the German merchants were re-granted their special privileges in Lynn and obtained licence from the town to erect a Steelyard.[3]

The two ranges of warehouses to the north and south of the courtyard are of different size and construction, but both had the same kind of crown post roof and so are roughly contemporary. The short range linking them across the west end of the yard has a trussed roof with side purlins, a form of construction found more often in the early 16th century. The 15th century ranges are two storeys high on the south, and three storeys on the north, and about 100 feet long. The larger, northern one is built in brick, the one on the south, alongside St. Margaret's Lane is of timber.

The brick warehouse has been much altered internally and, in order to use the roof space, the collars, collar purlins and crown posts have been removed leaving only the rafters and the tie beams of the crown post trusses in which evidence of the former roof can still be found. One original door and several window openings still survive indicating that there was an entrance through a narrow pointed arch opening from the courtyard about 30 feet from the west wall of the house. How goods were taken in and out is not known, but it was probably from the quay through an opening in the west gable. Since this warehouse was later extended westward the evidence for this has now disappeared. Window openings were made only in the south wall where they looked into the courtyard. The north wall was once entirely blank. As they survive today, the window openings were made without an arched head, with the wooden window frame acting as a lintol. In spans of more than 18 inches this was supported by the insertion of a wooden mullion. Window openings vary in width by several inches and were erratically placed in the wall. Internally the present building is still used as a warehouse; there are long uninterrupted floors with shoots at intervals to move grain down through the building. There is no evidence of the medieval warehouse having been divided internally.

The two-storey timber warehouse on the south uses the same method of construction as the east range of Nos. 37-9 Chapel Street. The first floor is jetteyed out into St. Margaret's Lane, but on the north, or courtyard, side the wall is built up in one plane. At present the ground storey is brick built, and brick replaces the original wattle and daub infill between the timber studs. Internally, parts of the first floor and the whole of the ground floor have been remodelled, but there is a section in which the original crown post roof survives and evidence of two window openings in the first storey facing into St. Margaret's Lane. When it was built this warehouse, too, may have consisted of long floors uninterrupted by permanent partitions.

The Hanseatic Steelyard would almost certainly have had a dwelling house attached to the warehouses, probably located, as was customary in merchant houses in Lynn, at the street end of the complex. The present house on this site was newly built in the 18th century, and contains no visible evidence of its medieval forerunner. The dwelling house, however, has now encroached into the eastern ends of both warehouses, again, a not uncommon feature in Lynn where the practice of building house and warehouse as one continuous range under the same roof made such encroachment a simple, not a major structural alteration.

Warehouses in the 16th and 17th Centuries

The mid-16th century marked a new period of expansion of Lynn's trade and an increasing volume of heavy, bulky goods had to be laid up in the town's warehouses. Almost all Lynn merchants dealt in grain and in smaller quantities of other crops like peas and beans, grown in the rich farming hinterland and brought to Lynn by barge. From Lynn, these were sent out by vessels either overseas to the Low Countries or coastwise both along the east coast to London and the south-east, and to Newcastle and the north-east. When, in December 1573, a search was made of Lynn warehouses in an attempt to control the illegal export of grain, only 250 quarters were found in store,[4] but the Licences issued to Lynn merchants between 1568 and 1589 show that most of them were handling quite considerable quantities even under restriction. In 1579 the licence permitted the export of 40,000 quarters over three years,[5] most of which was taken up by Lynn merchants in batches of about 300-400 quarters on average per year.[6] Although the export of grain naturally fluctuated according to the harvest, in unlicenced periods Lynn could expect to have to handle between 20,000 and 40,000 quarters annually from 1550 to the end of the 17th century.[7]

Kings Lynn's major import was coal, brought coastwise by lighter from the north-east, particularly from the Newcastle coalfield, and trans-shipped at Lynn into barges for the journey up river to the towns of the hinterland. By the 1680's the East Anglian ports were importing more coal even than London and the greatest quantity was handled by the merchants of Lynn.[8] In 1561-2, 4955 chalders (8,671 tons) were imported into the town and a peak was reached in the 16th century when in 1586 the town handled 9582 chalders (18,685 tons).[9] By the 1680's Lynn was handling up to 16,543 chalders of coal a year, the largest amount of any provincial port.[10]

Of the other bulky cargoes handled in Lynn, only fish and timber were of major importance by the 16th century. Wool had disappeared almost entirely from Lynn warehouses by that time and even cloth, which in the first half of the century was still coming to the town from Suffolk, was of very little importance in the trade of the town after 1550. Fish, however, was a staple item in most people's diet, and although Lynn merchants seem to have abandoned the annual voyage to the Greenland fisheries by mid-century, large quantities of codling, herring, sprats and whiting passed through the town, particularly in the February mart. Timber was imported into Lynn mainly from the Baltic and sent up river to supply the building industry inland.

Apart from bulky goods that were likely to require considerable warehouse space, many other commodities in smaller quantities came into Lynn mainly from overseas for distribution inland; groceries and household furnishings, iron nails, millstones, paper, glass, salt and many others it would be tedious to list.[11] Special accommodation was not, it seems, required for these.

Evidence of the commercial prosperity of Lynn in the 16th and 17th centuries is to be found in the scale of warehouse building carried out from the mid-16th century. Between 1550 and 1700 practically every warehouse along the Ouse bank was rebuilt and spacious new warehouses were added alongside. Many of these still survive today.

Warehouses of this period in Lynn are simple buildings without any of the complications either of planning or structure found in contemporary domestic work. Basically they are single-cell buildings, often of very considerable length, but limited by the span of roof and floor timbers to a width of around 20 feet. None of the surviving examples exceeds two storeys in height, although the West Prospect of the town engraved in 1725 seems to show the occasional three storey building along the water's edge. (Plate 3A.) These were almost certainly exceptional, since the problems of raising loads to any height were considerable; moreover, there was always plenty of space on building plots to extend buildings lengthwise rather than upwards. From 1550 warehouses were invariably built of brick, but some of the earlier ones used materials taken from the sites of the suppressed monastic houses and this included the occasional lump of dressed stone. They had tiled roofs to minimise the danger from fire, but wooden floors and, where they were used, wooden internal partitions. The 'corn chambers' and probably the upper floors were rendered internally with plaster, or perhaps lined with deal boarding, but otherwise the brick walls were left exposed both on the outside and the inside of the building. Many of the surviving examples still retain their original windows and it appears that they were well lit and ventilated, often from both long sides by means of mullioned windows with iron bars that could be closed with shutters. No form of permanent heating arrangement seems to have been used.

The layout of warehouses depended on the size and width of the building plot. Where the tenement was long and very narrow, as at St. George's Hall, the successive ranges of warehouses extended in a long line down one side of the plot right up to the waters edge and were entered from a passageway left down the remaining land at the side. (Plate 31B.) Where building plots were wider, warehouses, along with other outbuildings, were often arranged to enclose a number of small open courts and yards, as at Clifton House in Queen Street, thus giving space for storage of wares as could be left in the open. Coal for instance was stored in such yards, usually the ones nearest the waterside. In all cases, the lines of warehouse buildings were brought right up to the edge of the river so that at at least one point on the merchant's land it was possible to unload goods under cover. In many cases there was an opening in the gable end of a warehouse, known as a watergate, with a small slipway inside which, at high tide, made it possible to bring small boats in under the ground floor of the building. A succession of such openings in the warehouse walls for the whole length of the waterfront are shown in the West Prospect (1725) (Plate 3A) and can only have been made for this purpose. The only one to survive is in the west gable end of the St. George's Hall warehouses in King Street. (Plate 31A.) Another probable reason for bringing the warehouse forward to the waterside was to provide a firm anchorage for a hoist or crane. Privately owned cranes were used in Lynn in the 16th and 17th centuries although many people also used the public crane on the Common Staithe. There is, however, no archaeological evidence for these and it is not possible to tell exactly how they worked. Much of the waterfront has been rebuilt since the beginning of the 18th century especially to the south of the Purfleet where the new South Quay was made in 1853. This has obscured much of the earlier evidence.

The best preserved complex of warehouses is that which belonged to Clifton House in Queen Street. (Figs.42-5; Plate 32.) The property is bounded on the north by King's Staithe Lane and lies between the river Ouse on the west and Queen Street to the east. Originally, in the early medieval period, the tenement may have been divided into at least two and possibly three separate properties, but by the 16th century these had been thrown into one, leaving, as evidence of the earlier division, two parallel ranges at right angles to the street on the northern part of the plot containing both house and warehouse. The house lay to the east, fronting onto Queen Street and the warehouses behind stretched down to the river. There were thus parallel ranges of warehouses beside King's Staithe Lane and a considerable area to the south which appears from the 1889 Ordnance Survey to have also been laid out with warehouses around a large open courtyard. One warehouse lay parallel to the Ouse bank at the west end of the King's Staithe Lane buildings, the western wall of which still survives inside the modern shed which now occupies this site. The courtyard lay to the east of this building and was closed in on the south and east by ranges which have now disappeared. The eastern range continued to the line of the tower which today marks the junction between the domestic and the warehouse accommodation. All the warehouses were built in brick except the one on the south side of the court. The walls of this building have almost disappeared but the remaining parts show a widespread use of stone mixed with brick. The fact that much of the stone is carved with medieval mouldings and other decorative forms suggests that this building, at least, owes much to the fabric of the one of the suppressed monasteries in Lynn.

Of this large complex of warehouses only the double range alongside King's Staithe Lane still stands complete. They were built, on archaeological evidence, probably towards the end of the 16th century, when the whole property belonged to the Walden family, merchants who dealt in many different kinds of cargoes including grain and coal. The warehouses are two storeys high but had a ceiled roof space which gave extra second floor accommodation. Beneath the present ground floor are two parallel semi-excavated cellars with brick barrel-vaulted ceilings. The one under the north range connected with the medieval undercroft of the house. These are mostly 18th century in date but at their western end may mark the line and depth of the slipway to bring boats into the warehouse at high tide. In the southern range there is still a trap door in the ground floor which led into the cellar, through which goods could be handled.

The main structural walls of the warehouses were built in a reddish brown brick, probably manufactured locally, and were roofed in tile. The floors were made of timber and were constructed in a way that is characteristic of warehouse design in Lynn into the 19th century. The first floor was made in the usual way by laying beams across the width of the building at convenient intervals for the span of the joists, the second, attic, floor was more economically made by standing posts on the centres of main beams of the floor below to support a beam running lengthwise down the building. The second floor joists then crossed from wall to wall, the span having been halved by the lengthwise support. This left a central row of posts on the first floor but in a warehouse this was no particular disadvantage. Many warehouses in Lynn were floored in this way and a particularly good example can still be seen in the Steelyard warehouses in St. Margaret's Lane. (Fig.26.) In the warehouses in King's Staithe Lane the roof was made very crudely from timbers of all sizes, many of them re-used. There was no proper system of trussed and common rafters and no lengthwise support. Such a roof must have needed attention very early on in its life, and has been patched up subsequently in various ways. Some pairs of rafters now have collars and parts of the roof has side purlins tacked on with nails. The fairly spacious area in the roof was ceiled beneath the rafters with boarding and it may be that a part of it was used as a dormitory for apprentices. The will of Margaret Miller, who died in 1556 in a house in King Street, mentions accommodation of this kind for her servants.[12]

The warehouses were lit and ventilated both from the north and south by means of small irregularly-spaced, iron barred mullioned windows that could be closed from the inside with shutters. The main entrance to the building was from the waterfront although there was probably a way through from the house and also a door into the courtyard. The main entrance now is in the middle of the King's Staithe Lane front where a high doorway has been made and part of the first floor demolished to make way for a passage through for loaded carts to the yard beyond. This is probably a later arrangement since the passageway also breaks through the line of the semi-excavated cellar roofs.

The King's Staithe Lane warehouse are typical of their kind, and exactly similar buildings can be found either in single or double ranges elsewhere in the town. Many of them are visually very attractive although it is doubtful whether this was intended by their designers. In King's Staithe Lane, however, the band-courses of brick which decorated the walls of the house were continued along the warehouse wall, and where they were exposed to view in this way it is possible at least that their appearance was considered.

In addition to private warehouses, there was also in Lynn, in the 16th century, and probably in medieval times, some provision of public warehousing, built, maintained and leased by the Council. These buildings were located in two principal areas of the town: at the mouth of the Purfleet where there were public landing stages both on the north and south bank – the King's Staithe to the south and Purfleet quay to the north – and on the east side of the Tuesday Market on the Common Staithe.

In the 16th and 17th centuries, King's Staithe was a large open space beside the river Ouse bounded on the south by King's Staithe Lane and on the north by the Purfleet. The Council acquired the site with the Fee Farm of the Bishop's manor but they seem to have done little to develop it in the course of the 16th century. There was no crane there or undercover storage space. It appears to have been a landing stage used chiefly for coal and timber, where merchants could lease a coalyard by the year.[13] Exactly how a coalyard was constructed is a matter of conjecture but presumably it had a wall around it to keep it secure even if it had no roof.

Purfleet quay was more extensively developed. There was a wharf made with 'lime and stone' in 1547,[14] and warehouses were being leased by the Council there in 1622.[15] They also leased six ships' berths in the Purfleet river to merchants, but whether or not they built them is not known. There were no coal yards there leased to the public and very little is known about the layout of the quay. A crane was installed in 1623.

Because of its proximity to the Tuesday Market, the most important public landing stage was the Common Staithe. Here the Council initiated a major rebuilding programme in the 1580's which was completed over the next half century. The accounts of this work are unfortunately incomplete but from those which survive it is possible to gain some idea of what the layout of this important area was.[16]

The Common Staithe seems to have been the property of the Trinity Gild and it was only acquired by the Council after the dissolution of the Gilds and Chantries in 1547.[17] At that date it had already been partly laid out with warehouses and had a crane bequeathed to the gild in 1528 by John Burdy.[18] It occupied the site on the Ouse bank to the west of the Tuesday Market, and was bounded on the north by Pudding Lane (now Water Lane) and on the south by Common Staithe Lane both of which lanes were closed with gates. The main entrance to the staithe was by a gate lying between the two lane ends; the Custom House was either just beside the gate or in the gate-house over it; and the weigh-house stood beside it to the north. The Common Staithe yard itself was probably largely open ground. Along the waterfront it had a series of steps and mooring for boats, with a public coalyard at the foot of the Common Staithe Lane. The exact location of the crane is not known but it must have been right beside the water. It was not only used for hauling out heavy cargoes from boats, but for stepping masts. It was rebuilt in 1568. From the crane, and from the landing steps, goods were moved by labour controlled by the town's Company of Porters.

The yard was lined with buildings on the north, south and east. Facing outwards from the yard were various cottages and sheds entered from the lanes or the market-place; facing inwards in two rows, one on the north and one on the south, were the public warehouses which backed onto and sometimes interconnected with the cottages. This whole complex was rebuilt by the Council after 1585.[19] Their first new buildings were the 'fish warehouse', a group of three at the east end of the southern warehouse block, and in 1587 they began on the northern range.[20] When the rebuilding of the warehouses was complete there were nine on the south and seven on the north of the yard. They were built in brick and were all two storeys high with the upper rooms plaster rendered. These were used for storing grain. The ground storeys were used for storing a great variety of wards from dairy produce for the Mart to textiles, dried fish and iron and each section was fastened with an iron lock to which the tenant kept the key. Warehouses were mostly leased by merchants from other towns, although occasionally a Lynn merchant leased one temporarily. Unfortunately nothing now remains above ground of this area.

Shops

In pre-industrial towns a shop was not only a place where goods were sold; often it was also the place where they were made. In many small market towns there can have been only a few shops which specialised entirely in retail trade since so much of the food, clothing and equipment they sold was made locally. But in a town like Lynn where imported wares were handled from earliest times the proportion of retail shops to workshops must have been much greater. Thus in discussing shops in Kings Lynn we are considering two quite different kinds of accommodation: one housed the tools and equipment of craftsmen and provided the space for them to work in; the other housed the stock-in-trade of a retailer and the equipment needed to store this stock over long periods, together with some means of dividing and measuring the stock for re-sale. What they had in common was the fact that in both kinds of establishment the public came to make purchases, and this had to be accounted for in the layout and design of the accommodation.

Unfortunately, very little is known, from documentary sources of craftsmen's shops in Lynn or of the processes that were carried out there. There are, however, some 16th century lists of the contents of retail shops which give some idea of the kind of businesses they were. In 1574 an attempt was made by the Council to prevent either the chandlers on the one hand, or the linen drapers, grocers and mercers on the other, from gaining the major part of the town's retail trade and they issued an Ordinance setting out what each group was permitted to sell.[21] The contents of such shops were very various. Both groups were allowed to sell soap, vinegar, resin, hops, honey, nails, birdlime, wax, bottles, strings and ties, bowstrings, fine flax, shoe horns, trenchers, cords, points, ink, paper, pins, shirt string, needles, combs, nails, clasps, eyes, sacking, wool-cards, cotton wool, stringing, pots, and straw hats. The chandlers in addition could sell a number of other miscellaneous articles like bread-grates, house scales, shovels, lanterns, skips, and whetstones and an inventory of the contents of a chandler's shop in 1611 shows the range extended from groceries – figs, raisins, cloves, ginger, pepper, liquorice, coarse sugar and white sugar candy, dyestuffs (madder, indigo and powdered blue) – to brimstone and gunpowder.[22] These latter were probably the encroachments on the grocers' businesses the 1574 Ordinance was designed to prevent.

The equipment in a 16th century retail shop was primitive and limited to the simplest storage facilities and weighing and measuring machines. Richard Dichard, a tailor, bequeathed a shop-board in his will in 1557, probably a hinged counter which let down in front of the window and at night could be raised to act as a shutter.[23] Other wills and Probate Inventories mention weights and scales, measuring jars and vats, and chests for storage. Thomas Some, for example, a mercer who had two shops in Mercer Row in 1567, bequeathed two great beams with scales and three and a half hundred weights.[24] Thomas Langlie, a chandler, had in his shop in 1611 three pairs of old brass scales, brass weights up to five and a half pounds, and pewter measures of pint, half pint, and quarter pint. He also had two shop chests for storage and a lead vat to store oil in.[25] Smaller shopkeepers, like Agnes Bell in 1524, had only the odd coffer in the shop worth mentioning in her will.[26]

So few structures known to have been used as shops now survive that it is difficult to be precise about their siting, planning or construction. It has always been assumed that in medieval times, if not later, the shop was a part of the dwelling house, but although this is so in a number of cases in Lynn there is also some evidence that shops were built separately as distinct building types without the attached living quarters. The earliest documentary references to shops occur in the Red Register where a clear distinction is drawn between the shop with a hall and the shop and solar.[27] The former had an attached room which could be heated, the latter had not, unless an expensive stone chimney were installed; this difference seems to suggest a different purpose was intended in each case. Shops with solars often seem to have been built in groups of three or more and in 1349 there is mention of 11 together in Briggate (High Street). This suggests these were not built by single craftsmen for their own occupation but may have been built together as a speculative venture. It is most unfortuante that as yet it is not possible to tell what kinds of people would lease buildings of this kind; a parallel may perhaps be seen in the food retailers who, in the 16th century, leased semi-permanent stalls in the market places and clearly must have had living accommodation elsewhere.

The average size of a medieval shop is also unknown. Some of them were apparently very large. The Red Register mentions one in 1321 which measured

2½ rods long, 3¼ rods wide at the west end, and 3¾ at the east (42 ft. x 57 ft. x 60 ft.).[28] In the 16th century, the Council built temporary booths 24 feet by 12 feet and these were often divided by the tenants into two.[29] Much clearly depended on how the shop was to be used, and some craftsmen and retailers would need more space than others.

There is archaeological evidence of two types of medieval shop. Nos. 30 and 32 King Street are shops attached in the usual way to dwelling houses and form an integral part of the whole dual function complex; and in St. James' Street there is a row of about five medieval shops and solars unfortunately now very much altered internally.

Nos. 30 and 32 King Street are very probably medieval workshops despite their location in one of the busiest commercial streets in the town. (Figs.27 and 35; Plate 10.) The two shops are on the ground storey of a two storey timber range fronting onto the street and roofed parallel to it. Behind the northern shop is a hall, the stone side wall of which is built up to the street on the ground floor indicating that hall and shop are of one build. It is, in fact, only the front wall (in its entirety) and the gable ends of the building on the first floor upwards that are of timber, as was usual in Lynn where side walls were of stone to prevent the spread of fire. A hall in a similar position probably once stood behind No. 32 but this has now disappeared.

Both shops measured about 14 feet square and are over 11 feet high. The front wall of each shop carried the first floor sill on four timber posts and these are unevenly spaced to form one wide opening in the centre and one narrow opening to No. 30, and a wide opening and two narrower openings on either side to No. 32. The narrow side openings have lintels inserted and were probably door openings, one into the shop and, in the case of No. 32, the other opening into the side passage to the house behind. In medieval times there can have been no permanent infill between the timber uprights and the whole of the shop was open to the street. It is still possible to see the flat chamfer on the outer edges of all the vertical and horizontal members of the ground-floor timber framing. (Plate 11A.) At night there was probably some form of wooden shuttering to close the shops.

If the whole of the shopfront was open to the street some kind of protection from the weather was essential. It was usual to provide this by means of a pentice roof cantilevered out from the front wall of the shop, and there are many 18th century illustrations of English towns which show this arrangement, including one of the Lynn Saturday Market with such a shop beside the Gildhall.[30] On the facades of the shops in King Street it is still possible to see the mortice holes where the pentice was joined into each upright with a small notch of carved timber marking the foot of each brace. The first floor of this building is not jetteyed outward. Such a jetty might in itself in some instances have provided enough protection from the weather.

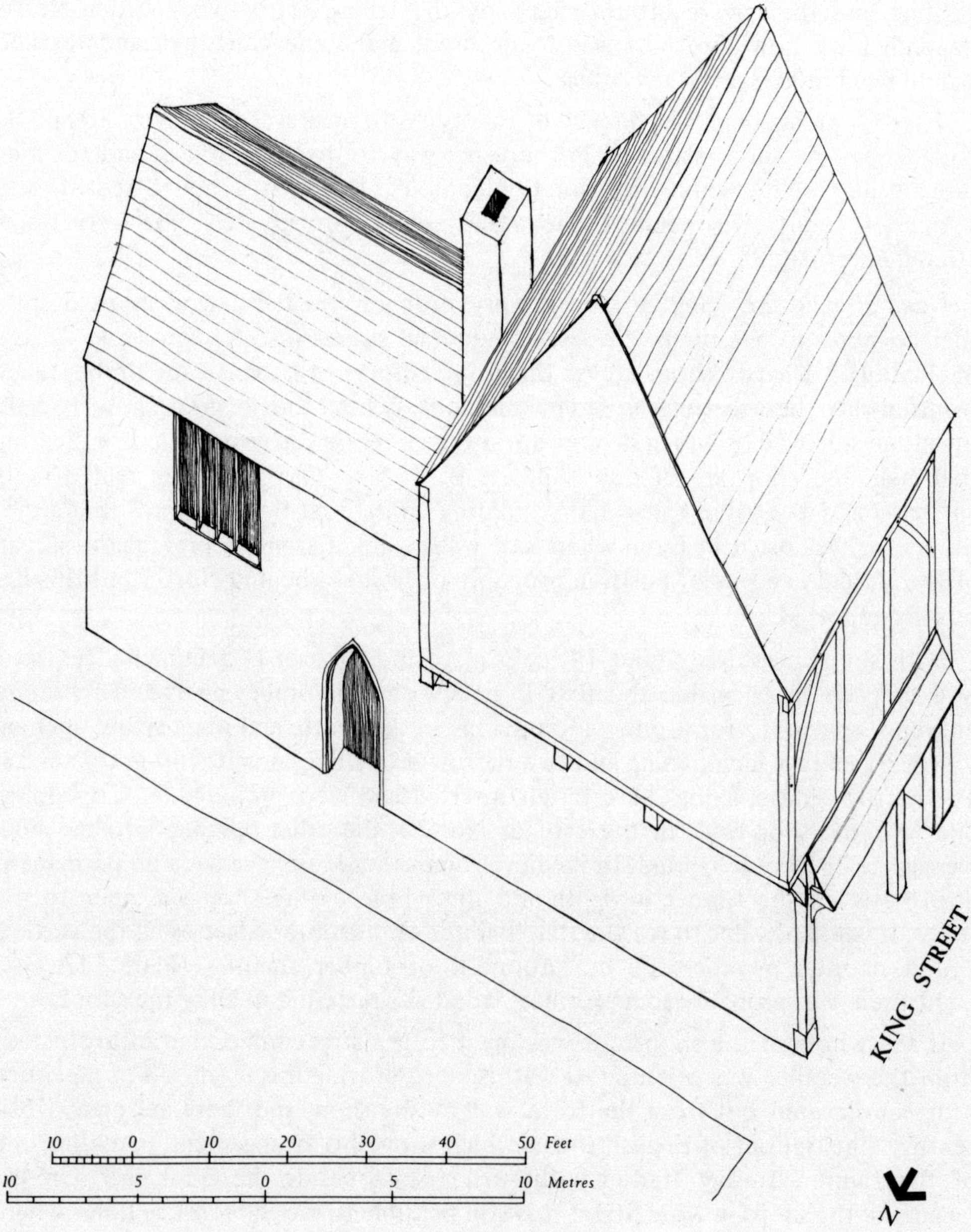

Fig 27 *No. 30 King Street: reconstruction*

The row of shops in St. James' Street consists of about five units under one continuous crown-post roof and they were probably erected in the course of the 15th century. (Plate 9A and B.) Each unit was two storeys high and had a ground floor room which measured about 10 feet square. They were constructed in timber throughout, and like the King Street shops, they may once have been open to the street. On the other hand if they were retail shops, and their size suggests this, they were more likely to have a much smaller window, sufficient only to light the inside of the shop and perhaps to use a counter with the shutter let down as a shop-board. There are good examples of this kind of shop window in Lavenham in Suffolk and at Thaxted in Essex, but none survives in Lynn.

None of the St. James' Street shops has a hall behind and the present chimneys, built along the back walls of some of the shops, are all comparatively modern. Each unit thus had only a ground floor shop, and a solar which was unheated. If the solar was used as a living room, cooking must have been done elsewhere, perhaps in a detached kitchen of which all traces have now disappeared. It may, however, have simply been used for storage, in which case the shopkeepers must have lived elsewhere.

There are some accounts for the 16th century of the kind of semi-permanent booths and stalls which complemented the function of the permanent shops. From earliest times these must have been erected in the market places for the benefit of those traders whose goods attracted a limited or seasonal demand in the town. Stalls which could be leased on a temporary basis were used particularly by people bringing limited quantities of fresh produce from the countryside; but they were also used by people like cutlers, potters and iron workers at certain times of the year, for in Lynn the normal level of demand was not sufficiently high to employ many of them permanently in the town.

Temporary retail accommodation was provided in Lynn in the 16th and 17th centuries by the town Council chiefly in the Tuesday and Saturday market-places and in Damgate, the ancient site of the annual mart or fair. In the Saturday Market the Council collected rents in 1557 from nine butchers' stalls located near the north porch of St. Margaret's Church, and from a number of standings held by fish-sellers and people selling dairy produce.[31] In 1587 the Council built a new row of pentices and stalls at the east end of the church, and these were converted into closed shops in 1630.[32] In such a manner much retail accommodation, originally put up for temporary use, encroached on the market places and streets and became permanent.

In the Tuesday Market the Council had both permanent booths that were used all the year round by butchers and other food retailers, and temporary standings that were put up each year for the annual February fair.[33] In 1537 the Council decided to lease permanently the 'perpetual booths' to burgesses but shortly after this they appear to have been cleared away. They were not replaced until 1594 when the Council decided to build a new row of 12 stalls on the site. A 'plot' was drawn and submitted to the Council before work began, and they were built by the town carpenter at a cost of £50.[34] This was a very remunerative investment since £40 was collected in rents for these within the first two years. A 17th century print of the Tuesday Market shows these stalls sited on the east side of the square facing the *Duke's Head.* (Plate 40A.) They were of timber construction and each unit had a ground floor section that was entirely open between the upright posts, and a section of roof space closed in and made secure for storage. In fact, each little stall was given its own gabled roof, instead of placing one continuous roof over them all, presumably to provide the necessary secure storage room. These stalls stood until the end of the 17th century and were cleared away when the new Market Cross was built.

The Council also provided the booths for the annual mart. In 1559, when this was first held after a considerable lapse of time, it was in Damgate that the booths were erected. In 1584, however, it was decided to move the mart permanently to the Tuesday Market and in 1609 standings were being let at 12d. a foot to 'strangers', 8d. a foot to non-burgesses of the town, and 6d. a foot to burgesses.[35] The 17th century mart accounts indicate that the fair was patronised by all kinds of craftsmen as well as by large merchants from London and the East coast ports. Craft stalls were set out systematically each year in the same places, the timbermen, basket makers and chairmakers around the Cross, the potters, iron merchants and nailmakers to the north, the linen weavers and glovers to the west, woollen weavers to the south and the cutlers, haberdashers and upholsterers to the east. The ubiquitous pedlars and chapmen were mainly on the southern side.[36] All their stalls and standings were cleared away when the mart ended.

Inns

Kings Lynn, like many ports, has always been well supplied with inns, many of which can be traced back to the early medieval period. The oldest inns are probably those at the west end of Damgate (now Norfolk Street), the *Saracens Head*, the *White Lion*, the *Green Dragon*, the *White Horse* and others, crammed into that short stretch of road between Listergate (Chapel Street) and Mercer Row (the north end of High Street), which was known in the 16th century as Gressmarket. It was here that the merchants bringing wares by road congregated on the edge of the market place and where, at the end of the street, they could find the cook's booths. The Tuesday Market itself was also well supplied with inns; significantly, most of them lay on the east and south sides which were developed before the waterfront areas to the north and west; and in the old town nucleus around St. Margaret's Church there were a number of medieval inns on the north side of the Saturday Market. By the 16th century, inns had spread from these early centres of trade to most of the main streets of the town and by the 19th century there were over 400 inns and public houses in the three square miles of the built-up area.[37]

Buildings that have remained in constant use as inns since the 12th century have naturally undergone constant renewal and rebuilding. There is no building in Lynn that can be confidently identified as a medieval inn which has not been for the most part rebuilt in the 19th or 20th century. It is thus impossible from archaeological evidence to reconstruct the accommodation that inns provided up to 1700, nor do we know at what date they began to be purpose-built in Lynn or to what extent they were planned and built like ordinary houses.

The earliest evidence of the kind of accommodation offered by the town's inns comes from two late 17th century inventories, one of 1670 and the other of 1690. Unfortunately, the name of the inns to which these refer are not given and there is no means of knowing whether or not they were typical of the period. The earlier of the two refers to an inn belonging to Francis Swayne, and this simply reads like the inventory of a typical town house of the period.[38] It had a gatehouse (and so was probably L-shaped in plan with the entry to one side), a hall, parlour and kitchen on the ground floor and bedrooms on the floor above. None of the ground floor rooms were furnished even with occasional beds, which is surprising in view of the limited number of bedrooms. The hall had only a trestle table with a settle and a 'screen to hang linen on' and the parlour was fitted up as a sitting room with chairs and tables. In the kitchen were the usual cooking utensils, and in outbuildings there was a scullery full of pots and pans, and a brewhouse. All the six bedrooms were provided with chairs and tables as well as beds.

The second inventory refers to a larger inn belonging to Thomas Hardy.[39] This also had a gatehouse and thus was probably L-shaped in plan. On the ground floor it had a hall and great parlour furnished with chairs and tables for daytime use. In addition to this and the usual domestic offices – kitchen, pantry, back kitchen and outbuildings – it had a billiard room and a dining room, the former containing 'one billiard table King port Balls and sticks' worth £3. On the first floor there were six bedrooms, one of them over the gatehouse, each designated by a name. Two of the bedrooms were heated and contained several beds each as well as chairs and tables. The stable, a vital part of an inn's accommodation, is also mentioned but there was no brewhouse.

The most interesting of the 17th century inns was the *Duke's Head* on the east side of the Tuesday Market. (Plate 34.) This replaced an earlier Inn on the site called the *Griffin* and was newly-built in 1683 by Sir John Turner who probably employed Henry Bell as his architect. The splendid facade of this building is one of the major architectural features of Lynn, but very little of the interior now remains and the inn has been very much extended recently to the rear. There is an inventory of the property made in 1773 which describes it as it was then.[40]

The *Duke's Head* was laid out round an internal courtyard, as were many of the most celebrated early inns like the *George* at Southwark and the *New Inn* at Gloucester.[41] On the internal facade of the building, looking into the courtyard, was a series of galleries giving separate access to each of the chambers on the three floors. These galleries were probably constructed of timber and framed independently of the load-bearing brick of the main structure. This arrangement made it possible to make the chambers the full width of the building and yet provide independent access to each room. Access to the gallery at first floor level was by a very fine carved oak staircase in the north-west corner of the court; (Plate 34B) the west staircase wall probably marks the line of the back wall of the front range. This range would thus be 20 feet wide and this is a likely width for the other three wings round the courtyard. The main public rooms of the inn were on the ground floor; the 'Great Parlour', the 'Great Dining Room', the 'Little Dining Room', the 'Wainscot Room' and others, the kitchen, the 'barr' and a cock room with 'deal furniture for fighting cocks'. Only 11 chambers are mentioned in the inventory, although the stable included accommodation for 25 horses. On the first floor the principal rooms overlooked the Tuesday Market on the west, and were panelled later in the 18th century.

The facade of the building is reminiscent of Henry Bell's work elsewhere.[42] It is stucco rendered, symmetrical in design, with the projecting central three bays of the nine-bay facade emphasised by rusticated quoins. The main entrance on the ground floor takes the form of two large openings with segmental heads side by side through which carriages passed to the yard beyond. The windows in the projecting central section above are decorated on each floor with plaster cartouches and this is capped by a giant scroll pediment through which an attic dormer projects. Over the rest of the front the mullioned and transomed windows have decorated aprons and the whole is finished with an attic balustrade.

Industrial Buildings

Kings Lynn was not an industrial town. The opportunity to develop as such by processing the raw materials carried through the town by merchants was never siezed by Lynn men in the period before 1700. But although there were no export industries to speak of in the town, there were nevertheless large numbers of people involved in industrial production. These were the craftsmen who catered for the limited demands of the town and its immediate hinterland, and whose production was organised on a small scale either within the family or with a few apprentices. Many of these people needed only very simple tools and no special equipment and worked either in shops attached to their dwelling houses or in sheds that were as flimsy and as temporary as their modern counterparts. Such people have left little or no trace of their activities above ground and because of the poverty of the early Probate Inventories for Lynn have left little trace in the written records either.

There were, however, two kinds of industrial building recorded in 16th and 17th century documents of the Corporation. Firstly these were special industries that required open space beyond that which could be found in the built-up area and needed facilities involving the use of public land or services. Secondly there were

Plate 26A *Nos. 30-32 Bridge Street*

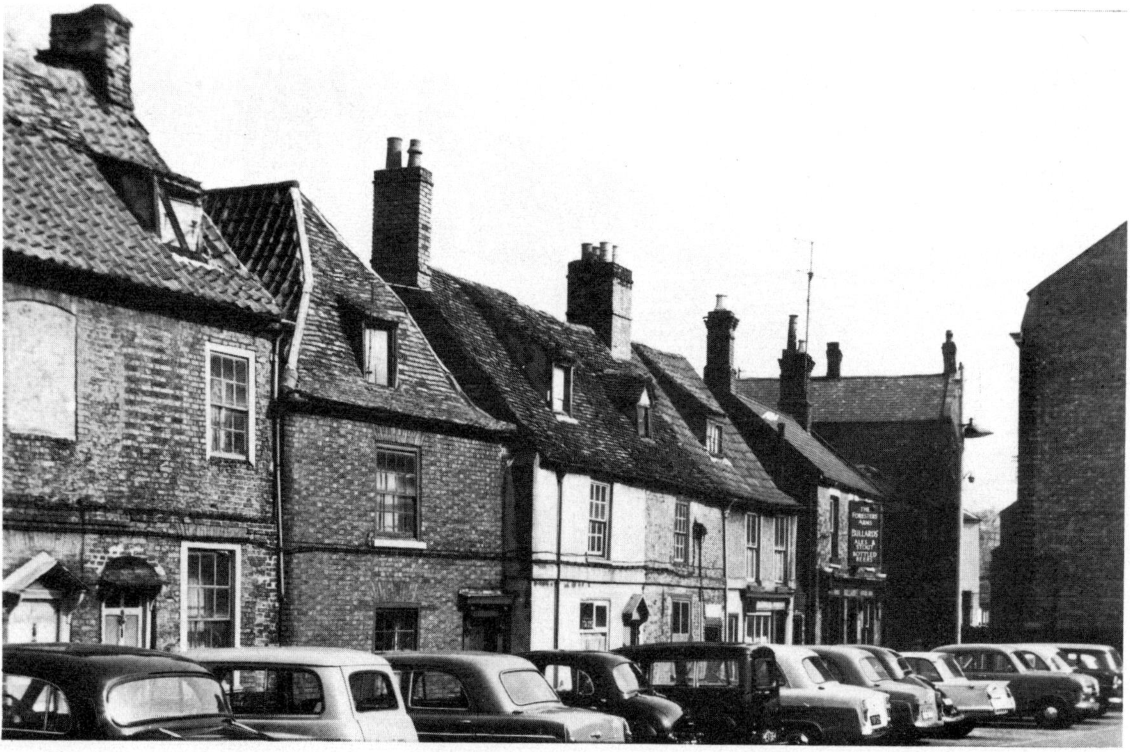

Plate 26B *Cottages in Sedgeford Lane*

Plate 27A *Thoresby College; gabled street front*

Plate 27B *St. Nicholas House; remains of east gable*

Plate 28A *Gable of cottage facing St. Nicholas churchyard*

Plate 28B *Stepped gables at rear of hall ranges, Nos. 23-25 King Street*

Plate 29 *'Hanseatic' warehouse on the south quay*

Plate 30A *Hanse steelyard; courtyard layout*

Plate 30B *Hanse steelyard; warehouse in St. Margaret Lane*

Plate 31A *St. George's Hall; watergate*

Plate 31B *St. George's Hall; warehouse on river bank*

Plate 32A *Clifton House; warehouses from above*

Plate 32B *Clifton House; warehouses in King Staithe Lane*

Plate 33 *The Kettlemill, c.1820*

industrial buildings requiring a major outlay of capital and which were, for this reason, often supplied and run by the Council. The picture of industrial building in Lynn derived from these sources will be by no means complete, not will it cover the medieval period, but this is one area where archaeological investigation below ground may eventually make a major contribution.

The town fields came into the hands of the Council with the fee farm of the Bishop's manor in 1536, and they became responsible for letting the land after that date. There were three types of industrial workers using these fields in the 16th century: clothworkers, who needed space to spread out cloths to dry after fulling; ropemakers who needed long narrow grounds to lay out and twist ropes; and the fisherman who used open ground for washing and drying fish. There were probably also some saltpans. There was certainly one at St. Anne's in 1587 from which a boatload of ash was bought for building work.[43]

The process of drying fish can be reconstructed from the descriptions of the town's 'Fish Ball' in the 1603-4. The first mention of drying fish in the town is in a will of 1525 where Richard Pepper bequeathed his 'stone called the Ball where I am accustomed to dry fish', but without mentioning the location.[44] It was, however, probably in the marshes of South Lynn, since before the fish were dried they had first to be washed and for this running water was required as well as open space on which to dry the fish afterwards. The process used in Lynn for washing the fish is still practised today at Overy Staithe on the north Norfolk coast. On the marshes there pits about six feet in diameter are dug within reach of the tide and lined with a trellis of thin twigs. Stakes are then planted around the pit to prevent the fish floating away and the fish placed in the pit and left to be washed as the tide runs in and out. In South Lynn a similar arrangement was set up by the Council at the beginning of the 17th century. In 1600 John Ferryer was lent £3 to provide shingle to spread on the towns fish ball and in 1604 he was given specific instructions on laying out and maintaining the premises. He was responsible for four acres of land in South Lynn, bounded on the north by the river Nar which provided the water for washing. The whole area was covered with shingle on which the fish were dried, except on the north where there were the 'fish pits', the flow of water through which was controlled by sluices. How long this practice persisted in Lynn is not known. Four acres of shingle is a large fish drying area and it seems unlikely that many private firms had their own 'fish balls' in addition. The land was farmed to Ferryer and there is no means of knowing what charge was made for its use.[45]

Whereas some industries required space which could only be obtained from the Council in the town fields, others required running water for driving machinery and fresh water for washing or mixing. Because the Council controlled the supply of water in the 16th century we know that there was a fulling mill set out on the banks of the Gaywood river in 1517 (although nothing further is heard of this building) and that the brewers absorbed quantities of fresh water from the town's pipe.

At the beginning of the 16th century, brewers had obtained their water by cart. By the end of the century practically all their premises, mainly located along the waterfront, were supplied with running water to the door and a special pipe known as the Brewers Pipe had been laid out down King Street. Brewing was often a side line to the main business of trade, and most big brewing establishments, like Thomas Some's in the 1550's, had grown out of a need originally to supply his own ships with victuals. The buildings and equipment needed for brewing were probably fairly simple. In 1647 an inventory of a brewhouse leased to John Lucas mentions a copper, two large vats, a 'double cooler' and a 'dandy' as well as the malthouse on two storeys, with windows that shut and locked, containing a corn screen, a rake and two shovels.[46] The scale of such business, however, is almost impossible to judge owing to the lack of any archaeological evidence.

The second group of industrial buildings to be recorded at least partially in the ordinances and leases of the Council, were those whose construction and maintenance were financed from public funds. In the 16th and 17th centuries the Council provided two important public services, equipment for grinding grain and a supply of fresh water pumped into pipes from the Gaywood river.

The public corn mill in Lynn was powered by water and was situated on the Millfleet. The first mill on this site in early medieval times was built by the Lord of South Lynn and the Bishop's corn mill was on the river Gay not far from St. Nicholas Church. (Fig.5.) By the beginning of the 16th century the Bishop's mill had disappeared and the Council was concentrating its resources on the building astride the Millfleet acquired for the town by the Holy Trinity Gild in 1448. A charge was levied on the townspeople, who had no choice but to take their grain there for grinding since private mills were forbidden, and from this the wages of the town miller were paid and any necessary building work financed. Grain sent in any bulk was collected by the miller's horse and cart and the meal delivered after grinding.

Unfortunately, there is no detailed description of the corn mill although it is illustrated on Raistricks map of 1725 (Plate 2). This shows a small single-storey building bridging the Millfleet a short distance to the south and east of St. James' chapel, with a two-storey extension to the north with a chimney, which was probably the miller's house. Both were built in stone. There is no evidence of a mill goit, or of any special construction to raise the head of water, and one of the most expensive problems in the 16th century was maintaining an even supply to turn the millwheel. The Millfleet alone had proved insufficient for this purpose and a channel had been dug outside the town walls in 1425 to bring additional supplies from the Gaywood river.[47] In 1554 it was decided to supplement this further from the river Nar to the south, and the Cockle Dike was dug running from the South Gates to a point on the Millfleet between the mill and Gannock Gate.[48] Even this, however, did not solve the problems, and the length of dike to be maintained was a constant drain on the town's resources.

In 1580, perhaps because of the difficulties with the water mill, the Council decided to build two windmills. These were also intended to grind grain but do not seem to have been a great success. Only one was built, after a lapse of almost 15 years, in 1595 by John Ferne, a millwright, at a cost of £38.[49] He was instructed to copy a mill in Barwick, belonging to Richard Bunting, built of 'white oak' and to equip it with 'going gears'. The Council undertook to provide the sails and the millstones when it was completed. It was first erected on the millhill in South Lynn but in 1596 it was moved, first to the Gallow pasture on the north bank of the Purfleet, only to be returned subsequently to its original site when the Council became aware of the cost of constructing a new millhill. There is no record of its being regularly supplied with millstones, and it was finally dismantled in 1652.[50]

Originally water had been drawn from the river by means of a 'kettlemill', built during the middle ages on the banks of the river at the north end of the town wall. (Fig.5.) This was in operation at the beginning of the 15th century. Powered by two horses, probably working alternately, it apparently consisted of a timber wheel hung with metal containers known as kettles. In 1557 a tinker was paid 2s. 0d. for repairing 15 of these, and in the same year the horses received new collars and halters and 7s. 2d. worth of horse meat and drink, the latter probably a form of gruel. A load of sand was also supplied 'for the path where the horse goes'.[51] By the mid-16th century the Council had made several additions to the town's fresh water supply, and the old kettlemill was clearly proving inadequate. In 1578 it was decided to construct a new pump, designed and erected by a carpenter, Richard Brown. The account of the early stages of its building have survived.[52]

There were six pumps made of elm sunk in a pit specially dug for the purpose, and the pistons were moved by a waterwheel turned by the river. As projected it was a much more sophisticated device than the old kettlemill, but it had one basic defect, lack of water power, particularly in the summer. It proved to be in need of constant repair and attention and eventually had to be partly converted to being driven by a horse.[53]

Notes to Chapter V

1 Map, unsigned, in Borough Surveyor's Office, Kings Lynn

2 K.L.M./Bc 7. Part 4, p.8, 9.

3 H.L. Bradfer Lawrence, *Merchants of Lynn,* 151, n 6. See also M.M. Postan 'The Economic and Political Relation of England and the Hanse', in *Studies in English Trade,* ed E. Power and M.M. Postan.

4 P.R.O./S.P.D./XCIII/3

5 K.L.M./H.B.V./168

6 K.L.M./H.B.IV/473d *et seq.* to H.B.V/387d.

7 N.S.B. Gras, *The Evolution of the English Corn Market,* (Harvard 1926), 290.

8 Williams, *East Anglian Ports,* 162-74.

9 *Ibid,* 163-5.

10 T.S. Willan, *The English Coasting Trade 1600-1750,* (1938), 210.

11 Williams, *East Anglian Ports,* 81; P.R.O./S.P.D./XXII/132.

12 P.C.C. F6, Ketchyn.

13 e.g. K.L.M./H.B.V./182, 318d, 372, 320d.

14 K.L.M./H.B.IV/1547.

15 K.L.M./H.B.VII/187d, 232.

16 K.L.M./Db 27 (1595-1655).

17 P.R.O./E178/7046.

18 P.C.C. 2 Jankyn.

19 K.L.M./H.B.V/296d.

20 K.L.M./H.B.V/366d.

21 K.L.M./H.B.V/100d.

22 Nor. Rec. Office: Norwich C.C. INV/24/357.

23 Nor. Rec. Office; Archdeaconry of Norwich Wills, 1557-8/215.

24 Nor. Rec. Office: Nor. C.C. Wills, 40 Bunne.

25 Nor. Rec. Office: Nor. C.C. INV/24/357.

26 P.C.C. 21, Bodfelde.

27 *Red Register* I. 75, 142, 144, 174, 177, 182.

28 *Red Register* I. 51.

29 K.L.M./H.B.IV/337d.

30 B.M. Prints and Drawings. B. Farringdon 1787.

31 K.L.M./Bc 8.

32 K.L.M./H.B.V/339d; H.B.VII/28d, 334.

33 K.L.M./H.B.III/313. See also A. Everitt, 'The Marketing of Agricultural Produce' in J. Thirsk (ed) *Agrarian History of England and Wales,* IV, (1967), 480-6, for examples of similar activities in other towns in the 16th century.

34 K.L.M./H.B.VI/42, 51d, 52, 57.

35 K.L.M./Dd (1609).

36 K.L.M./Dd (1609).

37 G.H. Anderson, 'Inns and Taverns of Lynn', *Lynn Advertiser* February 17th – March 24th (1933) reprinted. On the proliferation of inns from the 17th century see A. Everitt 'Change in the Provinces', 25-26.

38 Nor. Rec. Office: Nor. C.C. INV/56/66.

39 Nor. Rec. Office: Nor. C.C. INV/65/15.

40 H.L. Bradfer Lawrence, *The Merchants of Lynn,* Supplement to Blomfields Norfolk, IX, 157.

41 W.A. Pantin, 'Medieval Inns', *Studies in Building History,* ed Jope, 166-177.

42 H. Colvin, and L.M. Wodehouse 'Henry Bell of Kings Lynn', *Arch. Hist.,* IV, 1961, 41-62.

43 K.L.M./Ed 3, 1587.

44 P.C.C. F 24 Porch.

45 K.L.M./H.B.VI/203, 294, 330d.

46 Appendix II, Schedule of Lease. p.190.

47 Hillen, *Kings Lynn.*

48 K.L.M./H.B.IV/224d, 521d: H.B.V/33d, 46d, 68.

49 K.L.M./H.B.V/200d. H.B.VI/77d, 100d, 101, 111d.

50 K.L.M./H.B.VIII/348.

51 K.L.M./Ed 3/1557.

52 K.L.M./Bc 7.

53 K.L.M./H.B.VI/68d, 347, 357.

VI

Public Buildings

BY THE END of the 17th century Kings Lynn was provided with an important endowment of public buildings many of which had been inherited from an earlier period and adapted to new uses as the requirements of the community changed. There was a town wall, by then almost unnecessary, but once of much greater importance; three churches, one of them in South Lynn; a number of secular public meeting places, most of them a legacy from the medieval gilds; commercial buildings like the market halls, the Custom House and the Exchange; and provision for education, the poor and the sick. Many of these buildings are known to us from contemporary descriptions and illustrations even where they do not survive today.

Kings Lynn acquired its public buildings in a variety of ways and over a long period of time. Like other plantation towns it was provided by its founder with buildings and services designed to foster the expansion of the settlement and attract people to it.[1] The Bishops of Norwich gave the town its two most important churches, St. Margaret's, the building of which was begun at the end of the 11th century, and St. Nicholas' chapel begun 50 years later in the new settlement to the north of the Purfleet. The Bishops also helped fortify the town by building and maintaining one of the wooden towers or 'bretasks', and encouraged the growth of trade by laying out two public landing stages, one on the waterfront to the south of the Purfleet, and one beside the canal at Littleport bridge. They built the Stewards Hall in the Tuesday market place and a public corn mill on the banks of the Gaywood river near St. Nicholas Chapel.

As Lynn expanded in the 12th and 13th centuries, the gilds, particularly the merchant gilds, became increasingly important in the running of the town. It was they, both because they could mobilise financial support through their own organisation, and because they had also a vested interest in the fabric of the town, who were mainly involved in public building work in the later Middle Ages. The Trinity gild, for instance, made itself almost wholly responsible for the town's defences; it built a gildhall in the Saturday Market and a chapel attached to St. Margaret's Church and maintained a public staithe to the west of the Tuesday Market. The gild of St. Giles and St. Julian built and maintained an almshouse and other gilds like St. George and Corpus Christi built semi-public halls, warehouses and staithes for the benefit of their members.

By the 16th century the great days of the gilds were over in Lynn and authority was increasingly vested in the new town Council, set up by the Charter of Incorporation of 1524, and at that time consisting mainly of the officers of the Holy Trinity gild. The Bishop of Norwich surrendered all his rights in the town and the fee farm of his manor along with the lands and income of the suppressed gilds and chantries were all granted to the Corporation by 1548. Here, then, was the chief source of public building in the 16th and 17th centuries, and during this period much greater efforts were made to improve the public buildings and services of the town than had been possible in the past. The Council not only had a wider interest in the community as a whole, but much larger resources than the individual gilds, and was able to be more constructive, for example, about the critical problems of poor relief and the control of infectious disease. The rate of public investment in building was stepped up rapidly in the second half of the 16th century on the workhouse, schools, almshouse and, more particualrly, on providing a water supply and other necessary services of this kind. The late 17th century, however, was their great period of prestige building, when public buildings were designed to 'beautify and adorn' the town as well as to fulfil functional requirements. The Market Cross and the Custom House are the products of this age.

Because of the problems of finance, public building was more likely to be undertaken by groups of people rather than by individuals. Nevertheless, Lynn was not without its private benefactors. Thomas Thoresby, for example, founded, at the end of the 15th century, a chantry college attached to St. Margaret's Church and a school; and during the 17th century much of the hospital and almshouse accommodation was built from private bequests. Even the Custom House was financed mainly by Sir John Turner, and in the 16th and 17th centuries the projects of the Council were often saved from ruin by timely gifts and legacies.

The Town Walls

From the time Lynn was founded to the end of the 17th century the town wall remained an integral part of the built environment. This, in an English town at least, was somewhat unusual, since many of them had no walls to start with and others quickly outgrew the original circuit and failed, for one reason or another, to build extensions. The men of Lynn, however, clearly found a use for a ring of defences, and from time to time spent considerable sums of money on keeping it in repair. There are probably several reasons for this. In the first place, Lynn, unlike the majority of English new towns, was founded at a time when the political situation in England was such that defences were still needed to protect a settlement from outside attack. Thus one of the first public works was the setting up of a ditch and bank with controlled entry points to the built-up area, protected by wooden towers called bretasks. The line of this bank was determind in the case of Lynn not by a rough estimate of the likely limits of the built-up area in the future, or by the size of the already existing town, but by the line of the old sea bank at Gannock which provided the natural foundations of a system of defence.[2] This was well to the east of the original settlement and at no time did the town even approach this line, much less spread beyond it, except where ribbon development brought buildings along the main roads to the gates.

There were other reasons too for maintaining the wall around Kings Lynn. Strong though the English monarchy was in comparison with other European kings and princes, it was still unable to protect its subjects from all unlawful elements at all times. Even in the 16th century the uprisings of the 1530's and 40's prompted the Council to take measures to secure the town against attack. Lynn was also vulnerable to invasion from overseas. The Mayors Roll, a chronicle of the main events of the 15th and 16th century records the disaster which befell Sandwich when it was attacked and taken by the French in 1461.[3] In the 1580's the expected invasion of the Spanish fleet led to a strengthening of all the East Coast defences in the south including those of Lynn, and in the late 16th century Lynn shipping was being constantly harassed by pirates.[4] Strong fortifications, however, were not always an advantage in times of war since they put upon a town the obligation to fight. Lynn merchants must have regretted their walls in 1643 when Cromwell's army under the Earl of Manchester had to take military action against the Royalist faction entrenched in the town.[5] They were in a state of siege for over a month and many Lynn merchants subsequently complained of considerable damage to their property from cannon fire.[6]

One of the main advantages of a wall, though, was that it defined an area within which the town authorities governed, and made their work easier by providing them with a system of controlled entry and exit points. There were only two main entrances through the walls into Lynn, the South and East Gates, both of which were manned permanently by gatekeepers in the 15th, 16th and 17th centuries. All other points of access, like the old Gannock gate, had a bar which was kept locked at night. This system could be exploited by the town Council in a variety of ways. For example, the gates were used to stop, for the collection of tolls, merchandise passing in and out of the town by road. In 1436, it was one of the duties of the Keeper of the East Gates to see that after the Tuesday and Saturday markets no 'victuals or grain of any of the foresaid markets' left the town 'to the hurt of the corporation'.[7] To carry out his duties effectively, he was permitted to carry a club. Vehicles whose iron wheel rims might break up the town's pavement were stopped at the gates in by order in 1449,[8] and in 1516, when there was a bad outbreak of plague, the influx of beggars was controlled by closing the gates at 6.00 p.m.[9] Thus the Council, and probably the town's feudal overlord before, had good reasons for maintaining the wall not only for warding off attack from without, but also in the interests of keeping order within.

The circuit of walls shown on the Bell 'Groundplat', (Plate 1), indicated the maximum extent of the fortifications and includes the mid-17th century extensions to the north of the Gaywood river and to the south of the river Nar. They ringed the town in a great arc to the east, from St. Anne's Fort to the White Friars, the western or riverside part of the town being protected by the harbour walls and the river itself. The fortifications enclosed not only all the built-up part of the town, but at least twice as great an area again of marsh and pasture. The East Gates were located where the causeway from Gaywood and Norwich entered the circuit and the South Gates were at the end of the Hardwick causeway bringing a road from Cambridge and Ely. Gannock Gate, by then disused, stood to the north of the Millfleet and probably marked the site of a very early entrance to the original settlement around St. Margaret's Church.

The early history of the town's defences is not at all clear since the walls have not yet been excavated and the earliest documentary references occur only at the end of the 13th century.

The town received three grants of murage, in 1294 for six years, in 1300 for seven years, and finally in 1339 a grant for three years.[10] Much of the work on the medieval defences, then, was probably carried out in the first half of the 14th century. Originally, the town appears to have been defended by four wooden towers or bretasks. The Bishop's bretask is referred to in a deed of 1270 and stood near St. Annes Fort; and a century later we hear of four of these bretasks to the north, south, east and west of the town. The north bretask was the Bishop's, the west bretask stood beside the Ouse on the north bank of the Purfleet; the exact location of the other two is unknown although they were probably near the South and East Gates. They presumably reinforced the important points of access to the town.

When the early settlement around St. Margaret's was laid out, the part of the town most vulnerable to attack was the east. On this side the old sea bank to the south of the Purfleet was an already existing foundation to some kind of defensive earthwork. The line of this bank was, in fact, followed from the Purfleet to the South Gates by the later fortifications which took the form of an earthern wall and ditch. It is not known when this was made although the South Gate itself was in existence by the beginning of the 13th century. No wall was apparently contemplated to the north of St. Margaret's since this side of the settlement was protected by the Purfleet.

The extension to the north of the Purfleet, made in the 12th century, was given defences on its eastern side while its northern approaches were protected by the Gaywood river. The former were designed to link up with the line of the sea bank to the south of the Purfleet, but here, apparently, either there were no earthworks already existing, or they were later removed, and a strong rubble wall, faced with stone, was erected, pierced by the East Gate towards its northern end. This wall still survives in part today and at the beginning of the 18th century stood to its full height. (Plate 36A.) It had crenellations along the top and presuambly a gallery to allow men to circulate at that level. Lower down, niches were let into the thickness of the wall with thin slits to fire through, and an earth ramp provided the access to them and another circulation route at this level. One unexplained feature of the surviving stretch of wall is the series of arches at ground level on the eastern side forming niches which would surely have given protection to attackers as well as seriously weakening the wall itself. These are not only shown on the 18th century engraving but are referred to as 'les buttys' in a lease of 1426.[11] They must, then, be a part of the original structure.

The two main gateways were both substantially rebuilt in the 15th and 16th centuries, the South Gate in 1437 and 1520, and the East Gate in 1542. The former was designed by Richard Hertanger of London, but was finally finished in the 16th century by Nicholas Harmer of East Dereham and Thomas Herman of Benwell, both freemasons.[12] Still standing in its original position at the head of a bridge across the Nar, the South Gate is roughly square on plan, is two storeys high and has three openings at street level – a high carriage opening in the centre and two smaller pedestrian entrances on either side. The room over the gate, used during the 16th century for civic receptions for visiting dignitaries, was lit by two three-light mullioned windows in both south and north walls. The gate is crenellated and has turrets at each corner, hexagonal on the south and square on the north. It was constructed mainly in brick, but the south face is ashler rendered and ornamented at intervals with moulded string courses. (Plate 36B.)

The East Gate was demolished in 1890 and the stones partly incorporated into the Victorian gatehouse to Hillington Park. It appears from 18th century drawings to have been a much less impressive building than the South Gate. (Plate 35.) Two storeys high, with corner turrets and crenellation round the top, it had a single entry over which the town coat of arms had been carved. The room over the entry had one pointed arched window facing west, and what appears to have been a small house with a chimney had been incorporated into the west wall. This was probably the gatekeeper's dwelling. Parts of both the inner and the outer surfaces of the external walls were faced with ashlar. Both gates had drawbridges across the town ditch, and portcullises, as well as wooden gates that could be locked and barred.[13]

Two extensions were made to the medieval walls, one in 1587 when the Spanish Armada was expected and again in 1642/3 during the Civil War. These later fortifications have not yet been fully investigated but they account for the extensions north of the Gaywood river and to the South of the river Nar, illustrated on the Bell 'Groundplat'.

Public Buildings to 1500

The most important public buildings in the medieval town of Lynn were those which functioned as meeting places, either for religious worship, or for the social and business functions of the numerous gilds and fraternities who played such an important part in the organisation of the social, economic and political life of medieval communities. In addition, there was the early accommodation for trade and traders, and finally the first steps towards providing shelter for the poor and the sick.

The churches were by far the most splendid of the town's public monuments. There were three of them in medieval Lynn excluding All Saints Church in South Lynn which was not then a part of the borough. The earliest and subsequently the largest of them was the church of St. Margaret founded by Herbert Losinga, Bishop of Norwich at the end of the 11th century and given by him to the monks of Norwich Cathedral Priory. The first building on this site was financed by the Bishop, but the church was partly rebuilt several times in the 13th, 14th and finally in the 18th century, largely from public funds and private benefactions. To the east of St. Margaret was the chapel of St. James, founded in the first half of the 12th century. By the beginning of the 16th century it was ruinous and after being altered and adapted for various purposes it was finally demolished in 1910. This stood in what must clearly have been a populous part of the early town and the church's subsequent decay was the result of depopulation in this area in the late Middle Ages.[14] The 'new' town to the north of the Purfleet also had its own chapel, dedicated to St. Nicholas, which was in existence at the end of the 12th century, and, like St. Margaret's, was probably built by the Bishop of Norwich. It, too, was rebuilt, the tower and spire in the 13th century, and the rest at the beginning of the 15th century. Neither St. James nor St. Nicholas succeeded in separating from the parish church of St. Margaret and today St. Nicholas is still a chapel of ease to the main church.

Architecturally, St. Margaret and St. Nicholas still dominate the town and the twin 13th century west towers of the former and the slender spire of the latter are characteristic features of the skyline of Lynn. Early work in both was carried out in a rubble mixture, although the 15th century work at St. Nicholas is brick, and both were faced with stone brought by barge along the river Nene from the quarries around Peterborough.[15] St. Margaret's stood beside the Saturday Market and was in constant use, not only as a shelter and meeting place for traders, but as a ceremonial centre where the celebrations of civic dignity were given added religious significance. St. Nicholas was the medieval focus for the religious life of the northern part of the town and, like St. Margaret's, the gilds made use of it both for social and ceremonial occasions.

The medieval town was also served by a number of secular public meeting places. These not only housed the gilds and fraternities but were used as courtrooms, tollbooths and places where merchants gathered for a variety of purposes. The names of three public halls occur in the records of Lynn, in addition to the grander semi-public halls of the great merchant gilds. The three public halls were all located beside the market places, the natural foci for the economic life of the town and for much of its social and political life. The Stewards Hall, built in stone and with a stone undercroft, stood in the Tuesday Market on the north corner of

Jews' Lane (now Surrey Street). All traces above ground of this building, provided by the Bishop of Norwich as a tollbooth and courthouse, have now disappeared, although a part of the undercroft is said to survive beneath the present building on the site. The Monday Hall and the Sparrow Hall were both in the Saturday Market. The Monday Hall stood near the north porch of St. Margaret's Church and is recorded in the 16th century as an upstairs room over a row of shops on the ground floor.[16] It seems likely that this was built in the early 15th century from the ruins of the old Trinity gildhall burned down in 1421. No trace of this building survives today. The Sparrow Hall is mentioned first in a deed of 1376 and stood on the site of No. 3 St. Margaret's Place, at the west end of the church, bounded on the north by Leadenhall Lane.[17] The present house on this site may incorporate part of the hall, although the building is planned as a typical domestic layout with a two storey range dating from the 15th century parallel to the street and a hall at right angles behind. Unlike the Monday Hall, which was still used in the 16th century as a cloth hall and courtroom, the Sparrow Hall is not mentioned after the 14th century and may have been completely rebuilt.

The gildhalls were the most spectacular of the medieval public halls in Lynn and two survive, the Trinity Gildhall in the Saturday Market and St. George's Hall in King Street. Other gildhalls, like that of the Corpus Christi gild, also built in King Street, have unfortunately now disappeared, and there were probably others for which there is not even documentary evidence today. In the 14th century there were over 30 gilds in Lynn all of which needed a place for periodic business meetings and festivities, although only a very few can have been rich enough to build their own hall. The gild of St. Anthony, for example, a small fraternity whose membership was drawn largely from the town's victuallers, met in each others houses, members taking it in turns to offer hospitality. On the gilds General Day, then they had their annual feast, breakfasting off ribs of beef, bread and ale, they leased St. George's Hall, and this was probably common practice among the lesser gilds of Lynn.[18] The small merchant gild of South Lynn made similar arrangements for meetings in each others houses and leased the Trinity Gildhall for their feast; others are recorded using the churches and chapels for gild affairs.

There were at least three gilds and probably a handful more who were wealthy enough to build a gildhall. The return of Gild and Chantry property in Lynn, made in 1561, lists three halls that were standing then, belonging to the Holy Trinity Gild, St. George's Gild and Corpus Christi Gild.[19] These were all associations of wealthy merchants. The Trinity Gild was probably the oldest, whose existence was regularised by the Charter of 1204. Its leaders were inextricably involved in the running of the town in the medieval period, the Mayor was the gild Alderman, and the town and gild officers were invariably the same. It was also extremely rich, both from the fees of its members and the profits from its extensive properties and trading monopolies. The history of the Corpus Christi Gild is not well documented but it was apparently in existence in 1380;[20] St. George's Gild was not granted

Letters Patent until 1406.[21] Both had extensive properties at the Dissolution.

The Hall of the Holy Trinity Gild stands in the Saturday Market, the ancient economic centre of the monastic town beside St. Margaret's Church. (Plate 37A.) This part of the town was later to decline in importance as the facilities to the north around the Tuesday Market drew traders away, and the siting of the later Gildhalls was further towards the north. The choice of the Saturday Market as a site for its Hall is thus an indication of the relatively early development of this Gild. Its first Hall, of which nothing now survives, stood near the north porch of St. Margaret's Church. This was badly burned in 1421, along with the adjoining tenement, and the fire was recorded by Margery Kempe.[22] She speaks of sparks falling through the lantern of the church threatening to set fire to St. Margaret's itself before a timely fall of snow put out the blaze. In the following year work was put in hand on a new hall on a different site on the north-west corner of the Market, and the old Gildhall was abandoned. Its remains were still standing in 1548.

The new Gildhall took 16 years to finish at a total cost of £220, about half the annual income of the gild.[23] The plot on which it was laid out was long and narrow, so the Hall was planned at right angles to the street and an entry passage left down the west side. (Fig.28.) The plan was a simple one giving the Gild maximum flexibility in the use of the building. The hall was two storeys high, the main room or hall on the first floor being raised on a vaulted undercroft and entered by an outside staircase from the west at its southern end. Originally the Hall was six bays long (now somewhat shortened) and roofed in a single span with scissor braced rafters trussed at intervals by massive tie beams. The hall was a single space internally with a stone flagged floor strewn with rushes, and with built-in seats in the panelling of the lower parts of the walls. The upper walls were hung with cloths which, when there were renewed in 1635, were of red and green say.[24] Originally it does not seem to have been heated, but its windows were glazed, and by the 16th century some kind of stove or brazier was in use. A chimney was recorded in 1557, and in 1570 a 'pot baker' was employed to set up a 'new hot stowe' in the Hall at a cost of 46 shillings.[25] Furnishings were rather sparse. In 1579 a new wainscot table inlaid with the Queen's Arms was made for the Hall, and there was probably another large table for feasting and Council meetings. There was also a bench covered with green cotton. Two 'treasuries', wainscot cupboards that could be kept locked, were located in the undercroft.[26]

The undercroft was six bays long with a central row of piers and had a stone ribbed vault. In medieval times this was the gild's warehouse in which they stored their wine and occasionally millstones; when it ceased to be used for this purpose it became the town gaol and the gaoler's lodging.[27] It was originally entered in the south gable end through a double doorway in the centre later blocked and made into windows.

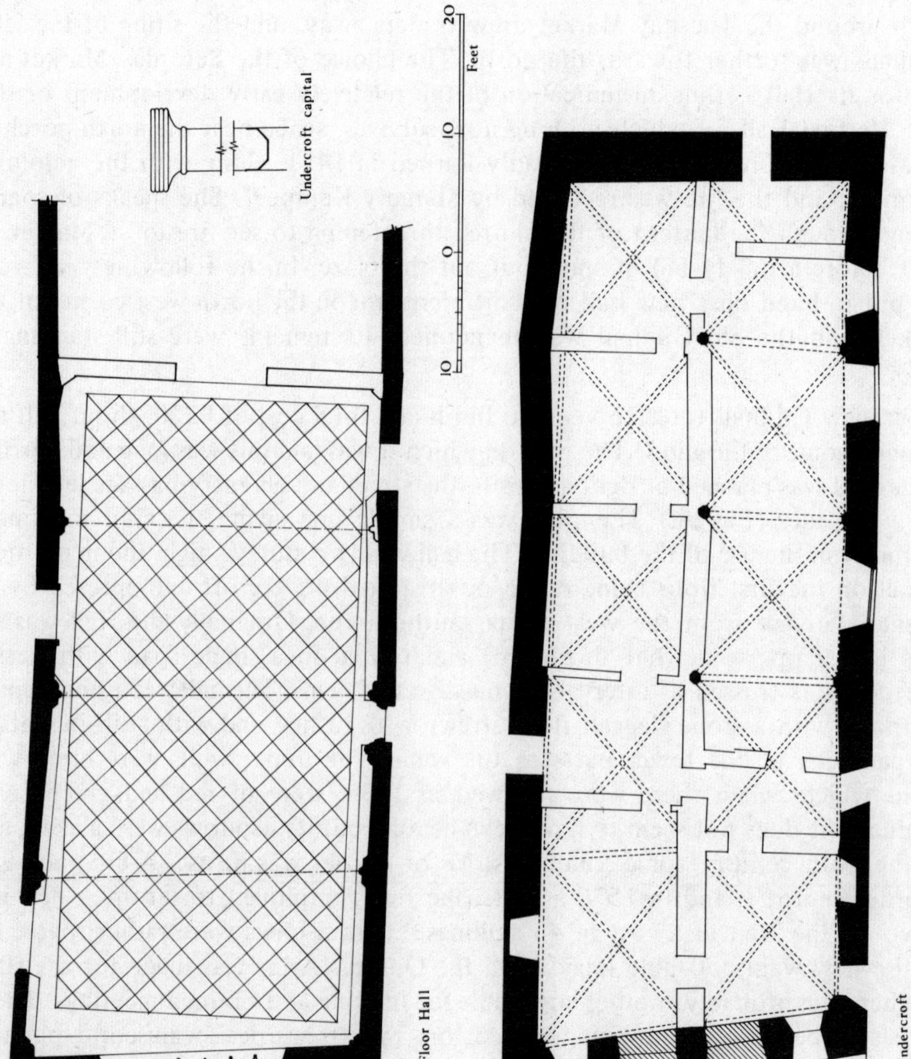

Fig 28 *The Holy Trinity Gildhall, Saturday Market: plans, c.1422*

With the exception of the vault of the undercroft, the hall was built in brick with door and window openings in dressed stone. Since the Hall was hemmed in on either side by buildings, only the south gable end was visible from the street and it was this facade alone that was given a decorative facing in the early 15th century. (Plate 37B.) In the centre of the upper floor was the great eight-light south window of the hall with its pointed-arch traceried head and horizontal transom near the sill. Beneath the sill were the wooden shutters to ventilate the room, the rest of the window having been filled with fixed glazing. Below this window there was a moulded stone bandcourse and in the ground storey the double doors with pointed arched heads into the undercroft were linked to two windows on either side by a continuous stone dripmould. The great beauty of this facade is its fine flint-flushwork facing, covering the surface centre wall with a regular pattern of small dark and light squares from the narrow ground floor plinth to the tip of the gable. It was once further adorned with statues, one on the top of the gable and one on a niche between the undercroft doors.

The porch which now protects the staircase on the west, fronting the Saturday Market, was built in 1624. Like the hall it was faced with flint-flushwork and its designer used a curious mixture of gothic and classical motifs on its south facade. The door has a round arched head and a Doric doorcase, the window above is mullioned and transomed, and the design is capped by two stone-carved Coats of Arms, one above the other. Originally the work may have been intended to stop with the lower of the two emblazonments, but the Chamberlains made the mistake of placing there 'the late Armes of England' taken, without the authority of the Council, from the facade of St. James' Workhouse.[28] This celebrated the reign of Elizabeth and was out of date. The Chamberlains were reprimanded and a new coat of arms was set above. This was apparently renewed in each reign. At the Restoration in 1664 the Chamberlains were instructed to 'take care to have the King's Armes cut in stone as formerly and placed on the outward door of the hall as the same were formerly placed.'[29]

The stair inside the porch is contemporary with the rest of the building and, mounting from directly inside the entrance, makes one and a half turns to enter the hall through the west door. The baluster shafts and handrail are of turned oak and the gallery is supported on large Ionic columns.

The gild of St. George was first licensed by Letters Patent in 1406, although it may well have been in existence before that date. At that time it owned a divided tenement in the King Street with the main part of the property to the east of the road, facing a quay to the west on the waterside. There is no mention of any building to the west of the street where the hall was later to be built,[30] so the present Gildhall must date from around the early 15th century at the earliest.

St. George's Gildhall occupies a long narrow plot between King Street (the Checker) and the river Ouse, bounded on the north by a lane with an open gutter known in 1406 as Corn Lane. (Fig.29; Plate 38.) Although smaller and less elaborate than the Trinity Gildhall it was planned to provide similar accommodation. The two-storeyed hall was built with its gable end fronting the street and so laid out on the plot that narrow passageways were left down both side of the building. These were not for access to the quay at the rear – the way to the back was through the undercroft – but to leave room for the great brick buttreses used to support the roof, and to provide light-wells on either side of the Hall. As in the Trinity Hall, the main room was on the first floor above an undercroft, the wooden ceiling of which was carried on massive timber beams. The hall itself was not divided and cooking for gild feasts was done in a separate kitchen mentioned in descriptions of the gild's property in 1561. By 1602, however, a chimney had been inserted on the north wall.[31]

The roof of the hall was similar to that of the Trinity Gildhall in that each pair of rafters was scissor braced and collared, but at St. George's the designer had managed to do away with the clumsy tie-beams by supporting the walls from the outside with brick buttresses. Between the buttresses large windows with four centred arch heads lit the hall from north and south and there was a further large window in the east gable looking into the Checker. Access to the hall on the first floor must have been by an internal stair in the north east corner. The door in the south wall, at present approached by an outside staircase, can hardly have been sufficient as a ceremonial entry such as the Gild would require.

The low undercroft has now been partly rebuilt with a brick barrel-vaulted ceiling but was originally timber ceiled throughout. On the southern side a passageway led through from the street to the rear of the plot and this part was partitioned off by a brick wall which also served to reduce the span of the ceiling beams. The passage was lit from the south side but the undercroft proper had no windows. It was probably used by the Gild as a warehouse and although dark would have been safer from theft.

The hall is built throughout in brown brick with carved stone frames in the window and door openings. The street front was left unadorned. The east hall window was six lights wide with a single transom and the heads of the lights were once cusped. Beneath the window were three openings. The principal entrance was on the north and led probably onto a stair to the hall; it had a simple cut brick four-centred arch head and was echoed by a smaller door on the south which led into the passage through the undercroft. The central opening, which had a flat wooden lintel, led into the warehouse in the undercroft.

When the Gilds were suppressed in Lynn, the King Street property of the Gild of St. George was described as a hall with a cellar, pantry and kitchen annexed, and had numerous outbuildings in the yard behind. It was acquired by the Council along with the rest of the Gild's property in 1547, but a suitable use was never found for it, the demand for this kind of large accommodation having apparently declined. It was used by Elizabethan travelling players from time to time and in 1588 was leased by George Waldon to start a school for learning

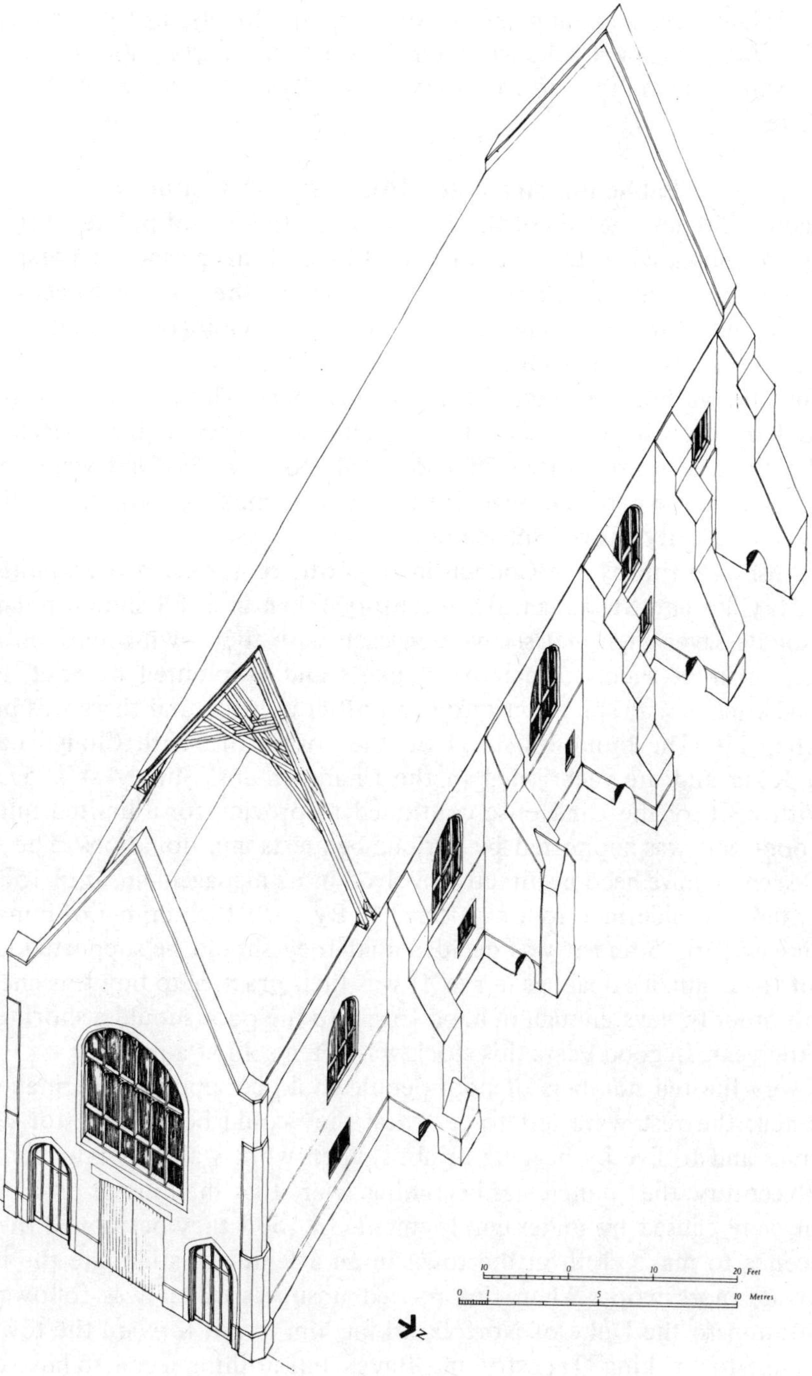

Fig 29 *St. George's Gildhall, King Street: reconstruction*

French.[32] It later became a sailmaker's workshop and finally, in 1653, a merchant's Exchange. When the new Exchange (later the Custom House) was built at the end of the century, the Hall became ruinous and was later revived in the 18th century as a theatre.

Public Building in the 16th and 17th Centuries

Between 1550 and the end of the 17th century the rate of public investment in building was increased in Lynn, as in other towns at this period, as larger responsibilities were assumed by urban authorities towards the poor and needy. This is not to say that town Councils were becoming increasingly philanthropic. The poor were a serious threat to the order and stability of urban communities in this period and the authorities ignored them at their peril. This problem was probably aggravated by the disappearance of the monastic houses in the 1530's and the Gilds shortly afterwards. From then onwards town authorities were forced in many cases to anticipate national legislation, and make provision for the poor where private charity proved inadequate.

The almshouse run by the Council in the 16th century had been built by the Gild of St. Giles and St. Julian. An inventory taken in 1488 shows that it could accommodate seven men and six women each with their own room containing a mattress, a pair of sheets, a pair of blankets and a coloured coverlet. It had a communal kitchen with spits, a gridiron and other utensils, and there was probably also a chapel.[33] The buildings stood on the corner of South Clough Lane and London Road and are mentioned in the Chamberlains' Survey of 1557. In the early 16th century the almshouse continued to provide for a limited number of town's poor and was supported by various bequests and donations. The Council does not seem to have become directly involved in its management until 1581 when it appointed two aldermen to look after it.[34] By 1611 the number of inmates had been increased to 15 and it was decided that they should be supported from the profits of the Council's dealings in rye. It was their practice to buy this cheap each August in order to have enough in hand to sell to the poor should a shortage occur later in the year. In good years this stock was often sold at a profit.[35]

Only very limited numbers of poor people could be supported permanently by the Council; the rest were left to get what they could be working for wages in good times and to live by begging or alms when work was unobtainable. By the mid-16th century, the Council was becoming aware that their major problems with the poor were caused by under-employment. In 1565 they petitioned the Crown for a licence to make cloth in the town in an attempt to stimulate the industry and provide more work. When this proved unsuccessful, it was followed by a representation to the Duke of Norfolk asking him to put forward the town's case for a licence for making 'Tapestry and Bayes' but nothing seems to have come of this. In the following decade the Council also tried to persuade experienced weavers to come and set up shops and train the people of Lynn to make cloth. Men from

Colchester making bays were given a loan of £200 to set up businesses in the town in 1573,[36] and in 1576 Thomas Freeman, a clothier from Northampton, was brought by the Council 'to live in Lynn and set the poor at work'.[37] He, too, was lent £200 but his business failed. He was arrested for debt in 1579 and ended his life in Lynn in poverty.

Having failed to stimulate employment of the poor by these means, the Council decided in 1580 to build a workhouse and to run an industrial venture themselves. This was not an entirely new idea. In 1548, the Mayor had been given a small sum of money and instructed to buy hemp to set people at work making canvas, and in 1568 a loan was raised in the town to buy wool to 'put the poor to work'.[38] These enterprises had not entailed a major outlay of capital on buildings and equipment but the project of 1580 was to cost the Council £600 on the building alone.[39]

The Council chose the linen and canvas-weaving industry as the one most likely to flourish in Lynn, and, since this did not involve the use of power-driven machinery, the choice of a site for the workhouse did not present any particular problems. The Council, therefore, chose to adapt an already existing building as a workhouse, the disused chapel of St. James. This had been founded at the beginning of the 12th century and was originally cruciform in plan with an aisled nave, unaisled transepts and an octagonal tower over the crossing. By the beginning of the 16th century its condition was ruinous and in 1548 the nave had been pulled down. In 1559, brick, stone and lead were taken from the church, leaving only the transepts and one bay of the chancel still standing. It was these ruins which, in the winter of 1580, the Council decided to convert. Work began in January 1581 and the new workhouse was finished except for the spire by the following October.

The work was directed by William Overend, a merchant and alderman, and the final scheme had no great architectural pretensions. This 16th century workhouse was depicted in an engraving at the end of the 17th century, before it was further altered by Henry Bell, and the illustration views the building from the west. It shows that little more had, in fact, been done than to make the building weatherproof and arrange a new system of lighting the interior. The workhouse had occupied the transepts and the crossing which together made one long rectangular workroom. This, however, had not apparently been floored and was lit by a row of new windows on the ground floor only. The lower part of the tower beneath the crossing arch had been walled in leaving the arch itself still clearly visible, and the tower had been capped with a squat broach spire. Rather surprisingly, in view of the failure of other industrial ventures in Lynn in this period, the workhouse seems to have done well for the next two decades, although nothing much is known of its activities in the 17th century. Probably it declined. The Bell engraving of 1680 suggests that it was ruinous by that time.

In 1681 the Council decided to renovate the old workhouse and make it suitable for the employment of pauper children. Henry Bell was on the Committee appointed by the Council to supervise the work so it is likely that he himself made the designs which were carried out within the year. This building was drawn in the 1820's by the Reverend Edward Edwards and was visually a considerable improvement on the old workhouse. (Plate 39.) It had been designed symmetrically about the central tower which had received a classical cupola in place of the broach spire and an elaborate classical doorcase forming the main entrance in the blocked off part beneath the crossing arch. A floor had been inserted and an attic made in the roof; it was lighted by new regularly placed mullioned and transomed windows of six lights, two on each floor on either side of the tower with two dormer windows to light the attic. Whether or not this building succeeded in housing an efficient work-house for children is not recorded. By the mid-19th century it was ruinous and the last vestiges of it were removed about 1910.

As well as trying to solve the problems of the poor, it also fell to the Council in the 16th century to take responsibility for education. By the end of the century there were two schools in Lynn, the Grammar School refounded by the Council in 1538 from the remains of the Charnel School,[40] and the French school run by George Walden in St. George's Hall. A school to teach children to write and 'cypher' was founded in 1630 by Nicholas Donne.[41] The Council took an interest in all these establishments, provided accommodation for them and supplied them, when necessary, with books. Only the Grammar School, however, was provided with a new building. Until 1548, it had been housed in the Charnel priests' school attached to St. Margaret's Church, but after that date it was moved, it is not known where, but probably into some other part of the complex of buildings surrounding the church. The new building to house 24 pupils was built in 1582.[42] It is clear from the Articles of the Common Free Grammar School drawn up in 1606 that the children were not expected to board but to attend the school only for the purpose of instruction.[43] The building was, therefore, not a large one. It stood at the west end of St. Margaret's Church facing the Trinity Gildhall and an indistinct aerial photograph, taken before it was pulled down, shows it to have been a single range rectangular building, one storey high, lit by tall four-centred arch windows in the long sides. It was furnished with benches and stools.

There was no permanent hospital for the sick in Lynn in the 16th and 17th centuries and the Council seems to have relied mainly on attempts to prevent rather than cure sporadic outbreaks of plague.[44] They tried to keep disease under control by cleansing the town's streets and watercourses, by keeping down the number of animals in the built-up area and, when plague did break out, by sealing off infected areas.[45] In the bad outbreaks of 1587 and 1636 they also built temporary timber 'pesthouses' for plague victims outside the town walls.[46] Beyond that, illness among poor people was dealt with by the Aldermen in charge of each of the town's wards. They were instructed by the Council in 1524 to carry out periodic inspections of their areas and to distribute alms to those in need. In addition the Council employed a qualified medical man to deal with special cases from 1580.[47]

The last group of public buildings to be discussed comprises those which, in the 16th and 17th centuries, were provided to improve the facilities for trade in Kings Lynn and thereby to encourage its growth.

Few English towns went to the lengths of providing market halls in the medieval period, unlike the towns in south-west France for instance, where almost invariably a large timber shelter was erected as soon as the town showed any signs of prosperity.[48] In Lynn no proper covered area was provided in either the Tuesday or the Saturday marketplaces until the end of the 17th century, but a series of makeshift arrangements probably protected traders from the worst of the weather. For example, even in the medieval period the town seems to have maintained semi-permanent boothes or shops in the market places leased on a temporary basis to visiting traders. A shelter was provided for the market people in the Tuesday Market in the 15th century, although nothing is known about this early 'cross' except that like its successors it was probably built around the conduit pool which stood in the northern half of the market square.

In 1580 the Council proposed to rebuild the old cross as 'a place . . . in some part of the Tuesday Market for persons resorting to the market to stand and walk dry'. This project seems not to have been completed because in 1601 it was proposed again that 'a convenient market house for market folk to sit in' should be made around the conduit pool and roofed with lead.[49] This was built and is illustrated in a print made of the market place in the late 17th century. (Plate 40A.) It was a single storeyed building, square in plan, out of the centre of which rose a square lantern with pinnacles on each corner, capped by a broach spire. The main entrance was from the south and the large window shown in the east wall may possibly have lighted a shop. All the details of door and window openings were gothic and the whole effect was somewhat curious, although similar to one built in the same period in Norwich. It apparently remained standing until the end of the 17th century when it was pulled down to make way for a new and much more elaborate building built in 1707.

This was the 'beautiful and ornamentall' market house put up to combine the functions of the 'present decayed Cross and the old Shambles' and to enhance the visual qualities of the Tuesday Market. (Plate 40B.) It was financed by public subscription which, according to Hillen, raised £596 10s. 0d. and the work was supervised by Charles Turner and Henry Bell.[50] Before it was pulled down in 1829, several drawings and engravings were made of it, including one by William Stukely, the antiquarian, in 1711. They show an unusual layout. The central feature was the new 'cross' from which three quadrant-shaped rows of stalls radiated into the market place. The centrepiece was a two storeyed octagonal building encircled by a peristyle of freestanding Ionic columns supporting a first floor balcony. It was domed and surmounted by a cupola. Inside, Stukeley mentions a 'fair octangular room' lit by windows in four sides of the octagon, the remaining alternate sides being ornamented with niches holding statues. The market stalls were contained in freestanding arcades of Doric columns, whose pedimented ends were decorated with emblems representing the produce sold there. They were probably built of timber but the Cross was stone. The whole layout was almost certainly designed by Henry Bell,[51] who also designed the celebrated 'Custom House' at the south end of King Street.

The original Custom House had been in the Common Staithe yard. In 1568 the Comptroller of the Customs leased a chamber over the Tollbooth Courthouse there, and in 1621 he had moved to new premises astride the main gate to the yard. These were in the centre block of a row of houses the Council were already rebuilding. They faced the Tuesday Market on the west side between Common Staithe Lane on the south and Water Lane on the norht. The King was petitioned for 100 marks towards the cost of the Customer's new accommodation. The row in which the Custom House was built was two storeys high and divided into seven dwelling houses with shops. The facades were designed in an exactly uniform manner on the specific instructions of the Council and little distinguished the Custom House from its neighbours. (Plate 41.) Like the market house, it was two storeys high and three bays wide with a bandcourse beneath the sills of the first floor windows, and had mullioned and transomed window openings with cut brick pediments above. All the houses were roofed parallel to the street and had tall pointed dormer windows facing east. The place of the dormer in the centre of the Custom House facade was taken by a statue of Charles I in an ornamental niche 'fairly cut in stone' and painted and gilded. This was the centrepiece of the row. The Custom House was further distinguished by a large covered porch at the front of the building lined with seats.

In 1682, Sir John Turner, a prominent citizen of Kings Lynn and Member of Parliament for the town, petitioned the Council for a grant of land for the erecting of an Exchange or place for the meeting of Merchants'. He was granted 40 feet of ground westward from Purfleet bridge on the north bank of the fleet and in the following year work on the new Exchange was begun.[52] This was the building later to be known as the Lynn Custom House, but not originally designed as such. Indeed, it was badly sited for the collection of customs dues, being away from the main landing stage at Common Staithe where the bulk of Lynn's goods was handled. It was apparently built at a time when the site of the old Custom House was wanted for re-development by Sir John Turner's younger brother Charles, and the Customer was offered alternative accommodation in the first floor of the new building. Since the Exchange seems never to have been popular, the whole building was leased by him shortly after its completion.

The building of the Exchange was financed almost entirely by Sir John Turner and was designed by his fellow Alderman, Henry Bell. Bell's career as an architect has been fully discussed by H.M. Colvin.[53] He was an amateur and probably self-taught, but gained a considerable reputation for his architectural designs not only in Lynn and the surrounding country, but in Northampton. Born in 1653, he was a native of Lynn where his father was an alderman and a merchant, and, as a young man, he travelled for the business, visiting the Netherlands probably in 1676. When he returned to Lynn he became, like his father, involved in the government of the town and was Mayor twice, in 1692 and 1703. As a member of the governing body he was associated with most of the public works of the last two decades of the 17th century, and seems also to have undertaken a number of private commissions in and around Lynn, of which the *Duke's Head* in the Tuesday Market, the street front of Clifton House in Queen Street and No. 29 King Street are said to be examples.

The design of the Exchange was very much more sophisticated than anything that had been built in Lynn hitherto. In the first places it was a free-standing structure and designed three dimensionally, whereas most buildings in Lynn had only one wall visible from the street and were treated with flat, two dimensional, decorative patterns. In the second place this was the first building in Lynn, as far as we know, to use the grammar of classical architecture correctly. Bell did not take only the decorative details of classical building, as for example the architect of the Trinity Gildhall porch had done, and use them as applied ornament. He understood that the whole design had to be guided by a rigid system of proportions of which the orders and other classical details were the key.

In plan the Lynn Custom House is a rectangle of which the sides are in the ratio of 4:5. The height of the building to the top of the attic balustrade is also four units making the short sides square in elevation; the long sides have a height to length ratio the same as the plan, 4:5. Finally, the steep pitched roof of the original design, illustrated in a contemporary engraving by Bell himself, was surmounted by an cupola and an obelisk, on the top of which was a statue of Fame. (Plate 42.) This gave the building a total height of twice its length and thus elevation fitted within a double square. The obelisk and the statue fell in the gales of 1741 and were not replaced.

The design of the exterior wall surfaces was regulated by a superimposed order of flat pilasters, Doric on the ground floor and Ionic on the first storey. The entablature of the Doric order, with a plain frieze, forms a bandcourse beneath the sills of the first-floor windows, and the modilion cornice of the Ionic entablature hides the eaves of the roof. The attic balustrade, which once partly hid the pitched roof, has now disappeared. Pilasters divided the short and long sides into four and five bays respectively but their spacing was not entirely even. The three centre bays of the long side and the two centre bays of the short sides were to be left open on the ground storey and were wider than the rest. These openings were given semi-circular heads with mask keystones. The main entrance to the Exchange was in the centre of the north front. Here emphasis was achieved by bringing slightly forward the orders of that particular bay and surmounting the Ionic entablature with a pediment. On the first floor a semi-circular headed niche held a statue of James II, while immediately over the door was a cartouche and an inscription. Each bay on the first floor has a glazed casement window, some of which are blind, and the attic was lit by dormers in the roof. The platform on top of the roof, from which the cupola springs, was surrounded by a balustrade with obelisk finials on each corner. These finials have now been removed. (Plate 43.)

Access to the first floor was by means of a dog-leg stair set back against the south wall. This had turned oak balusters and a thick, square-section handrail similar to the stairs in the *Duke's Head*. The interior does not seem to have been lavishly decorated. Each of the rooms on the first floor had a simple wooden box cornice, but no panelling or plasterwork. The ground floor arcades were walled in when the Customs Officer took over the whole building.

Notes to Chapter VI

1 Beresford, *New Towns,* 142-78.
2 Beloe, 'Making of Lynn', 329.
3 K.L.M./Roll of the Mayors of Lynn.
4 e.g. K.L.M./HB.V/143d, 252, 350d, etc.
5 A. Kingston, *East Anglia in the Great Civil War,* (1897), 134-9.
6 *Ibid,* 139.
7 W. Taylor, *Antiquities of Lynn,* (1844), 157.
8 K.L.M./H.B.I/29; H.B.II/286.

9 K.L.M./H.B.III/1516.

10 *Cal. Patent Rolls,* 1292-1301, 74, 491; 1338-40, 240. J.C. Tingey, 'The Grants of Murage to Norwich, Yarmouth and Lynn', *Norf. Arch.,* XVIII, (1912), 137.

11 K.L.M./H.B.I/123.

12 K.L.M./H.B.I/23; H.B.III/225d.

13 The drawbridges were renewed in 1642: K.L.M./H.B.VIII/103.

14 See above p.30.

15 It is not proposed to examine in detail the archaeology of Lynn churches here. This will be the major part of a forthcoming volume in this series.

16 K.L.M./H.B.V/76d, 87, 192.

17 K.L.M./Be550.

18 K.L.M./Gd 78.

19 P.R.O./E178/7046.

20 K.L.M./Gd33; Gild Book begins in *c.*1493 *Blomefield's Norfolk,* VIII, 518.

21 K.L.M./Gd 34; *Blomefields Norfolk,* VIII, 505-9.

22 *The Book of Margery Kempe,* ed. W. Butler-Bowden, 213-15.

23 K.L.M./Ea. 58, 59, 59a, 60.

24 K.L.M./H.B.VII/423.

25 K.L.M./Bc 7 Chamberlains A/c.; Ea/1557.

26 K.L.M./Ed3/1586.

27 K.L.M./H.B.V/49.

28 K.L.M./H.B.VII/223d.

29 K.L.M./H.B.IX/165.

30 *Blomefield's Norfolk* VIII, 505.

31 P.R.O./E.178/7046; *Blomefield's Norfolk* VIII, 506; K.L.M. Ed4/1602-5.

32 K.L.M./H.B.V/365.

33 Richards' *Kings Lynn,* I, 434-5.

34 K.L.M./H.B.V/220d.

35 K.L.M./H.B.IV/487; H.B.V/159; H.B.VI/61.

36 K.L.M./H.B.V/83d, 86.

37 K.L.M./H.B.V/132, 138d, 139d, 169; H.B.VI/68d.

38 K.L.M./H.B.IV/98d, 510d.

39 K.L.M./H.B.V/215, 218d, 220d, 223d, 230, 230d, 240.

40 K.L.M./H.B.III/1538.

41 K.L.M./H.B.VII/333.

42 K.L.M./H.B.V/243.

43 K.L.M./H.B.VI/374d; K.L.M./Bb12.

44 In 1582 the Council purchased the Hospital of St. Mary Magdalen in Gaywood from the Crown, but this does not appear to have been used as a Leper House as formerly, but rather as an almshouse.

45 K.L.M./H.B.VI/161d; H.B.V/300d.

46 K.L.M./H.B.VII/445, 450. In the plague of 1598 victims were housed in the workhouse. K.L.M./H.B.VI/155.

47 K.L.M./H.B.V/290, 301d. In January 1580 Thomas Surflete, surgeon, was given the Freedom if he agreed to treat the poor and the needy at the request of the mayor. K.L.M./H.B. V/190.

48 Beresford, *New Towns*, 167, 177.

49 K.L.M./H.B.V/198d.

50 Hillen, *Kings Lynn*, 564.

51 Colvin, 'Henry Bell', 51.

52 K.L.M./H.B.IX/1683.

53 Colvin, 'Henry Bell', *passim.*

VII

The Urban Environment in the 16th and 17th centuries

MOST OF THIS BOOK has been concerned with analysing and describing the individual elements of the fabric of the town of Kings Lynn, the street plan, and various building types – houses, public works, commercial and industrial buildings and other special-purpose buildings. Yet a town is not just a random collection of individual units, but a complete organism, living and changing. The community of Lynn, and in particular the governing body, naturally took an interest in their town's development. It is from their contemporary comments, as well as from the remaining visual evidence both on the ground and in prints and illustrations, that it has been possible to reconstruct some of the problems of the physical environment as a whole – its problems of circulation and drainage, and the visual qualities of its streets and open spaces.

If an interest in altering and improving their environment was shown by the people of Lynn in the medieval period, the evidence of this has not survived and we have very little knowledge from contemporary sources of the state of the town at that time. In the 16th century, many of the physical problems of the built environment came within the scope of the activities of the Town Council, and from about 1550 the record of the meetings of the Council in the Hall Books contains numerous references to discussions and enactments covering this subject. The Council, as might be expected, was mainly interested in solving the practical problems of a town entering a new period of commercial expansion with a stock of buildings and a pattern of communications still basically medieval. But the Renaissance idea of ordering the built environment for visual effect was not entirely ignored in Lynn in the 16th and 17th centuries. The example of the Dutch towns was sufficient to demonstrate the important link between an attractive townscape and a commercially successful town. Their clean paved streets, regular building lines, and tidy brick buildings were known to attract merchants who welcomed the improved facilities they offered.[1]

The Council, the body who made all the important planning decisions in 16th and 17th century Lynn, was newly constituted in 1524 as a closed, self-elected group consisting of a Mayor, 12 Aldermen and 18 members of the Common Council. The original 12 Aldermen were nominated by the Crown. It was the Aldermen who chose the Mayor, elected annually from one of their number, and nominated members to the Common Council from among the burgesses of the town. Vacancies among the Aldermen were then filled from the Common Council.[2] This completely closed system of selection to the governing body lasted in Lynn, as in some other towns, until 1835. The Council had wide powers particularly after 1536 when it acquired the fee farm of the Bishop's manor from the Crown. In 1547 it became heir to the properties and privileges of the gilds as well, and thus there came under one hand the fragmented political authority of the medieval community. In exercising this authority the Council was bound to reflect the interests of its members almost exclusively, since the community as a whole had no representation and, therefore, no say in the way in which the affairs of the town were handled. The town was, in fact, run by its most wealthy citizens and until 1700 these were the merchants.

A merchant had a clearly defined status in Lynn. In 1547 a local act clearly separated the great overseas and wholesale trader from the shop-keeper and pedlar, reserving the designation of merchant for the former group alone.[3] By this act a merchant paid a substantially greater fine than others to receive his grant of Freedom. This gave him the right to 'buy and sell freely in the town as a merchant', that is, to deal directly with merchants from other towns rather than indirectly through a middleman, and to 'adventure to the sea by ship'. He was also free of the usual tolls at Lynn and in other towns where the Corporation had negotiated special privileges. All other occupations were excluded from this, the most lucrative branch of commerce, the wholesale and overseas trade, so a merchant by definition was a member of Lynn's plutocracy. Although there were people in Lynn whose wealth was derived from land rather than trade, they were so few in number that they created no really effective challenge. All the important places on the Town Council went almost invariably to the merchant class. From 1550 to 1700 only five of the Mayors were non-merchants, and although some Common Council members were from other occupations, it was rare to find any except merchants attaining the office of Alderman. Thus, from the mid-16th century, it was the merchants, as members of the Council, who were chiefly involved in the problems of the urban environment, raising money by taxation to initiate specific building projects like the new layout of the Common Staithe, or exerting their powers through the Council to regulate at least some aspects of private development. It was their approach to these problems which determined much of the kind of work done to improve the town of Lynn in the 16th and 17th centuries.

In the mid-16th century, the growing interest in the quality of the urban environment in Lynn coincided with the expansion of trade, particularly the coasting trade in grain and coal, which is so marked a feature of the town's economic development from 1550 to 1700. The growth of trade was an important influence on the progress of town planning in Lynn for two reasons. In the first place it was from the profits of trade that wealth for investment in the fabric of the town came. Secondly, and perhaps more importantly, it provided the major incentive to improvement at this time. When trade was hindered, or held up, by some deficiency in the fabric of the town like the impassability of a street or watercourse, this was a spur to the town authorities to deal with the problem. It was the expectation of further growth in trade that stimulated both public and private building activity in this period.

When much of the business of a merchant was still conducted face to face and when many merchants still travelled with their goods, it was clearly of vital importance that the town could accommodate visiting traders in safety and comfort and offer them adequate space to display and handle their wares. By the 16th century, it is true, some of the larger merchant firms had already begun to conduct their business operations by letter and the number following this course was to grow in the 17th century. Nevertheless, the ability to attract an influx of 'merchant strangers', both from other English towns and from abroad, was a matter of serious concern until well into the 17th century. Lynn, in competition with other towns on the east coast, had to be careful that potential visitors were not put off by inadequate facilities for trade, even if the positive attractions of Lynn as a trading town with an impressively extensive hinterland still remained.

Principally, the merchants of Lynn seem to have worried about three aspects of their town which they knew to be harmful to their trading interests: the danger of fire, the prevalence of disease owing to the filthy surroundings in which people lived, and the inadequacy of the system of communications, both by water and road, in the town centre. Three times in the 16th century the complaints of visiting merchants spurred the Council to take action to clear the most offensive streets and watercourses: first in 1545 when the filth in the watercourses was released by unblocking them; again in 1569 when the Council accused the men of Lynn and South Lynn of living like beasts surrounded by filth and riddled with disease to the grave detriment of trade; and finally in 1585 after a bad outbreak of plague, when visiting merchants again complained and further measures were taken to clean up the town.[4] But, even when the specific complaints of visiting merchants are not recorded, the increasing number of attempts after about 1550 to improve the town must be seen against this background. The interest of the Council in the built environment of Lynn was not so much paternalistic, as has sometimes been suggested, as dictated by economic necessity. Lynn was then in competition with other towns like Norwich and Hull in attracting the vital personal contacts between merchant and merchant, which were the basis of trade. Plague, for example, could bring the whole economic life of a town to a halt, sometimes for weeks on end.

So, indeed, could fire, and the Mayors' Roll, or chronicle, gave prominent place in the 15th and 16th centuries to the fires that had paralysed the life of Lynn's competitors.[5] Clearly, very little could be done to check a major outbreak once the town's timber buildings were alight, but in 1581 the Aldermen were to have ready four leather buckets, and members of the Common Council three, to check minor outbreaks in the wards of the town for which they were responsible.[6]

Otherwise the Council in Lynn, as elsewhere, took preventive action wherever possible, though it is perhaps surprising to find no Ordinance forbidding the use of timber construction, even when brick had become more widely available, as it had by the 17th century. Thatch was forbidden as roof covering in 1572 and the stacks of 'sedge', used both for roofing and floor covering, were strictly confined to the public quays along the waterfront in 1591. Constables were instructed to take special care after the mart that unruly and 'evil disposed persons' with lighted torches were kept away from those areas.[7]

The worst health problem in Lynn, as in most towns, was caused by the accumulation of filth blocking the streets and watercourses, obstructing vital communications between one part of the town and another and making a fertile breeding ground for epidemics. In 16th century Lynn the Council believed that these blockages were caused partly by the habit, in default of a suitable alternative, of throwing out rubbish onto the nearest open space, and partly by bringing animals into the town centre and allowing them to run loose. Numerous Ordinances were passed excluding pigs, ducks, horses, cows and sheep from the town, but the very number of local acts suggests that they were largely unsuccessful.[8] Pigs, certainly, remained as a normal part of the street scene until the end of the 17th century and, in spite of an Ordinance of 1545 few people seem to have milked their cows in the fields, but continued to bring them to their houses at milking time.

The council also attempted to deal with refuse dumped in the streets by providing alternative places for disposing waste. They did this by appointing places where muckhills could be laid out, and by building public privies; both places were cleaned periodically by the Council's agents called 'Muckhill fowers'. In 1558 a survey made by the town chamberlains mentions five muckhills, one at the East Gates, one in St. Anne's Yard, one known as Purfleet dunghill beside Purfleet staithe, St. Margaret's muckhill at the end of St. Margaret's Lane to serve the Saturday Market and one at the end of Pudding Lane to serve the Tuesday Market and the Common Staithe.[9] Muckhills were usually located beside the river or the larger fleets so that they could be cleared either by barges from which they were dumped in the estuary or by throwing them into the water and letting the tide carry them out to sea. The muckhill at the East Gates was usually cleared by cart and the filth spread on the surrounding fields. It was recorded in 1630 that the great muckhill at the East Gate was taken to Mr. Pells pasture called St. Katherine and spread by men and women at the rate of 6d. and 4d. a day respectively.[10]

Some of the muckhill sites had probably remained the same since medieval times, particularly those by the market places where they were constantly in demand. Needless to say they were extremely unpleasant for those living nearby, and the sites were probably changed quite often in the centre of the town. In 1500, for example, it was one of the privileges of the mayor that he could demand the removal of a butcher's muckhill if he happened to live near one,[11] and, in 1579, there was an attempt to limit the number of muckhills to two – one at St. Anne's Yard for those living north of the Millfleet and one outside the South Gates for those living to the south.[12] A list of Muckhills of 1583, when their numbers had increased again, shows the use of several alternative sites.[13]

The survey of 1557 lists nine public privies, three in the vicinity of the Tuesday Market and Common Staithe, one on each side of Purfleet bridge, one in Leadenhall Lane just off the Saturday Market, one at Ladybridge over the Millfleet and two in the centre of the town at Baxtar Bridge and in Sedgeford Lane.[14] Like the muckhills, the privies were built beside or even over the town's fleets and were flushed out by the tide. They seem to have been timber buildings, repaired and maintained by the town's chamberlains, and swept out periodically by the muckhill fowers.[15]

The nauseous accumulation of filth in the town centre was by no means disposed of by these measures nor was the problem really solved until an adequate system of main drainage was laid out at the end of the 19th century. In the 16th century there was, at all events on paper, a system of watercourses which, had they functioned properly, should have provided each occupant of a tenement with his own drain. In a survey of the town's fleets in 1558 nine smaller watercourses were mentioned, in addition to the four major streams flowing through the town centre, and these were channelled to flow along the rear boundaries of tenements in all the main streets.[16] In Damgate (now Norfolk Street) an open gutter or fleet ran along the backs of the properties on both sides of the street, draining into the Purfleet. (Fig.7.) The fleet on the north turned south at Listergate (now Chapel Street) and drained the backs of tenements in Mercer Row (High Street north) on its way, and the fleet behind the properties on the south side of Damgate ran south down Webstar Row (now Broad Street) to enter the Purfleet at Baxtar Bridge. For most of the 16th century the fleet in Webstar Row was an open gutter down the centre of the road only finally bridged and levelled in 1586.[17] To the west of Mercer Row a fleet ran parallel to the river Ouse, draining the east side of Checker (now King Street) and continuing south of the Purfleet between Wingate (now Queen Street) and Briggate (now High Street South); it surfaced behind the Trinity Gildhall where there was a piece of open ground left for the muckhill when the fleet was cleansed. To the east of this a fleet ran between the Millfleet and the Purfleet draining the east side of Briggate, the Saturday Market and Stonegate Street. When first laid out, probably in the Middle Ages, these fleets may, like the Purfleet, have been fresh water streams but filled twice daily by the tide as well. In the 16th century most of them were blocked. Like the refuse in the streets, such blockages were not only a danger to health but fouled the communications. Many of the smaller fleets flowed into the Purfleet and the accumulated filth there obstructed shipping.

The river Ouse, too, in the 16th century was gradually silting up, partly because of the amount of rubbish tipped into it by the people of Lynn. As early as the 15th century the blockages to shipping were giving cause for concern, and in 1587 a local act made it illegal to tip rubbish into the Ouse for two years, presumably with the idea that in those two years the action of the tide would have scoured and deepened the shipping channels.[18] The dumping of ballast, too, was strictly controlled during the 16th century, in a vain attempt to check the deterioration of the Lynn harbour. More radical steps were needed to check the silting of the mouth of the Ouse: the problems were later shown to be aggravated by the towns's waste disposal system but not caused by it.[19]

The system of waste disposal in 16th and 17th century Lynn was probably superior to that of most towns because the waste could be carried by water out of the built-up area of the town. But it was totally inadequate for the needs of a community of five to six thousand people. This basic inadequacy went unrecorded by the Council, who were both unable through lack of funds, and probably unwilling to contemplate a radical solution. All they did was to try to patch up the old system at its weakest points. In 1516 and again in 1541 weekly sweepings, in which householders were enjoined to clean the streets, started, with those furthest from the fleet or drain sweeping the accumulated filth down towards the haven. In 1575 Saturday was the day when the sweeping took place under the supervision of the Aldermen, but, despite repeated attempts in the last quarter of the 16th century to get public co-operation, it was not a success, and the ordinance had to be re-inforced again and again. The levying of a rate to pay for this to be done by public officials, however, does not seem to have been considered, and the half-hearted weekly sweeping was still being done at the end of the 17th century.

At the beginning of the 16th century, the fleets, too, were ordered to be cleaned by those who held property along their banks, and the same system was adopted whereby filth was swept downstream towards the Ouse bank, or taken out of the fleets and laid on muckhills. But by 1608 the Council had taken full charge of this operation, and a special rate was levied periodically to enable the Council workmen to do the job properly.[20]

While the Council does not seem to have been able to improve the health of the town by a major reorganisation of the system of waste disposal it did, during the course of the 16th century, undertake to supply many of the householders in the main streets of the town with fresh water. This was a difficult problem in Lynn. To avoid contamination with salt water, fresh water had to be taken out of the rivers at some distance from the rown and it was difficult to gain sufficient head of water to ensure that it flowed through the pipes. At the beginning of the 16th century practically nothing had been done about a piped water supply, and most of the town was still supplied from the watercarts. The earliest pipe, which was in existence in 1500, and may perhaps have been medieval, ran along Norfolk Street to a conduit head known as Harwoods conduit at the junction of Norfolk Street and Chapel Street, the old site of the 'grassmarket'. This took its fresh water from the river Gay near the East Gate by means of a 'kettle mill', a big

Plate 34A *Duke's Head; street front, c.1700*

Plate 34B *Duke's Head; main stair, c.1700*

Plate 35A *East Gate from the west*

Plate 35B *East Gate from the east*

Plate 36A *Town wall near the East Gate*

Plate 36B *The South Gate*

Plate 37A *Aerial view of the site of Trinity Gildhall*

Plate 37B *Street facade of Trinity Gildhall*

Plate 38 *North elevation of the Gildhall of St. George*

Plate 39 *The St. James's Workhouse, c.1820*

Plate 40A *The 'Old Cross' in the Tuesday Market in 17th century*

Plate 40B *The 'New Cross', 1707*

Plate 41 *The Old Custom House and adjoining cottages on the west side of Tuesday Market, c.1620*

Plate 42 *The engraving by Henry Bell of 'The Exchange', 1682-3*

Plate 43 *The Custom House, Purfleet Quay*

wheel to which buckets were attached and turning in a vertical plane. The mill was driven by a horse.

Sometime around 1530 the Council began to extend the piped water supply and work continued on this throughout the rest of the 16th century. A second pipe was laid from the Kettlemill's supply down Hopman's Way (now Austin Street) into the Tuesday marketplace and this was later extended down into Checker Street (now King Street) to a conduit pool there. The new pipe along Woolmarket (now St. Nicholas Street) was laid in 1525 and the extension into Checker was made in the 1580's. In the Middle Ages the religious houses had been well in advance of the town in laying on supplies of fresh water to their conventual buildings. After the Dissolution, the Council acquired all these supplies, including the pipes and aqueducts, and was able to incorporate them in the town's supply system. The Blackfriars' pipe, which took water from the Middleton river, was extended in 1551 to the banks of the Purfleet in Fincham Street (later named New Conduit Street) and from this source a new system of pipes was laid out to take water to the area to the south of the Purfleet, to Briggate (High Street South), Wingate (Queen Street) and the Saturday Market.[21]

By the end of the 16th century between 40 and 50 households were being currently supplied with water from the town's pipes.[22] These were mostly the wealthy members of the community, since the supply was expensive to maintain and rents were high. In 1587 it cost an ordinary householder 6s. 8d. a year for his supply and those who used the town's water for brewing paid £3. 6s. 8d. a year. At the beginning of the 16th century, when only a few lengths of pipe were supplied from the Kettlemill, householders appear to have been able to drain off water from the main pipe whenever they needed to. By the end of the century the supply was becoming insufficient. In 1580 the Chamberlains were instructed to examine branch pipes for possible leaks, and all households supplied with water were required to build a cistern. Because the main pipe was usually laid down the centre of the street most houses took in their supply from the front of the house and built their cistern in the street. This was made of stone lined with lead and covered with a wooden lid to prevent people falling in.[23]

Another difficulty encountered during the latter part of the 16th century was in maintaining the supply during seasonal droughts. This was partly overcome by building reservoirs for each supply, in the Pinfold of the Austin Friars and at Kettlemills for water from the Gaywood river, and at the Red Mount and St. Margaret's for the water from Middleton. There is no record of how much this or any of the other installations cost the Council. The only figures that have survived relate to the cost of adapting the old Kettlemill to a 'pump mill' in 1578.[24] This work was carried out by a carpenter, Richard Brown, and seems to have involved the construction of six wooden vacuum pumps through which water could be fed in greater volume into the Kettlemill's pipe. The work originally cost the Council £35 plus the lead, but failed to work efficiently and a further £50 was needed later.

Maintaining good communications within the town was a serious problem in the 16th and 17th centuries, and yet it was clearly vital to the success of the settlement that the streets and watercourses should be kept free from obstruction. The worst problem that of the accumulation of rubbish, has already been referred to. Other causes of obstruction were the encroachments of buildings, failure to keep a reasonably level paved surface, and the habit of using the street as an extension to private property and cluttering it not only with animals but cargo, carts and other objects. The night-time darkness of the streets was a problem too, since in winter it must have meant business would cease in the early evening. From the early 16th century, innkeepers, victuallers and tipplers had to hang out a light from 6.00 p.m. to 9.00 a.m. during the February fair, and aldermen and common council members were enjoined to hang lights outside on dark nights, but these few sources of illumination can hardly have proved adequate.[25]

Throughout the medieval period in Lynn, the widths of the streets were probably being reduced by encroachments and even in the mid-19th century the last of the projecting porches were still being cleared away from the street line.[26] In the late 16th century attempts were being made to limit encroachment and to fix and maintain a building line for each street. From the 1560's the permission of the chamberlains had to be obtained for the line of the front wall of any new building project. William Killingtree's new house in the Tuesday Market, for example, had a projecting porch the line of which the Chamberlains approved before work started in 1569. In 1594 Arthur Dalton asked their permission to 'further beautify' his house in Damgate with a porch projecting two feet six inches into the street with 'seats closed in on both sides of the said door'. Again, in 1611, when John Grebby exceeded the agreed area of street frontage for his building on north side of Pudding Lane, he was ordered to pull down the offending building, as had been Francis Shaxton, who obstructed College Lane with a brick buttress in 1578.[27] The Hall Books contain many references to acts of this kind in the late 16th century and clearly to the town Council this was an important problem.

One form of encroachment which the Council usually authorised for a small fine was 'latching', the rebuilding of the ground storeys of timber buildings outwards to the same plane as the jettied wall of the first floor. This usually involved the taking in of about 18 inches from the street, but the Council made sure that the building line after the latching of several houses in a row was even. On the north side of the Tuesday Market, for example, the line of William Doughty's house, latched in 1615, was taken by Richard Brown when he latched his house in 1631 and by a Mr. Porter in 1637.[28]

Many streets in the 16th century seem to have been difficult to negotiate because of their uneven surface, and, in 1546, the Council ordered all the pavements throughout Lynn to be mended.[29] Some parts of the town had been paved in the medieval period particularly in the neighbourhood of the market-places where traffic could be expected to be heavy. The cobble paving in the Tuesday Market was maintained by the Council who, from time to time, employed people to keep down the weeds, but it did not extend over the whole area of the marketplace and much of the paving elsewhere in the town must have been similarly patchy. Most of the streets were partly paved and the paving maintained by private individuals who laid a surface in front of their own properties without reference to the street level as a whole. In the 16th century the Council, exercising its authority through the manorial Court Leet, was able to compel private individuals to keep the paving in front of their houses in repair.[30] The Council made their job easier by forbidding access to the town of vehicles most likely to damage the surface of the streets; brewers' watercarts with iron shod wheels and iron shod sleds in 1549, and later all carts with iron wheel rims except those making regular journeys outside the town.[31] No attempt seems to have been made to level already existing pavements but in 1571, it became an offence to build a new pavement above or below the general level of the street, an offence for which both the owners of the pavement and the paviours they employed were liable to be fined.[32]

The visual qualities that might have been though desirable in the townscape of Lynn are more difficult to determine, since the Council never formulated its views clearly on this topic. This, however, was the period when the Renaissance was spreading throughout northern Europe and the Council could hardly have been unaware of the growing importance attached to the appearance of towns, and the pressures on town authorities to lay out at least new developments in accordance with the classical system of town planning. The straight street, preferably with a monumental building or statue at the end of it; lines of buildings designed from the outset to weld together a number of small units for grand effect; the regular, geometrical shapes of open spaces, preferably circular or square; and an underlying symmetry of plan; these were the basic principles of the system. In towns like Lynn, with a basically medieval plan and a stock of ancient buildings, neither major rebuilding nor the laying out of a new area offered much scope for redesigning the urban environment. Councils, even if they were impressed by classical design principles, were unable to put the whole system into effect. Nevertheless, there are signs in the 17th century at least, of an endeavour to bring more order and regularity to the appearance of Lynn. Even if the Council was unable to formulate abstract aesthetic reasons why this should be so, the practical advantages of some feature of classical planning – the straight, wide street, for example – would have commended itself to them. Thus we find in Lynn, either for practical or for aesthetic reasons, but probably for a mixture of both, that the visual quality of the built environment was changing during the 16th and 17th centuries.

That the Council in Lynn was aware of contemporary town planning fashion is shown in their treatment of the one area of redevelopment carried out under their direct supervision in the early 17th century, the Common Staithe area in the Tuesday Market. All the early 17th century work there has now been cleared away, but illustrations survive of the facade of the row of cottages fronting onto the

Tuesday Market from Pudding Lane southward. (Plate 41.) These were built between 1612 and 1623, and it is most remarkable that, even though they were built over as long a period as 11 years, each facade was designed to correspond exactly with that of its neighbour in the arrangement of solids and voids, and in decorative details such as bandcourses and dormer gables in the roof. The cottages were laid out symmetrically about the new Custom House gate and porch, and the overall effect, with the statue of Charles I in the Custom House gable on the axis of the design, was a degree of classical regularity and monumentality, albeit somewhat reduced by the homely scale of the cottages. The intentions of the Council in this instance are clear and in 1623, when the last house was about to be built, it was their instructions that it should be 'builded this summer in a uniform fashion answerable to the Custom House and the rest of the tenements in that row'.[33]

When it came to dealing with the owners of private property the Council had very little power to compel them to undertake building work, whatever they may have thought desirable. For this reason an important element in the townscape – the street elevations of buildings – was largely beyond their control. Only by the Statute for the Decay of Towns (1541) were they empowered to make the owners of utterly derelict property repair their houses and outbuildings. This act was, in fact, invoked three times in the second half of the 16th century, in 1578, 1585 and 1595, to instigate repairs to, or the rebuilding of some 37 properties.[34] Unsound buildings were, of course, not only an eyesore but a danger as well. To try and reduce their number it was made an offence in 1553 to lease a house, without the Council's permission, to anyone unable to earn a living or to non-burgesses; leases were to be drawn up giving the owner the right to re-enter the property if the building was not maintained.[35]

Nevertheless, although not always the direct result of the Council's intervention, Lynn in the 16th, and more particularly in the 17th century, came to have a townscape that was more ordered and regular than before and thus more attuned to contemporary planning ideals. The improvements made by the Council to the town's streets and watercourses in the course of the 16th century could be appreciated not only for the practical problems they solved but for the neater and more orderly appearance they produced in the town centre. Clean, level and well-paved roads, lined by a regular street facade of buildings were primarily the result of the Council's activities to improve circulation and reduce the risk of disease. But the visual qualities of such an environment must also have been attractive, bringing Lynn nearer to the Dutch form of townscape which Lynn merchants know from experience provided an encouraging environment for trade.

As for the facades of buildings, these, too, were altering during the 16th and 17th centuries. In the medieval town most of the street facades of buildings had been timber framed and jettied on each floor into the street. Each house was built not as a part of a uniform and regular street but as an individual unit designed to fulfil the needs of a particular household and tailored to their requirements in terms of size and layout. No kind of formal design procedure was involved and many houses were ornamented in highly individual ways. Buildings were thus of different sizes, had different storey heights and were variously and ornamented. The resulting street scene was a picturesque jumble that can still be seen in those towns like York, Lavenham, and Thaxted where whole streets of medieval timber buildings still survive. To the trader attempting to use the streets of the town the effect must have often been confusing and traffic would have experienced the disadvantages of a limited range of vision as turns in the road and the projecting upper storeys of buildings blocked the view.

By the 16th century the straight wide street was being advocated in certain parts of Europe for abstract aesthetic reasons, but what the builders of Lynn were also likely to appreciate were the practical advantages of a systematic layout of streets and buildings with a regular building line, leaving vistas uninterrupted by unnecessary projections. The Council's work in attempting to organise a straight building line in each street must have helped towards this ideal, but individual buildings were still beyond their control. Nevertheless, from 1550 onwards great improvements were made in the facades of Lynn streets. Many houses were being re-built, not in timber but in brick and it was the growing use of brick in all construction work that was responsible for the marked changes in the townscape of Lynn up to 1700.

The use of brick did not at once reduce the townscape of Lynn to monotonous rows of exactly similar houses. The medieval divisions of property insured a wide variety of ownership in each street and although many houses were rebuilt in this period, formal classical design procedure was not sufficiently accepted in Lynn before the 18th century to determine the choice of an exactly similar design for each house. In addition, brick came from a number of sources each with its characteristic colour and texture. As great a variety was thus preserved in the street scene as in the medieval period, but it was more controlled. Houses were no longer built with the front wall projecting in stages into the street, but in one vertical plane. The confusing variety of ornament had gone, to be replaced by less obtrusive cut brick or plaster decoration, and buildings were more durable and more fireproof than before.

By the end of the 17th century Lynn had acquired the quality of 'neatness' so much admired by contemporaries as the visible sign of a town's efficient and vigorous economic life. In 1722 it was described by Defoe as a 'beautiful, well-built and well situated town' enjoying a flourishing trade carried along 'the greatest extent of Inland Navigation of any Port in England'.[36] The process of adapting the medieval town to the requirements of a new period of commercial expansion had involved no major rebuilding of the towns layout. Nevertheless, Lynn in 1700 was a very different place from the town at the beginning of the 16th century, not because its fabric had been altered in its essentials but because its outward appearance had been changed. The business of projecting the appropriate image of a thriving port was as important then as it is today, perhaps even more so, and this was largely derived from the appearance of a town's public places, its streets, market-places and quays and the parts of buildings visible from them. The Council at Lynn seems to have been well aware of this and both as private individuals rebuilding the front walls of their own houses and collectively as the governing body, they contributed towards the new environment in the 17th century town.

Notes to Chapter VII

1 L. Guicciardini, 'Description of Antwerp' *Tudor Economic Documents* III, ed R.H. Tawney and E. Power, 1924, 156.

2 Sir W. Savage, *The Making of Our Towns*, (1952), 74-75.

3 K.L.M./H.B.IV/81.

4 K.L.M./H.B.IV/32d, 512; H.B.V/300d. This problem was, of course, by no means peculiar to Lynn. For example see *V.C. H. City of York*, 119.

5 Roll of Mayors', K.L.M./H.B./VII/39, 41d. remarks the destruction wrough by a fire at Cley.

6 K.L.M./H.B./V/230d.

7 K.L.M./H.B./V/59d, 421d-422.

8 See for example: K.L.M./H.B.III, 180, 248, 293; H.B.V/116d, 204, 300d-301.

9 K.L.M./Bc7/Part 1, p.69/70.

10 K.L.M./H.B.VIII/337d.

11 K.L.M./H.B.III/1500.

12 K.L.M./H.B.V/171.

13 K.L.M./H.B.V/305.

14 K.L.M./Bc7, Part I/70d; H.B.V/305.

15 K.L.M./H.B.V/305.

16 K.L.M./Bc 7. Part I/71, 71d (Appendix I).

17 K.L.M./H.B.V/318d, 319.

18 K.L.M./H.B.V/347.

19 Badeslade *Navigation, passim.*

20 K.L.M./H.B.VI/415.

21 Numerous references occur both in the Hall Books and in the 16th century Chamberlains Accounts (Bc 7) to the town's water supply.

22 See the Water Rents in K.L.M./H.B.VI/13; Bc 7; Be 9.

23 K.L.M./H.B.V/207.

24 See above p.133.

25 K.L.M./H.B.III/225d, 227, 313d.

26 This, of course, was not a problem peculiar to Lynn; for example in Exeter in 1563, the Council tried to control the building of jetteys 'For the avoidance of sundry inconveniences which do grow by the excessive buildings in sailing themselves further out than it appertaineth it should be used'. W.G. Hoskins, The Elizabethan Merchants of Exeter' in *Elizabethan Government and Society; Essays presented to Sir John Neale* ed. Bindoff, Hurstfield and Williams, (1961), 179.

27 K.L.M./H.B.V/12d, 161; H.B.VI/41, 490.

28 K.L.M./H.B.VII/348d, 466.

29 K.L.M./Mayors Roll.

30 K.L.M./H.B.V/49d.

31 K.L.M./H.B.IV/105d.

32 K.L.M./H.B.V/49d.

33 K.L.M./H.B.VII/216.

34 K.L.M./H.B.V/6,612,297,298d-99; H.B.VI/85d.

35 K.L.M./H.B.IV/214; H.B.V/150.

36 Defoe, *Tour*, 73.

Appendix I

The Chamberlains' Survey, c.1557
(Kings Lynn Muniments, Bc.7)

The names of all stretis Lanes and wharffes then in Kyngs Lenne

ffirst the est strete ledying without dowshill gate to the Kettle mylls warde.
Item the west strete ther Leadinge to Dowshills
Item dowshill strete within dowshills gate leadynge to Saynte nycholas Churche
Item A Lane from St nycolas sowth stile into hopmans strete
Item A Crost strete from Dowshills strete Leadinge west to St Annes gates callyd drewes strete
Item St Annes Wharffe
Item the northe End strete leadinge from St Annes to woolemarket
Item A lane ther with A wharff on the west of St nycolas Churche
Item Lytstur Strete Leadinge from St Nycolas churche to gressemarkett
Item hoppmans waye strete
Item Dampgate strete
Item A lane ther on the sowth syd callyd Spynner Lane
Item A lane At the est end ther Leadinge to hopmans waye
Item A Lane ther leadinge by St Johns to blakffryers
Item lyttleporte strete
Item A lane ther Leadinge to Kettle mylls by the walls
Item A lane ther Leadinge to the mownte by the walls
Item webstarrowe Strete
Item A lane ther callyd Ratton Rowe
Item A strete ther from baxstar bridge to blakffryers
Item ffyncham strete
Item woolemarkete strete
Item Twesdaie market strete
Item Iron rowe ther on the north syde
Item Page stathe Lane ther and wharff
Item Pillory Lane ab antiquo called hobhouse lane
Item Puddinge Lane and wharff
Item Comon stathe yarde and wharff
Item Comen stathe lane and wharff
Item Jewes Lane
Item Cooke Rowe strete
Item Gressmarkett strete
Item Mersserrowe strete

Item Purflete strete
Item Cheker Strete
Item thymble Lane and wharff
Item Lyttle Lane by north wm bedous howse by purflete bridge
Item Purflete wharffe
Item Kyngs stathe yards and wharffs
Item Lyttle Cheker
Item wyndgate strete
Item A lane behynd Little cheker ledynge to purflete
Item A lane and with a wharff leadinge owt of wyndgate
Item A Lane ther called Colledge Lane
Item Bridgegate strete
Item Sedgeforthe Lane
Item A Lyttle Lane ther a callid sheepis Lane Agaynst A comen privie
Item A Lane ther called . . .
Item A Lyttle Lane with A wharff therto the flete over agaynst the same
Item Madd Lane ther is a madd howsse somtyme more lane
Item Saterday markett strete
Item Bull stake
Item Lathe Strete
Item Leadinge Hall Lane
Item St. Margarets Muckhill Lane
Item Stonegate strete
Item Pryorye Lane
Item the strete ledinge from stongate by ladie Bridge to the mills
Item Skynner Rowe strete
Item Codlynge Lane ther ledinge to Bevers Bridge
Item Basingley Baxstarrowe strete
Item ffuller Rowe strete
Item A Lyttle Lane and wharff ther ledinge to the fleete
Item the strete from blakfryers Clowe to the Almeshowse
Item St James End Strete conteyneth many old fletes and Lanes decayed whose names not knowen
Item Coulde Hurne Strete
Item A strete or lane from the sowthend of Ladie Brige from cold hurne Leadinge to the corne watter mylls
Item the croked Lane Leadinge from could hurne to the churche of All Saints
Item the Lane leadinge from the myll flete to the churche of All Sayncts
Item the strete wherein the vicarage howse of Sowth Lynn is Scituate beinge in Kings Lynne

The stone Sluses Clowes and fflape dores in Kings Lynne and Sowth Lenne at the Towne charge

ffyrst at Kettle mylls A sluss and Clowe
Item ther Another Slusse and two Clowe dores
Item ther Another Clowe dore
Item ther on the west syd of the howse A fflapedore
Item into dowshill fleete A flape dore for defenc of salt water
Item at Lyttle porte bridge A fflape dore
Item Barkars sluse clowe and flape dore in barkars flete
Item Blakfriers bridge A Clowe and flape dore
Item at the flete by thalmeshowse A Clowe
Item by the mownt bank A slwse and Clowe
Item without gannock A slwse and clowe beinge the lowest drawe of all
Item A slwse clowe and ii flapp dores by the south gate and damm
Item thre fflapp dores under sowth gate Bridge
Item purpoynts fflappe dore in sowth Lynne for defenc of Salt Water for ould Peweneye
Item A clowe at the Almeshowse fflete
Item A Clowe dore in madd Lane fflete

Comen previes in Kings Lenne

ffyrst one At Pagis stathe
Item one in Comen stath yard
Item one in Comen stathe Lane
Item one in Purflet strete leadede
Item one in Lyttle cheker
Item one by Bull Stak callyd ledinge hall
Item one upon Ladie Bridge
Item one in Sedgeforthe Lane
Item one at Baxster bridge

Voltes in stretis

ffyrst one in Cheker strete
Item one of either syd of stone bridge to the grates ther
Item one in Baxstarrowe
Item one in Skynner rowe
Item one in Webstarrowe
Item one in wyndgate
Item one madd Lane
Item in pagis stare Lane one

Stone Bridges in Kings Lenne and Sowth Lynne at the charge of maior and Burgesses

ffyrst dowshill Bridge
Item Kettle mylls Bridge
Item est gate Bridge
Item Lyttle Porte bridge
Item hopmans way Bridge
Item barkars clow Bridge
Item St. Johns Bridge
Item blakfryers Bridge
Item th almeshowse Bridge
Item baxterrow Bridge
Item Baxstar Bridge
Item webstarow Bridge
Item stone Bridge
Item Purflete Bridge
Item gannok Bridge without
Item gannok Bridge within
Item bevers Bridge
Item Ladie Bridge
Item whyt ffryers Bridge
Item all Sayncts Bridge
Item Sowth gate Bridge
Item Poorpoynts bridge by old peweneye
Item Tymber bridge over myddleton eye
Item Stone bridge upon hardwick cawsey

Cundittis ther

ffyrst St margarets Cundytt
Item the new Cundytt
Item Cheker Cundytt
Item Twesday markett Cundytt
Item harwoodes Cundytt
Item St Jhons Cundytt
Item Lyttleport Cundytt

Ffletis in and about Kings Lenne

ffyrst Dowshill flete Leadinge to Lyttleporte bridge in which fflete the ffreshe water dyssendethe from gaywoode throughe the Towne
Item one flete assendinge out of the same flete Lyinge on the bakesyd of Dowshill strete into hopmans waye

Item one other so to damgate flete and the Awgusten ffryers

Item one flete Leadinge under the towne walls to Lyttleport bridge called Barkers fflete

Item one flete ther lyinge betwene St Johns and blakffryers

Item one fflete Lyinge on the baksyd of gressemarkett webstarrowe and mercer rowe (and ther is a pece of Comon ground) to lye all the ffythe upon when the said fflete is clensyd the water dissends to purflete flete

Item one dry fflete is Pavyd parte lyinge betwen Cheker and mercer rowe and Purflete stretis the water therin dessendethe thorowgh Cheker in a voilte to the haven

Item Purflete flete Assendethe unto the Comen dyke thorowghe with the ffreshe water dyssendethe thorowgh the Towne in the myddis therof out from the said Comen Dyke into the haven

Item A flete (betwene purflete bridge and stone bridge) Leadinge Sowthe goyinge under wyndgate strete upto the bakesyde of the Trynytie Hall and Prison howse ther lyinge betwen Bridgegate strete and wyndgate strete (And a pece of the Comen grond) Lyinge at the northend of the said fflete to Lye uppon all suche fylthe as comethe when the fflete is Clensyd

Item a flete Leadinge from Baxstarbridge up to madd Lane so under Skinner Rowe strete and so up to stone gate strete clensynge Bridgegate Baxstarrowe Skynner rowe and stongate

Item A flete Leadinge from blakffryers Clowe bridge up to The Almeshowse and from thence westward to Baxstarrowe strete (to clense ffuller Rowe St James End strete and Baxstarrowe

Item The myll fflete (ebbynge andfflowinge) thoroughe the Towne from geywood and myntlyne by charture

Item A flete on the northe syd of whyte ffryers goynge thorowghe the Towne flowinge from Kings Lene to the haven

Item the whyte ffryers fflete dyssendinge from Setchey and Middleton on the sowthe syd of the towne wherein the ffreshe water dyssendethe to the haven in which ffleete it dothe bothe ebb and fflowe

Item myddletone fflete discendinge from myddletone unto Sowthe gates, and so thorowe into whygt friers flete and so to the haven of Lenne but most tymes tornyd to the Corne water mylls to serve the same as of Antiquitie

Item A fflete Comynge from Peweneye thorowe ould Peweneye by A stone bridge under hardwick causey Leadinge to Purpoynts goole in sowthe Lenne and so to the Myddleton flete dissendinge to Sowthe gatis and to the mylls.

Comen wharfes for Landynge of wares from the water

ffyrst at Lyttleport Bridge in damgate

Item one on the est and another on the west of dowshill bridge

Item one at St Annes yarde

Item one in the Lane on the west agaynst St nicholas Churche
Item one at Pagis stathe Lanes Ende
Item one at Puddinge Lanes ende callyd Puddinge Lane wharfe
Item A chese wharfe in Comen stathe
Item Comen stathe Lane wharffe
Item one at Thymble lane end in Cheker on the west syd ther
Item all Purflete wharfe
Item one wharfe and Two stares in Kyngs stathe
Item one at the Lane end and one the sowth syde of Kings stathe
Item one at College Lane
Item one at St Margarets muckhill
Item one at marys flete Lanes end in Lathe strete
Item one at the whyt fryers bridge
Item one at Sokon brydge on the same flete on the sowth syd of all seynts chuch
Item one at the Lanes end agaynst thomas blesbys howse next the same fryers
Item one at the Lanes end between henry fyshers ground and the land of Frances Knape in Sowth Lynne
Item one at the Lanes end ther betwen the said henry fysher howse on the west and the tenement of John glover on the est apon the said friers flete
Item one by the new dame ther now decayed
Item one at Bevers Bridge End
Item one on the north syd of ffuller Rowe
Item one on the north syd and one on the sowthe syde of Baxstarbridge
Item one the north syd of Segeforthe Lane to the flete agaynst a lytle Lane ther
Item one on the sowth syd on in fyncham strete Right agaynst next a tenement ther of Mr Robert Hullior on the est syd
Item one ther callyd fletchers wharffe
Item one at purflet stret end on the est syd of Purflett Bridge
Item one in Lyttle Cheker next the Privye ther

Appendix II

Robert Stonar's Inventory, 1613

(Norfolk and Norwich Record Office,
Norwich Consistory Court Inventories INV/26/122)

An inventorye taken the 18th daye of June 1613 of the goods and howshold stuffe of Robert Stonars latlye deseased in Kyngs Lynn by John Atkyn Robert Taylor Tomas Jags John Cony Robert Barnerd the younger a cooper: Robert Clark and others viz

Item in the parlour next the shoppe

a table and 6 Framed stoles		xx^{s}	
a lyvery cobberd a glase case a Frame to hange upp a towell		vii^{s}	
Item 2 lytell old coffers prayssed			xii^{d}
Item A cradle a bed settle and an old square table wyth Frame		vi^{s}	viii^{d}
Item an old chest and fyve old chayers		ii^{s}	vi^{d}
Item xxiiii peces of pewter lytell and great being in them xxii lb wayt at vi^{d} a pound		xi^{s}	
Item twoo lytell cushens and sixe other greater prayssed at		ix^{s}	
Item a payer of bellows and an old warmynge pan prayssed		ii^{s}	vi^{d}
Item an yron cradle a payer of gallows of iron 2 drawinge hooks twoe fyer pans a payer of tongs a tosting Iron a gred Iron and a payer pothoakes beinge 3 stonne wayt or therebye		vii^{s}	
Item a lytell hamper and 3 old boxes			xii^{d}
Item his apparell prayssed		xxvi^{s}	viii^{d}
Item a trondell bedsted a lytel fether-bed twooe bowlsters 2 pyllowes an old coverlett and 2 old blanketts prayssed at		x^{s}	
Item seaven payer of sheets 3 pyllowe bers and fower table napkyns praysed at		xx^{s}	
Item twooe shirts a paynted tablecloth sixe hand towells and an old table cloth		vi^{s}	
Item a dossin trenchers and other old tryfells in this Rowme prayssed at			xii^{d}
Some of thes things	vi^{li}	xi^{s}	iiii^{d}

Item in the Buttrye

Item three Cettls toe skellets and an yron pot		viii^{s}	
Item a Friange pan an yron slyce an old skouer			iiii^{d}

Item in that rome more 8 old dishes and platers of wood and other things			xii^{d}
Some is		ix^{s}	iiii^{d}

Item in the chamber over the parlor

Item a great old chest and a smaler chests		viii^{s}	
Item a lyvery bedsted and a thisteledowne bed an old coveringe		vi^{s}	
Item an old coverlett and an old carpeet		v^{s}	
Item a bowltinge hutch and a broken ansele and an old box and other tryfles			xii^{d}
Some of thes		xx^{s}	

In the chamber over the shoppe viz

Item an old trendle bedsted one sheet and a hapharlot and an old matres prayssed at		ii^{s}	vi^{d}
Item 3 C pyne hoops prayssed at		x^{s}	
Item in whyt hoops and other skatred hoops pryssed at		x^{s}	
Item butter firkins staves and heads fyve last pryssed at 13s. 4d. the last	iii^{li}	vi^{s}	viii^{d}
Item a bushell Ryme and other tryfells		ii^{s}	
Some is	iiii^{li}	xi^{s}	ii^{d}

Item in the shoppe viz

Item an old brase pot a morter wyth a pestell		iiii^{s}	vi^{d}
Item twooe newe soes a mylk tubbe and a churne 2 byts 9 newe ffirkins		viii^{s}	
Item a halfe bushell 9 paylls and loose hoops about the shoppe in all		iiii^{s}	viii^{d}
Item 3 axes 3 persers 4 shaves three crowses fower adses 3 howells and other tools in the shoppe and other tryffels		xii^{s}	
Some is		xxix^{s}	ii^{d}

Item in the yerd viz

Item xx clapbords at 4d apece		vi^{s}	viii^{d}
Item in kylderkyns staves and heads 3 last is at 12s.		xxxvi^{s}	
Item a grynestone and a trevett a C tubb staves and other tryfles in the yerd valowed at		vi^{s}	viii^{d}
Some is		xLix^{s}	iiii^{d}

Item in his warhowse viz

Item a di C pype hoops and 4 C hogshed hoops	xii^{s}	
Item tene hundreth and a half of barrell hoops	xxi^{s}	
Item sixe C½ of halfe barrell hoops	ix^{s}	
Item 8 C firkin hoops	v^{s}	iiii^{d}
Item one bere vessell hooped wyth 6 whyt hops and other loose hoops about the warhowse	iii^{s}	iiii^{d}
Some is of thes	L^{s}	viii^{d}

good detts

Item dewe ffrom John atkyn to hym at his death eyght pounds seaventene shyllyngs is saye	viii^{li}	xvii^{s}	
Item rychard Cudlyn of watton owe hym		xx^{s}	
Item mr Spence oweth hym a di last by		xiiii^{s}	
Item dewe ffrom Akers norroubou		iii^{s}	
Item dewe from nycolls of west wynch 2 paylls			xxviii^{d}
Item dewe from mr pygott for 6 fyrkins		iiii^{s}	
Some is	x^{li}	xix^{s}	vi^{d}
Some totallis is	xxx^{li}		vi^{d}

Thes Bothe wytnesses John Atkyn John Corny Thomas Jagge Robert Barnard the yunger robert Clark his mark

A prysement mad the fourth daye of September 1613 of such things as wer left out of the Inventorye of Robert Stonar, at the fyrst praysement, the prayssers then thinking thes goods did belonge to the wyfe: beinge her owen Cossen she maryed wyth stonar

Item A besteed wyth a tester and a fetherbed a bowlster a coverlett a blankett curtens and Curten rods of Irone prayssed at	iii^{li}	xii^{s}	
Item a cobberd and a presse under it prayssed at		xx^{s}	
Item a lyttell table of twooe leaves prayssed at		ii^{s}	
Item an eshinge Chayer prayssed at			xvi^{d}
Item a lyttell brasse pot prayssed at		iii^{s}	iiii^{d}
Item a latchpane prayssed at			xii^{d}
Item a payer of cobberns and a speet			xx^{d}
Item a wickker chayer prayesed at			xvi^{d}
Item 2 candlstiks of brasse			xxii^{d}
Item that the wydowe stonar had receyved in money beffore the fyrst Inventorye was made for detts	iii^{l}	ix^{s}	
Some is	viii^{li}	xiii^{s}	vi^{d}

John Atkyn John Cornay the ellder Thomas Jagge 3 martii 1613

Robert Ladiman's Inventory 1589

(Norfolk and Norwich Record Office,
Norwich Consistory Court Inventories INV/5/201)

An Inventory indented and made the 1 of march in Anno Domini 1589 of all and singular the goods chattells debts and implements of houshold of Robert Ladiman late of Kings Lynn Shipmaster deceased and prised by us George Nellson John Codling and Roger Scarbrough

Imprimis in the hall

A long table with a frame A forme and a benche		x^{s}	
iiii old charis and an old squartable		iii^{s}	
A liverye table		iiii^{s}	
A waynscot coberd and an old benche		vi^{s}	viii^{d}
A pare of fyre Irons a gallos a payre of tongs and vi old quotions		v^{s}	
vi newe quotions unmad upp		v^{s}	
		xxiii^{s}	viii^{d}

In the great parlor

A posted bedsted a fetherbed a pare of blankets a coverled a bolster two pilloes a payre of curtaynes and a vallance	iii^{li}	vi^{s}	viii^{d}
A trundle bedstead an old fetherbed ii bolsters and ii old dornex coverlets		xiii^{s}	iiii^{d}
A livery table and a payrof plaing tables		x^{s}	
A square table a vi stooles		xvi^{s}	
iii little grene stoles embroidered and v littell waynscot stools		iiii^{s}	
A chayre a bench a round coberd of waynscot and a little danske chest		xiii^{s}	iiii^{d}
A pare of galloes v hookes A fyre shovell a pare of tongs and a payre of fyre Irons		vi^{s}	viii^{d}
A pare of belloes			xii^{d}
	vi^{l}	xi^{s}	

In the little parlore

A livery bedstead ii old fether bedds ii bolsters iii pillos A pare of blanketts and an old coverlet		xx^{s}	
An old danks chest		ii^{s}	vi^{d}
		xxii^{s}	v^{d}

In the buttry

v pottle potts of pewter		vi^{s}	

iii quart potts		ii^{s}	vi^{d}
iiii pynt potts		ii^{s}	
xvii pewter platters		xxiiii^{s}	
xx pewter dishes		x^{s}	
ii little old basons			xii^{d}
xii trencher platts		iiii^{s}	
xii porengers and xiiii sawsers		vi^{s}	
ii pye plates			xvi^{d}
x latten candelsticks		viii^{s}	
ii mortars and A pestell		iii^{s}	iiii^{d}
A dosen of trenchers			iii^{d}
	3^{li}	8^{s}	5^{d}

In the Chamber

An old danske chest		iii^{s}	iiii^{d}
ii clokes an old satten doblet a payre of briches an old gowne and iiii sherts		xxvi^{s}	viii^{d}
A hatt lined with velvet		v^{s}	
An old trundle bed an old fetherbed and other old trashe		xiii^{s}	iiii^{d}
v table clothis plane		xvi^{s}	viii^{d}
ii old diaper table clothes		iii^{s}	iiii^{d}
v little course table clothes		v^{s}	
iii dosen of old napkins		viii^{s}	
vi handtowells			xviii^{d}
xii pillobears		vi^{s}	
viii pare of old shetts		xx^{s}	
	v^{li}	viii^{s}	x^{d}

In the fore parlore

A posted bedsted A pare of blanketts A bolster curtayns and fring		xxx^{s}	
An old square table and a forme		ii^{s}	viii^{d}
paynted clothes about the parlor		x^{s}	
	ii^{li}	ii^{s}	viii^{d}

In the kitching

An old square table and a pare of mustard querns		iiii^{s}	
ii pare of cobirons		iiii^{s}	
vi old brase potts and ii posnitts		xiii^{s}	iiii^{d}
ii chafens an old warming pann A scars and an old latten bason		v^{s}	
v old kettells		vi^{s}	viii^{d}
iiii spytts and A driping pann		vi^{s}	
A ston mortar and A bushall A cole mett and other trashe		iiii^{s}	

ii chamber potts			xii^{d}
ii pare of pott hooks			viii^{d}
iii spyning wheles		iii^{s}	iiii^{d}
	ix^{li}	xix^{s}	vi^{d}
Sum Total	xxii^{li}	xvi^{s}	i^{d}

Thomas Purdy's Inventory 1591
(Norfolk and Norwich Record Office
Norwich Consistory Court Inventories INV/8/188)

The Inventory Indented of all and singular the goods . . . and Chattells of Thomas Purdy late while he lived of Kings Lynn in the Countye of Norfolk deceased, Since valued and priced the xxixth daye of November in the year of our Lord God A thowsand fyve hondred nyntye and one And the yere of the reygne of our Sovereygne Lady Elizabeth by the grace of god of Inglond ffrance and Ireland Quene Defender of the fayth the xxxiiiith By Thomas Steele water bottman Thomas Gale Christopher Roper and others as followeth

The Parlor

Imprimis his Apparell	xx^{s}	
Item A posted bedsted coverlet fetherbed, with fethers blancketts shets and a pillow	xl^{s}	
Item a Cubbert	x^{s}	
Item three Candlestickes	ii^{s}	
Item Six peces of Pewter	viii^{s}	
Item A framed tabl and two long stoles	x^{s}	
Item a great Chest	iii^{s}	iiii^{d}
Item a Smal Coffer of chest	ii^{s}	vi^{d}
Item a form or stol		iiii^{d}

The Hall

Item A posted bedsted two fetherbeds a coverlett two boulsters and A pillow	xxvi^{s}	viii^{d}
Item a Trundle Bedsted A fetherbed boulster two coverlets and a Tromsone	xiii^{s}	iiii^{d}
Item a Smale Cubberd	iii^{s}	iiii^{d}
Item A chafendish		vi^{d}
Item three Pewter platters	ii^{s}	
Item three Pewter Potts and a . . .	ii^{s}	vi^{d}
Item a framed table and two long formes	vi^{s}	viii^{d}

Item two Smal chests		iiii^{s}	
Item A Wicker chayre		iii^{s}	iiii^{d}
Item fyer Irons		vi^{s}	viii^{d}
Item A Bacondebl			viii^{d}

In the Parlor Chamber

Item A Bedsted		vi^{s}	viii^{d}
Item A littl coffer			iiii^{d}
Item A Long Planke or Table			xx^{d}

The Hall Chamber

Item A coverlitt A Pike and A culver		xxiiii^{s}	iiii^{d}
Item three Tubbes and A churne			xii^{d}

The Kitchin

Item fyve Brasse potts		xxx^{s}	
Item fower Latten Basons		vi^{s}	viii^{d}
Item two great panes		vi^{s}	viii^{d}
Item three Smal Kittles		v^{s}	
Item a possnet or littl pott of Brass			xii^{d}
Item A payer coblrons		iiii^{s}	
Item two Spits A fryen pan rost iron and dripen pane		v^{s}	iiii^{d}
Item A new tubb and two Trayes		ii^{s}	

Obligations

Item one obligation of the Summe of xl^{li} for the trewe payment of xx^{li} at michaelmas next	xx^{li}		
Item one other of xl^{li} for the payment of xii^{li} in and uppon the seyd day	xxii^{li}		
Item one of the Summe of fower pounds for the payment of x^{l} vi^{s} viii^{d} in and uppon the first daye of may next		xliii^{s}	
Item one other of the Sum of six pounds for the triwe payment of iii^{li} vi^{s} viii^{d} in and uppon the seyd first of May	iii^{li}	vi^{s}	viii^{d}
Sum total	lx^{li}	xii^{s}	x^{d}

Inventory of Thomas Revett, Town Clerk, d.1633

(Norfolk and Norwich Record Office, Norwich Consistory Court Inventories INV/39/75)

	£	s.	d.
In the Shop and Study below			
Desks parchment paper and other implements	4	6	8
In the Hall			
1 long table and other household stuff	6	1	1
In the Parlour			
1 bedstead and other implements	18	10	0
In the Kitchen and Yards			
Brass pewter and other necessaries	16	19	10
In the Parlour Chamber			
Posted bedstead and other implements	8	10	0
In the Gallery			
Lynnen of all sorts and other household stuff and implements	68	4	6
In the Shop Chamber			
Posted bedstead and household stuff	8	4	4
In Hall Chamber			
Field bedstead and other implements	7	8	6
In Kitchen Chamber			
Wainscott bedstead and other necessary implements	4	5	0
Chamber called Mother Palmers Chamber			
A long draw Table of walnut tree and other implements	2	0	0
In the Study above			
A spanish nest of boxes books and other implements	9	13	4

	£	s.	d.
In good debts by bond	315	0	0
In ready money	40	15	0
In silver plate and gilt plate	38	13	8
In apparell	20	0	0

Total £358 3s. 10d.

Inventory of Valentine Thacker 1668
(Norfolk and Norwich Record Office,
Norwich Consistory Court Inventories INV/53/53)

A true and perfect Inventory of all and Singular the goods chattells and personall estate of Valentine Thacker of Kings Lynn: in the County of Norfolk Buttcher deceased taken and Apprised by us whose names are hereunder written, the fifte daye of January in the twentie yeare of the Raigne of oure soveraigne Lord Kinge Charles the second over England 1668:

	£	s.	d.
Imprimis his apparrell and Money in his purse	6	13	4
In the Hall			
Item one ffirecreadle a paire of cobirons two spetts A jack, ffirepane and tongs and other Irons ther	2	10	0
more ffor one pewter case with drawers ffull ffurnish with pewter	5	10	0
more one stone case ffurnish one towellcase ffurnish and other Earthingware, one lookeing glasse one hie Table sixe stooles sixe leather chayres sixe other chayres one dussen of cushins one carpett and a brasse candlestick	4	8	4
More one hie bedstead ffurnished A trundle bed; warming pann and other things ther	10	0	0
In the Kitchinge			
Item one ffirecreadle one brasse pote two irone pots three kettles one cubert one table, stooles chayres A muskett ffurnished, pewter, and other things ther	4	10	0

In the Parler chamber

	£	s.	d.
Item one hie Bedsteade ffull ffurnished a chist of drawers two tables two carpetts tenn chayres one ffirecreadle with a paire of brasse Andirons and other ffurniter, one glasse case ffurnished: one looking glasse and other things ther	20	13	4

In the shope chamber

	£	s.	d.
Item one ffirecreadle with one Irone one hie bed ffurnished one liverry cubert a carpett two cheists two boxes sixe chayres one lookeinge glasse and other things ther	12	0	0
Item in plate	6	0	0
Item in Lynnen	7	16	0
Item in good debts	10	0	0
Item in a out Rome two bedsteads ffurnished	3	0	0
In the slaughter house two beames, scooles, waits and other things ther	1	10	0
Item in the yeard one sowe two shotts more ffor a stable and other things ther	2	10	0

In the ffields

	£	s.	d.
Item ffor the one halfe part of sixtie fowre Neat Beasts	145	5	0
Item ffor the one halfe part of thirtie eight weathers, Ewes and shep hoggs	9	19	6
Item ffor the one halfe part of the haye, posts, deales, and bings	34	10	0
Item one horse and a Mare	9	0	0
Item other things not fformerly Remembred		6	8
Item more the one, thirtie two part of a Shipp	10	0	0

The sume Totall is £308 5s. 6d.

Thomas Beney
John Goddard

John Butler's Inventory, 1708

(Norfolk and Norwich Record Office,
Norwich Consistory Court Inventories INV/70/5)

An Inventory of all and Singular the Goods and Chattells and Household Stuffe of John Butler late of Kings Lynn in the County of Norfolk Woollen Draper deceased taken and apprised by us whose names ar herunto Subscribed the Seventh day of March Anno Domini 1708 as ffolloweth

In the Kitchen:-

7 stone of old puter at 7s per stone	02	09	00
4 Stone 7li of New puter	01	11	06
3Stone 7li of brass	01	04	06
1 Stone 11 li of pott brass at 4d. per li	00	04	02
9 pound of dyitt pott brass	00	08	00
2 old brass warming panes at	00	02	06
5 Stone 7li of old iron potts	00	06	00
1 old brass Sauce pann	00	00	09
1 old Cloth press at	00	10	00
1 fire Grate with other irons	00	12	00
1 iron jacke at	00	03	00
Schooles and Waites at	00	14	00
1 brass fryen pann at	00	01	06
table and dresser bords 1 old Cubbord	00	10	00
4 doson of Glass bottells and other lumber	00	12	00

Woolle in the Kitchen

64 lood from the Grower at 5s. per lood	16	00	00
16 lood of drest woolle at 6s per lood	04	16	00

In the Parler

18 Cheskwered Shirts at	01	16	00
4 paire of Cheskwerd drawers at	00	06	00
55 Yellow westcoates at 9d per peece	02	01	03
6 duson paire of Lether pockitts	00	15	00
1 boyes Suit at	00	05	00
7 Lades coates at 5s per peece	01	15	00
2 Menes and 3 Lades westcoates	00	15	00
12 Lades vests at	01	04	00
7 menes vests at	01	01	00
6 paire of britches	00	08	00
3 Menes dubll bristed Coates	01	01	00

5 Lades Coates at	01	01	00
2 lined Westcoates unmade	00	10	00
3 Menes great Coates and 3 Lades vests	01	10	00
2 Menes Cotes 1 Lades vest	00	10	00
4 Menes Cotes 3 Lades vests	06	04	00
3 dubll bristed Cotes at	00	18	00
2 Menes westcotes at	00	03	00
11 paire of Menes britches	01	13	00
4 Lades westcotes	00	12	00
4 Chelldren frocks	00	02	00
5 paire of Menes britches	00	10	00
1 boyes Suitt	00	05	00
1 womans pettecote	00	01	00
1 parcell of buttens in twoe baggs	01	10	00
9 bonnets	00	03	00
10 beuerett hates	05	00	00
21 Carsters	03	03	00
25 Carsters at 2s 6d per peece	03	02	06
275 Course hatts	13	15	00
35 Carrilana hattes at 2s 6d per peece	03	17	00
60 decayed wite hates	01	10	00
1 fire Grate and Shelves and 2 tables and one Looken Glass	00	15	00
1 paire of lether britches 8 skines	00	06	00
8 pee Jacketts	01	00	00
3 stufe Gownes	00	10	00
2 paire of boyes britches	00	02	00
1 riden Gowne 2 riden hoods	00	07	00
1 Seare Gowne at	00	02	00
Six ends of West Cuntrey Cloth at 29¾ yds at Eight Shillings per yard	11	18	00
Seventen Ends of Yorkesheire broad Cloth 154½ yds in all at 2s per yard	15	09	00
4½ yds of West Cuntrey Keirsey at 4s	00	18	00
five ends of Yorkesheire Mist Keirsey 43 yds ¾ in all at 2s 6d a yard	05	08	1½
Six ends of halfe thicke Keirsey 46 yds in all at 12d a yard	02	06	00
Eight ends of Penistone 44 yds in all at 9d per yard	01	13	00
Three ends of Cotton 8 yds in all at 6d a yard	00	04	00
7 yards of stript larting at 8d per yard	00	04	06
3 yards of fearenothing at 1s per yd	00	03	06

In the Seller

for Lumber	01	00	00

In the Kitchen Chamber

A Bed as it Stands	01	10	00
a Chist a Couch and a table	00	07	06
128 Bed Cords at	03	04	00
a fire Great at	00	01	06
for Lumber	00	05	00

Woole in the Garrett over the Kitchen Chamber

one packe of Course and Cullered Niles	01	10	00
4½ packes and 3 stone of Gray woole	04	13	06
3 packes and 3 stone fine bay woole	07	16	00
1 packe 3 quarters 1 stone fine wite Niles	04	11	06
3 packes 3 stone fine Cloathing woole	06	01	00
4 packes 1 quarter of Greasey Niles	04	05	00
1 packs of toppings	00	10	00

In the Greate Chamber over the Shopp

2 Stone of all sorts of Silk at 8s per pound	11	04	00
1 Stone 7 li of all sortes of threeds at	01	01	00
12 li of Mowhaire	03	00	00
a parcell of ribbenes in a trunke	02	00	00
a parcell of Silk Gowloones	01	10	00
3 Groose of Checke Gowlones	01	10	00
a parcell of Gunse Lase and a parcell of old wosted Lace	01	00	00
a parcell of Loamb worke Laces in paperes	01	00	00
a parcell of ferritts	01	00	00
17 ounces of Old Silver Laces	02	00	00
a remnant of old Statued Gowloones and wosted	00	07	00
Some Remnants of Silk	02	00	00
a box with old Colleres and peces of Stayes	00	02	06
a parcell of buttenes in a rapper	00	15	00
6 Small Oyle skines	00	02	00
a Neast of draweres	00	10	00
a Table and Chist and other Lumber	00	15	00

In the Parler Chamber

One Bed as it stands	02	10	00
6 Chaires 2 Stooles	00	15	00
one Cloase press at	00	07	00
4 old Chists at	00	06	00

In the Closett in the Parlour Chamber

A parcell of Old severall sorts of Apparrell	10	00	00

In the Garrett over the Parler Chamber

for lumber	00	02	06

In the Maids Chamber

a Bed. as it Stands	01	10	00
a Chist and boxis and other Lumber	00	10	00

In the Chamber Next to it

a Chist and boxis	00	06	00

In the Staire Case

one Bedstead and other Lumber	00	15	00

In the Shopp

(List of clothing and cloth similar to that listed under 'Parler' not transcribed).

In Clease and Money in his pockitt	03	10	00
In Money that came from Yarmouth	22	00	00
Plate and ringes	10	00	00
for Lumber in severall placeses	01	10	00
In good and bad debts due to the deceased	35	00	00

Summe total £905 01s. 04½d.

Robt Sparrow,
Stephen Baylor

Schedule Attached to a Lease in Possession of Messrs Bush, Solicitors, Kings Lynn

A Schedule indented conteyninge all those Brewynge vessells and ymplements for brewynge howsehold stuff and ymplements for howsehold menconed in a certeyne Indenture of Lease hereunto annexed, made betwene Richard Davy and Elizabeth his wief on thone part, and John Lucas on thother part as hereafter followeth videlicet

Imprimis In the Hall, One Bench And in the Clossett adioyninge a Table lyned with greene bayes and a Bench with a d . . .

Item In the gardeyn howse (beynge seeled) a Bench and a shelf to rise and fall

Item in the Seller Twoo Bere sooles; and shelves round: In the Little Seller Twoo shelves and a meat block

Item in the kitchyn One Jackrise One pewter case with ffowers drawers locks and keys: One white dresser under the wyndowe, and a shelf underitt and a Rack to lay Speets on: with one large fire Cradle a gallowbalk and twoo Cheeks

Item in the pantree ffowere dressers Three shelves whereof one a hanginge one

Item in the back kitchyn one dresser under the wyndowe: One Copper hunged with the ffier Irons

Item in the upper Roofe of the Capitall Mesuage Eleven poles, with a Table,

Item in the best Chamber Closset one dresser with ffyve Shelves and twoo Curtyn Rodds

Item The Hall Chamber Clossett. Seeled all ovirrownd about, with particions for writinge and allso Twoo Benches and ffyve shelves;

Item in the Meale Chamber One Large boultinge hutch with three particions

Item in the Brewhouwse One Copper, Twoo Large ffats. One underbeck A doble Cooler and One Dandy:

Item in the Malthowse, Shutt wyndowes to every Light with Sufficient Locks and Keyes: One to the dores And to the Chambers belonginge to the said Malthowse every of them shutt wyndowes with like locks and keyes: One Corne skreene Twoo Shelves One Large Iron peele a rake and twoo Iron purrs

Item To every dore belonginge to the Capitall Mesuage with in the Indenture hereunto annexed to be demised that is necessarie or needfull a Lock and Key

Item in the Yard. One good and Sufficient Pumpe with a Lead att the foote thereof

Item in the Gardyne Thirtene flower potts

Item in the Crane Chamber One hoystinge Crane and twoo Crane ropes one Iron hooke twoo slings

Appendix III

A Building Account of 1612
(Kings Lynn Muniments, DB27)

ffor buildinge the newhowse late in
thoccupacon of Barnard and Toppitowe
in the markett stead

Paid to Mr. Lease and Samnell Eastwood for a bargayne of stones att the Augustine friers	iii^{li}	iii^{s}	iiii^{d}
paid to make a way to fetch out the same and to lode them			xviii^{d}
paid for two keeles and about 3 quarters of a keel of Cambridge Clay	v^{li}	xvii^{s}	vi^{d}
paid to Mr. Woleman for two hundred and a quarter seasoned deales att v^{li} per hundred	xi^{li}	v^{s}	
paid for carriage of part of the said deales		ii^{s}	vi^{d}
paid to Tho. Clarke for 13 loads of Stone from the blakfriers		xix^{s}	vi^{d}
paid to Batholomew Wormell for furren stuff		xxxvii^{s}	vi^{d}
paid to Brian Lupton for a chest of glasse		xxx^{s}	
paid more to John Lease for 3 Loads of Ragge and one load of half bricks		vii^{s}	
paid to widowe Spooner for bricks		xi^{s}	xi^{d}
paid to her sonne in Lawe for bricks		xxxiiii^{s}	
paid to Sallebanck for v thousand bricks		xlvii^{s}	vi^{d}
paid to hym for half a thowsand of Chamfrett bricks		v^{s}	
paid to Longe for vi thousand of bricks	iii^{li}	ix^{s}	
paid to the women for carryinge up the same		v^{s}	
paid for iii thousand and a half of tiles		xlii^{s}	
paid for takynge up the same into the Coleyard			xii^{d}
paid more to Sallebanck for iii thousand bricks		xxxvii^{s}	vi^{d}
paid for a thousand chamfrett bricks		v^{s}	vi^{d}
paid for carryinge the same up from the waterside		iiii^{s}	vii^{d}
paid to widow Spooner for A table stone			xvi^{d}
paid to Horsebroke Myett for 9 Loads of Stone		xii^{s}	
paid to widowe Spooner for coapinge stone		xv^{s}	
paid for 46 Rouf tiles		v^{s}	iii^{d}
paid more for xi Rouf tiles			xvii^{d}
paid for fetching of staginge poales			viii^{d}

paid for ii Callys Lynes to stage with	xx^{d}
paid more for xx roof tiles	ii^{s} vii^{d}
paid to Mr. Hoos man for a load of half bricks	ii^{s} viii^{d}
paid for viii hundred pavinge tiles	iii^{li} xvi^{s}
paid for a bushell of Smithie Combe	vi^{d}
paid for 34 chalder a half and one sack of Lyme	vii^{li} xix^{s} ii^{d}
paid for carriage up therof att 8d per chalder	xxiii^{s}
paid for carriage up of all the Cambridge Clay	xv^{s}
paid to Robert Symmes Edmond May Robert Daniby and Mr. Beckams men for carting of stones sand silt Clay and Colder	iiii^{li} xv^{s} viii^{d}
paid for lxiii bushells of Tanners hare	xxxi^{s} vi^{d}
paid for carriage up of some of the same hare	viii^{d}
paid to the woemen for carryinge Colder out of the howse	iii^{s}
paid to the Plomer for shootinge and layinge the gutters	xii^{s}
paid for a Bote of Marsh manner	v^{s} vi^{d}
paid for carrying up part of the same	iii^{s} vii^{d}
paid for carryinge up Tiles out of the Coleyard	xvi^{d}
paid for Lamblack	iiii^{d}
paid for Reed to Hellowe and Tiler	ix^{s} ii^{d}
paid for Size and Spanishe white	iii^{s} iii^{d}
paid to Willson the Paynter	xxxiii^{s} viii^{d}
Paid to Ollyver Blackett for xx^{li} of small anchers att iii^{d} quarter the pound	xvi^{s} ix^{d}
paid to hym for a boat and a wyndinge	ix^{d}
paid to Widow Stokes for 4 Casements	iii^{s} iiii^{d}
paid for v hundred of 8d Nayles	iii^{s}
paid more to Blackett for small anchers	ix^{s} viii^{d}
paid more to Blackett for vi anchers and two bolts wayinge v stone ix cwt and a half at iii^{d} per pound	xix^{s} x^{d}
paid to Giles Waren for v hundred of Bradds	vi^{s} iii^{d}
paid to William Grene for 17 lb of Spikes	iiii^{s} iii^{d}
paid more to hym for one Thowsand bradds	x^{s}
paid to Joathan Matthew for two Snacks	xii^{d}
paid to Robert Kercher Junior for Nayles as per his bill	xxxiii^{s} ix^{d}
paid more to Blackett as appears by his bill	iii^{li} x^{s} ix^{d}
paid for 3 pricketts of Iron for the gable ends	iii^{s}
paid more to Blackett for one hundred bradds	xiii^{d}
paid for two hundred dishedd Nayles	vii^{s}
paid to a Cuntry Smith for v hundred of vi^{d} Nayles	
Paid to John Dawson Sam Estwood and their Laborers at severall tymes for all their wags	xvii^{li} v^{s} xiii^{d}

paid to William Grene John Park and Robert Wright and their Laborers att several tymes for all their wags	xxxv^{li}	ii^{s}	viii^{d}
paid to the Glasier for his wage		xlix^{s}	ii^{d}
paid for a brush for the Glasier			iii^{d}
paid for a pownd and a half of redd Lead			vii^{d}
paid for oyle for hym		ii^{s}	viii^{d}
paid for x lb of Soader		vi^{s}	x^{d}
paid for fetchinge the chest of glasse			iiii^{d}
paid to twoo Sawers for tenne dayes work		xxvi^{s}	viii^{d}
Paid to John Grebby for 31 foot and a half of firr		xv^{s}	ix^{d}
paid more to hym for 51 foot of furr		xxv^{s}	vi^{d}
Paid for Carpenters wags att severall tymes	xv^{li}	v^{s}	
paid for windowes and all other timber which was bought for the said Newe buyldinge	xvii^{li}	xvi^{s}	iii^{d}
paid for Tile pynnes		v^{s}	vi^{d}
paid for Shinks for the Masons and Carpenters		xlv^{s}	vi^{d}
paid for Candles for them to work by		iii^{s}	

Sum of the newe Building is £168 11s. 1d.

FIGURES IN THE APPENDIX

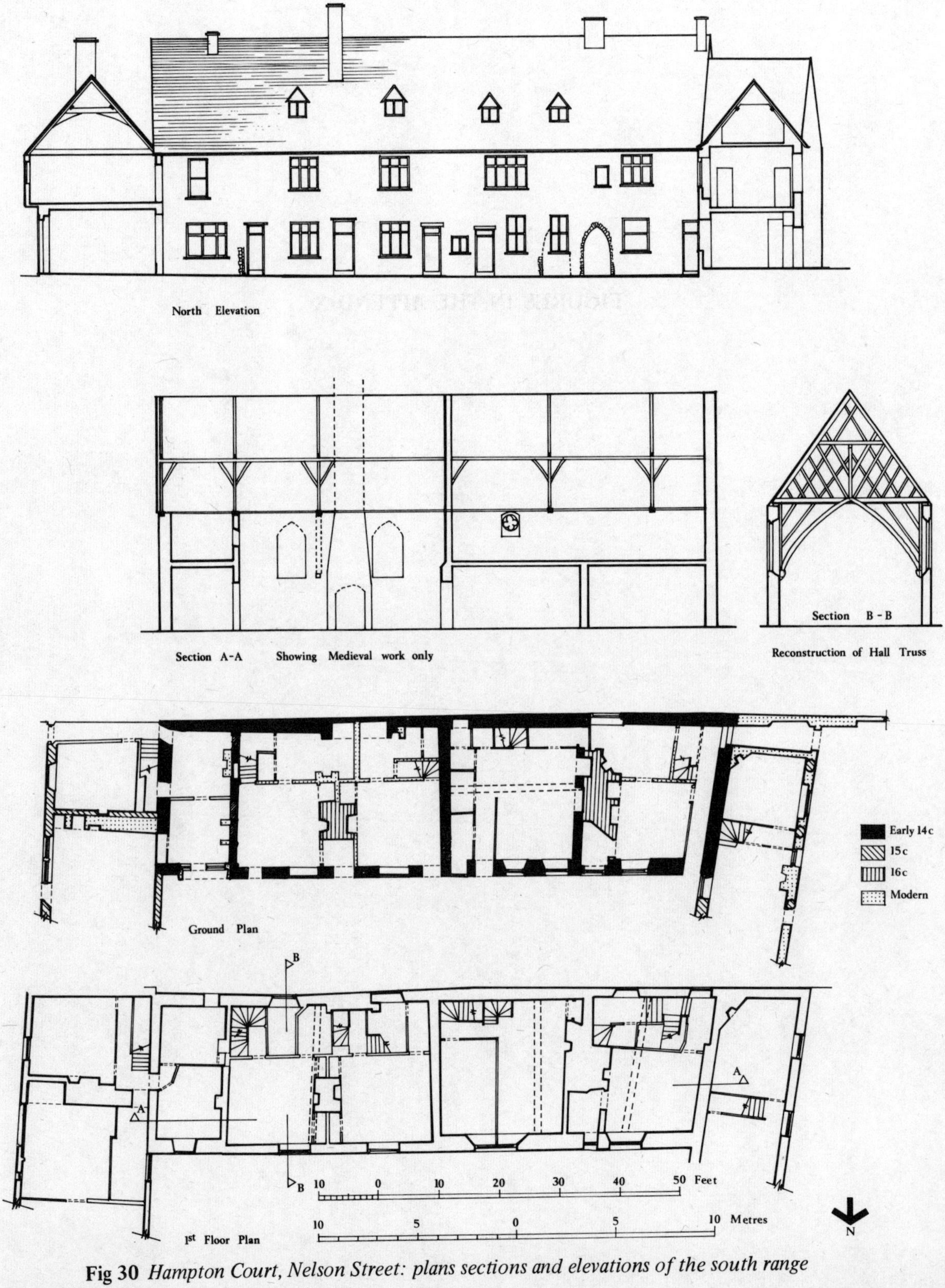

Fig 30 *Hampton Court, Nelson Street: plans sections and elevations of the south range*

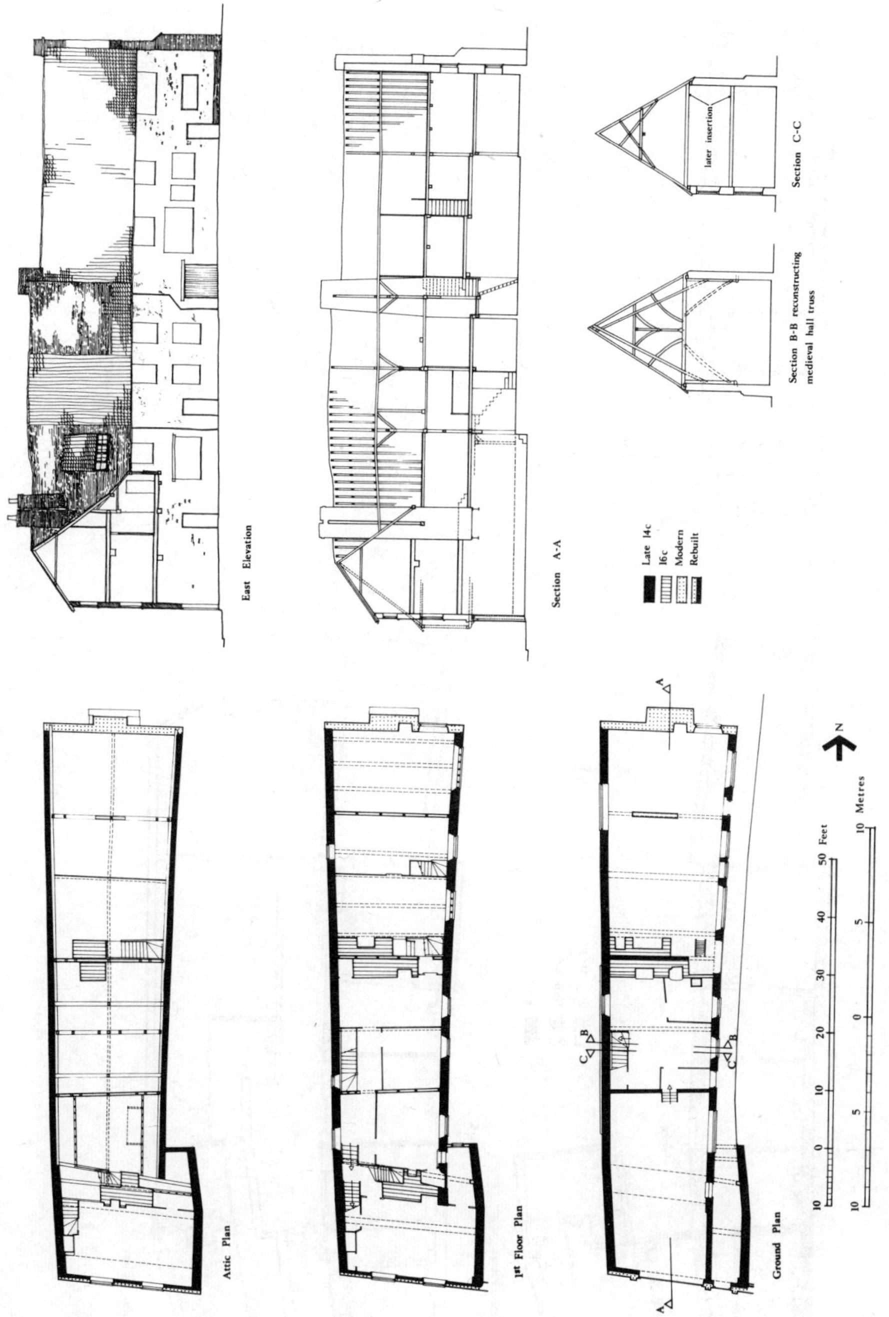

Fig 31 *No. 8 Purfleet Street: plans, sections and elevations*

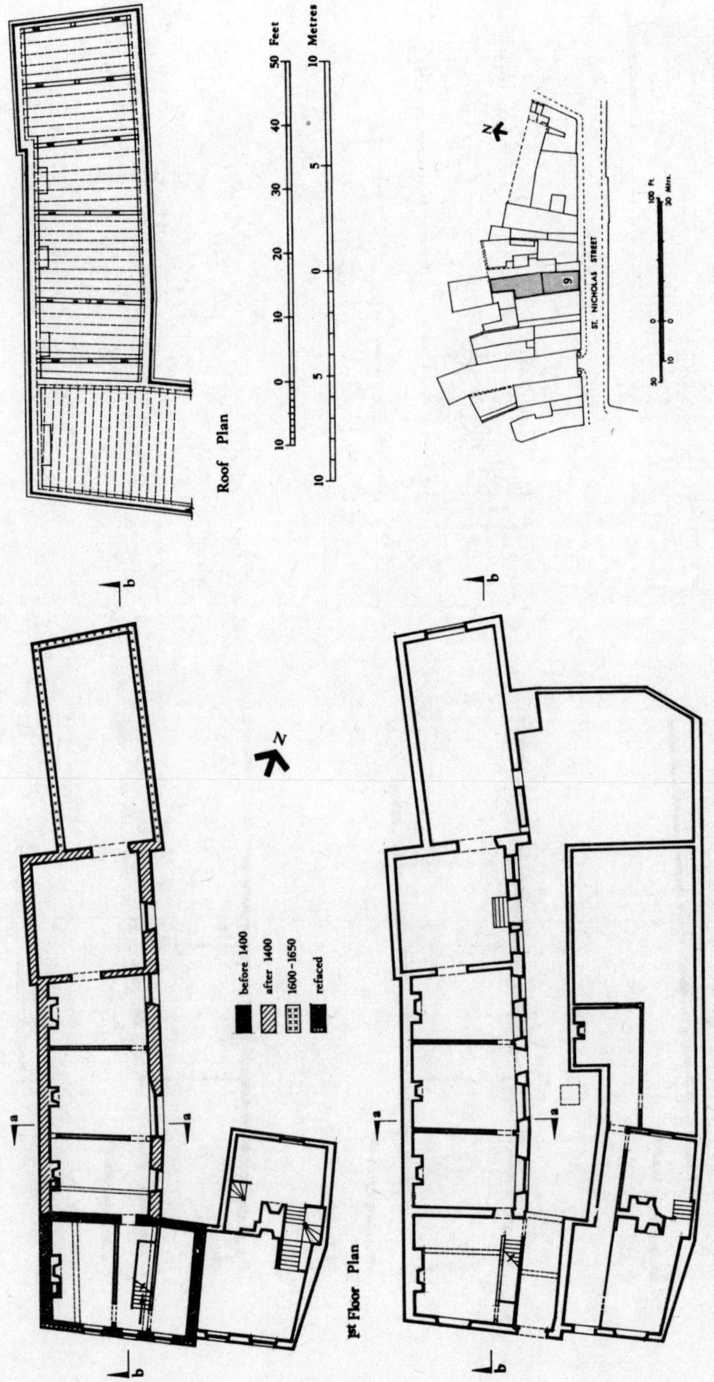

Fig 32 No. 9 Nicholas Street: plans

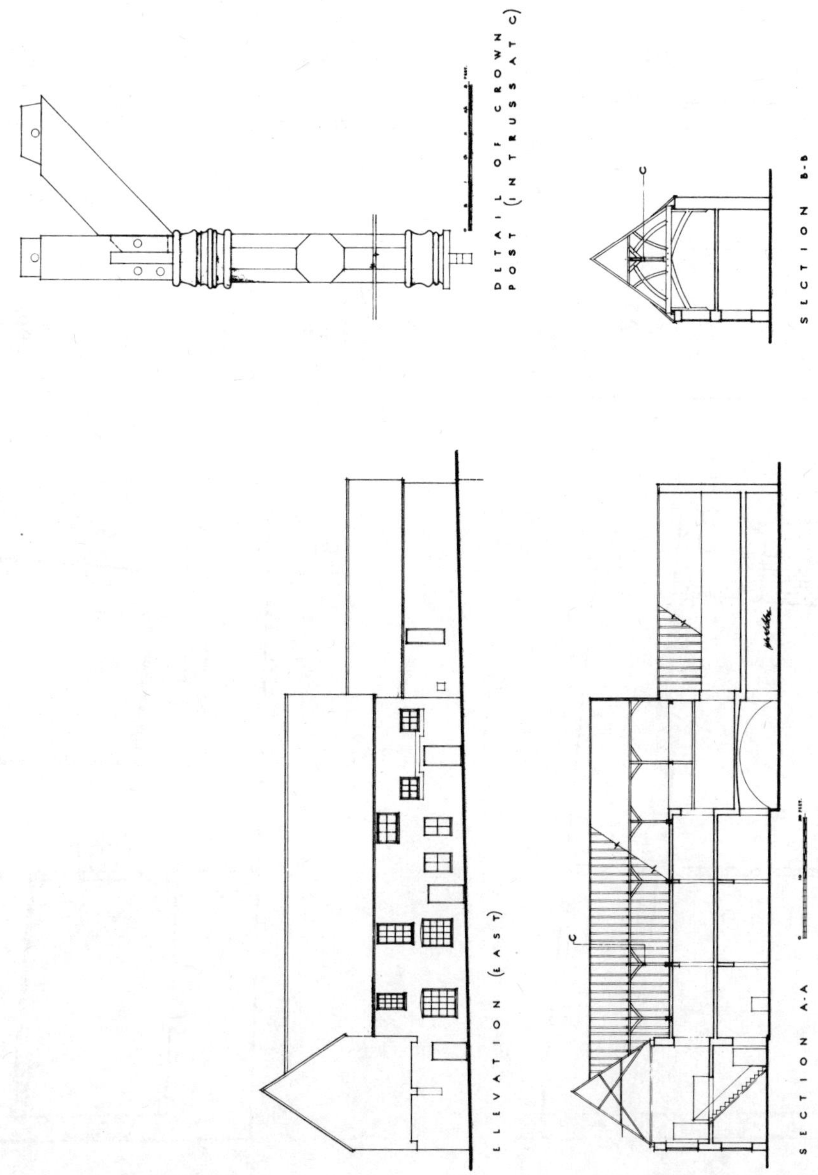

Fig 33 *No. 9 Nicholas Street: sections, elevation and details of hall roof truss*

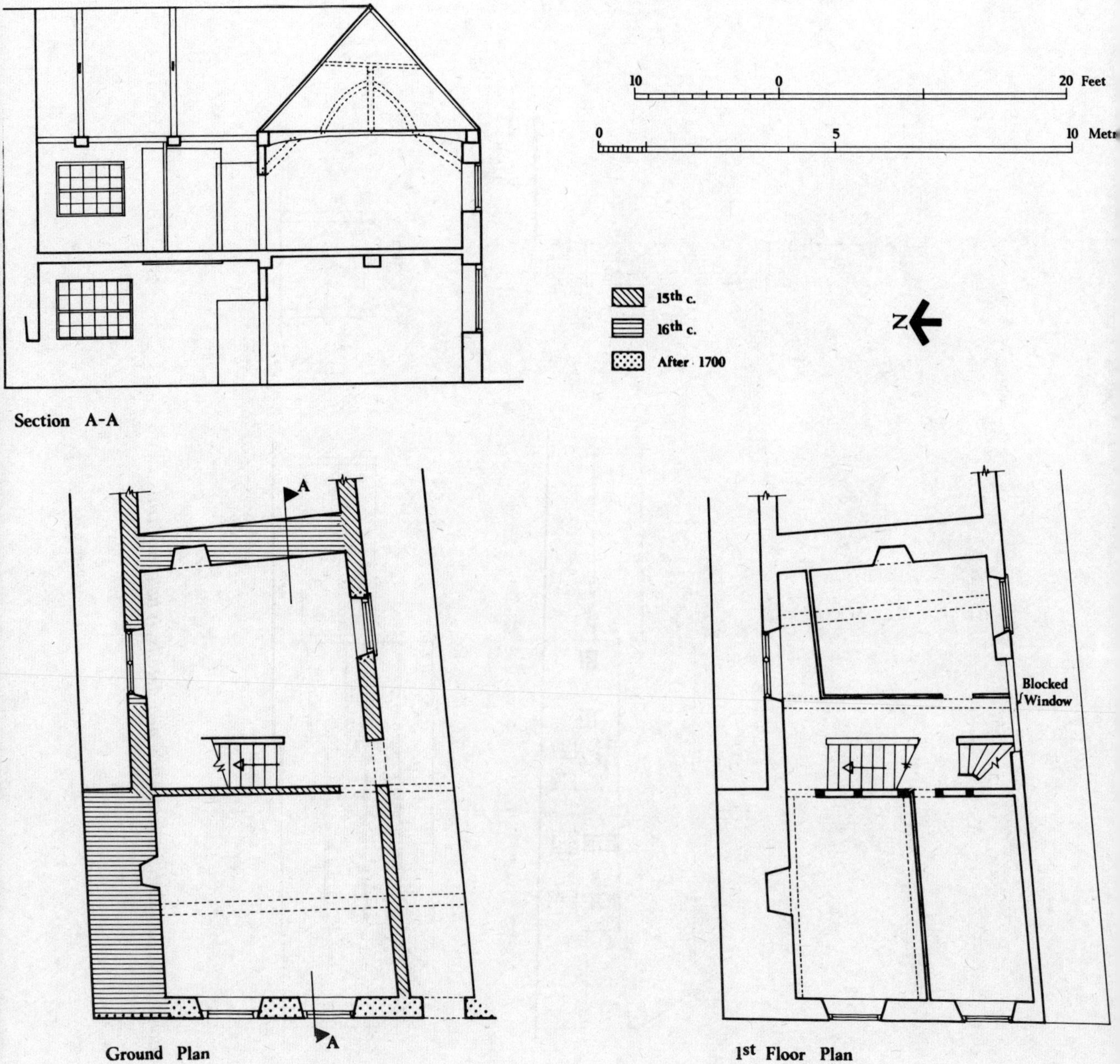

Fig 34 *No. 13 Friar Street: plans and section*

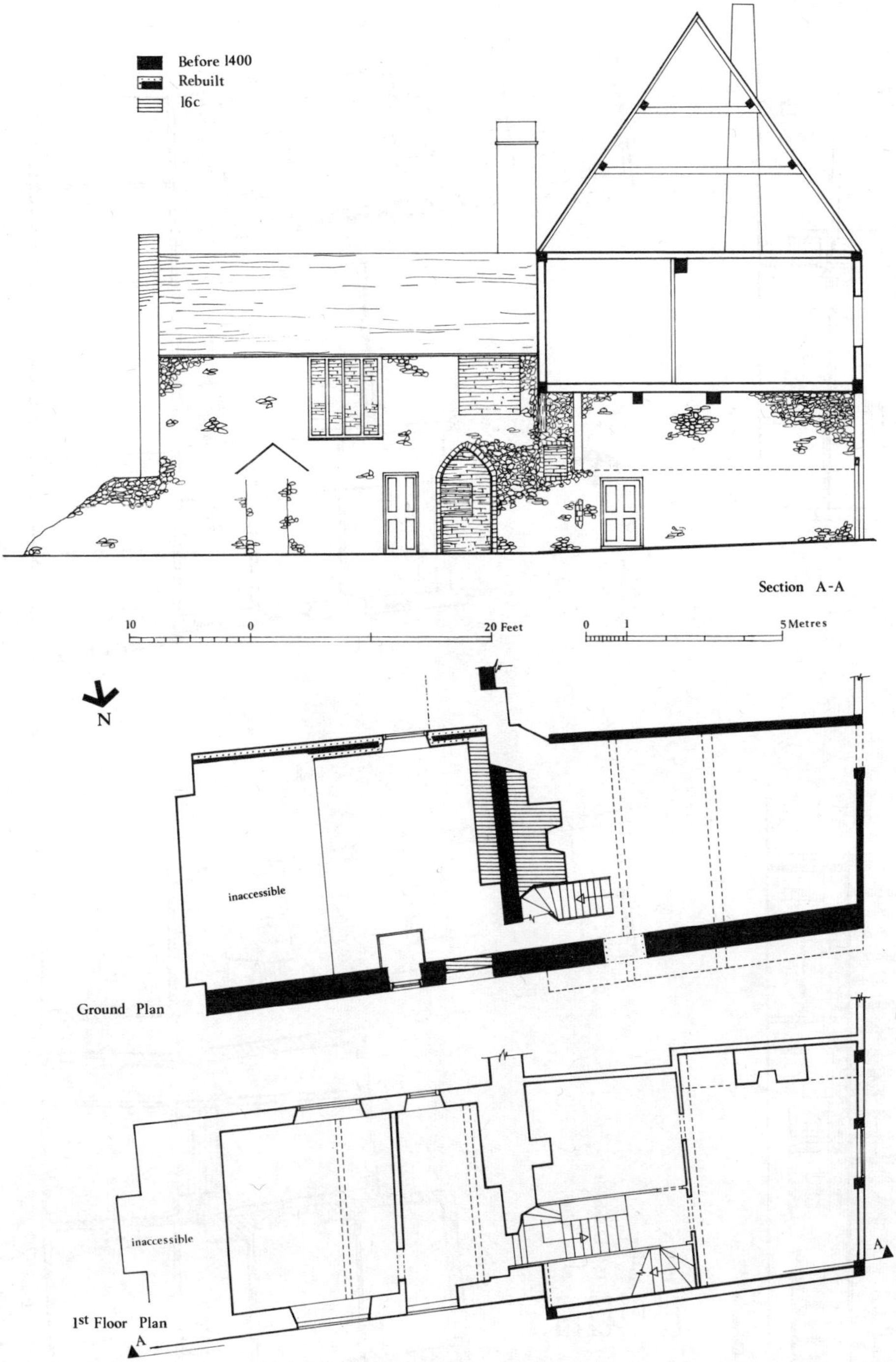

Fig 35 *No. 30 King Street: plans, section and elevation*

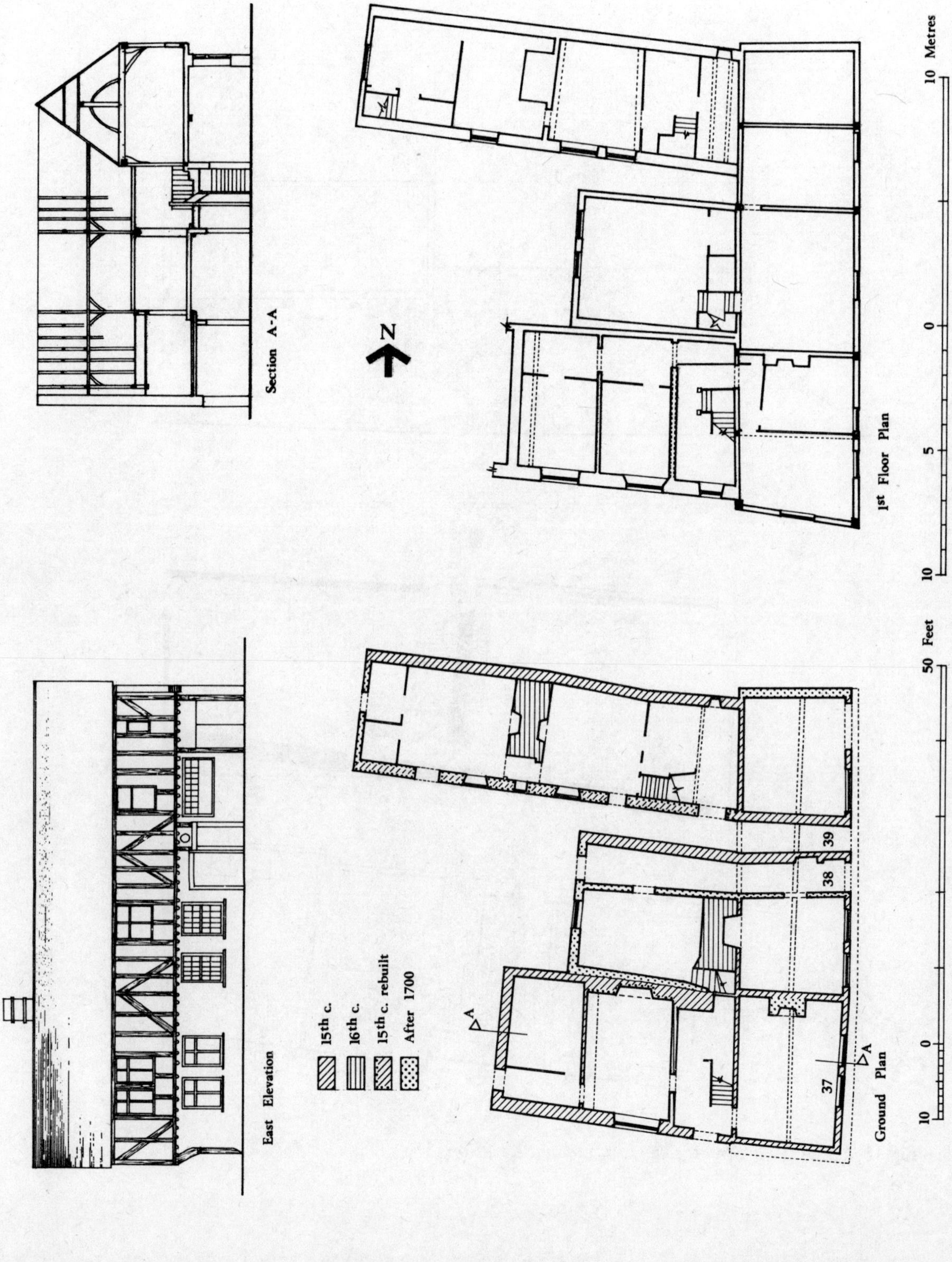

Fig 36 *Nos. 37-9 Chapel Street: plans, section and elevation*

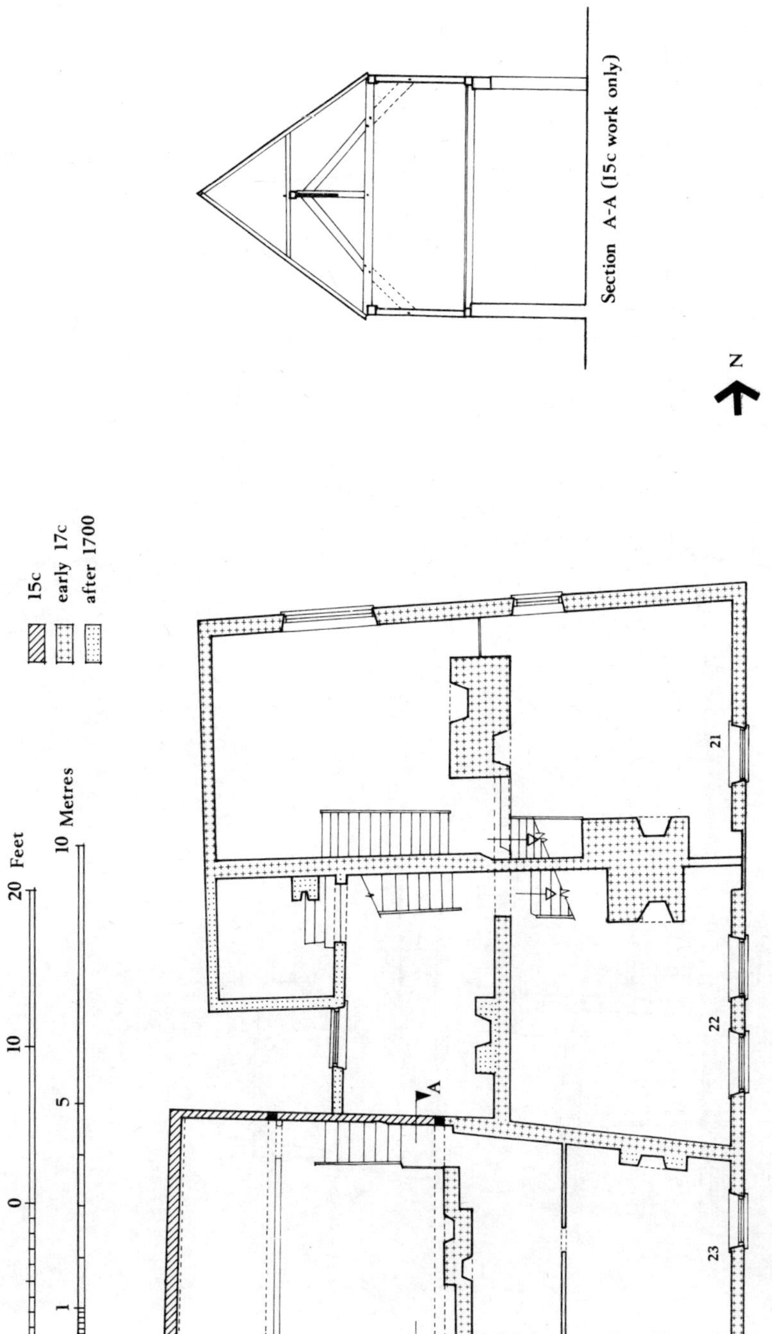

Fig 37 *Nos. 21-3 Broad Street: plan and section*

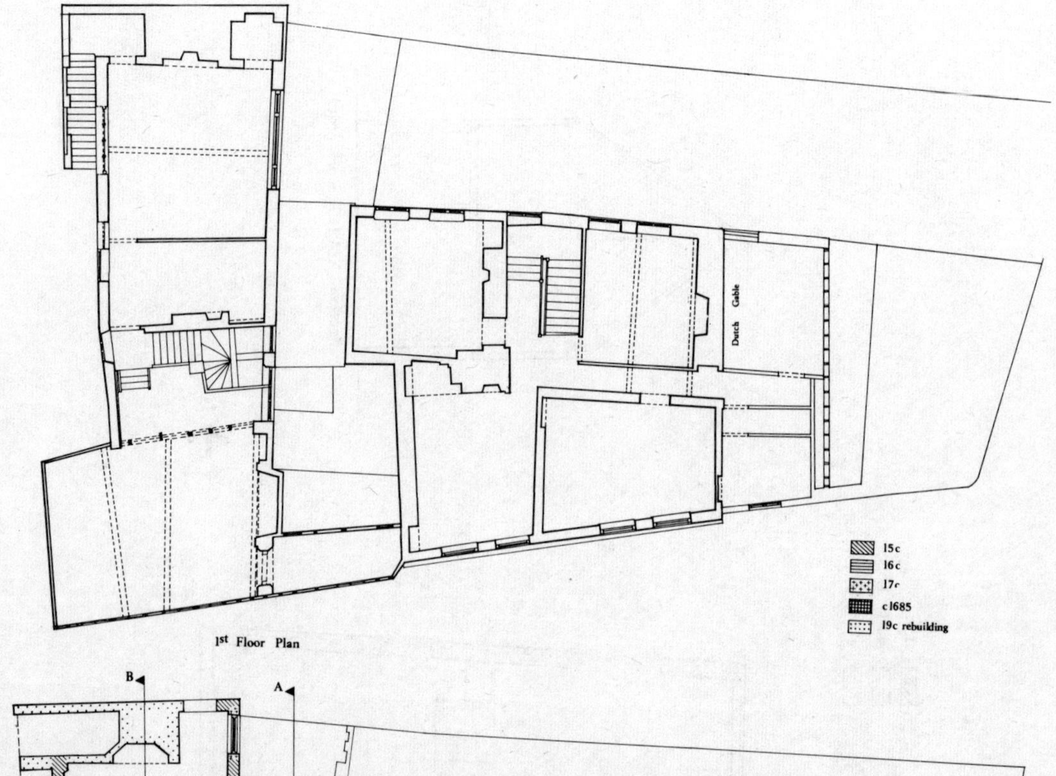

Fig 38 *No. 11 St. Nicholas Street and St. Nicholas House: plans*

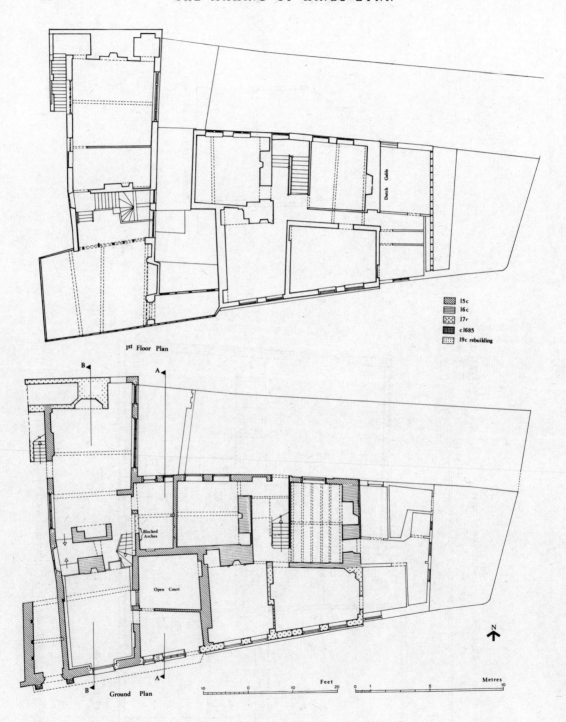

Fig 39 *No. 11 St. Nicholas Street and St. Nicholas House: sections and elevations*

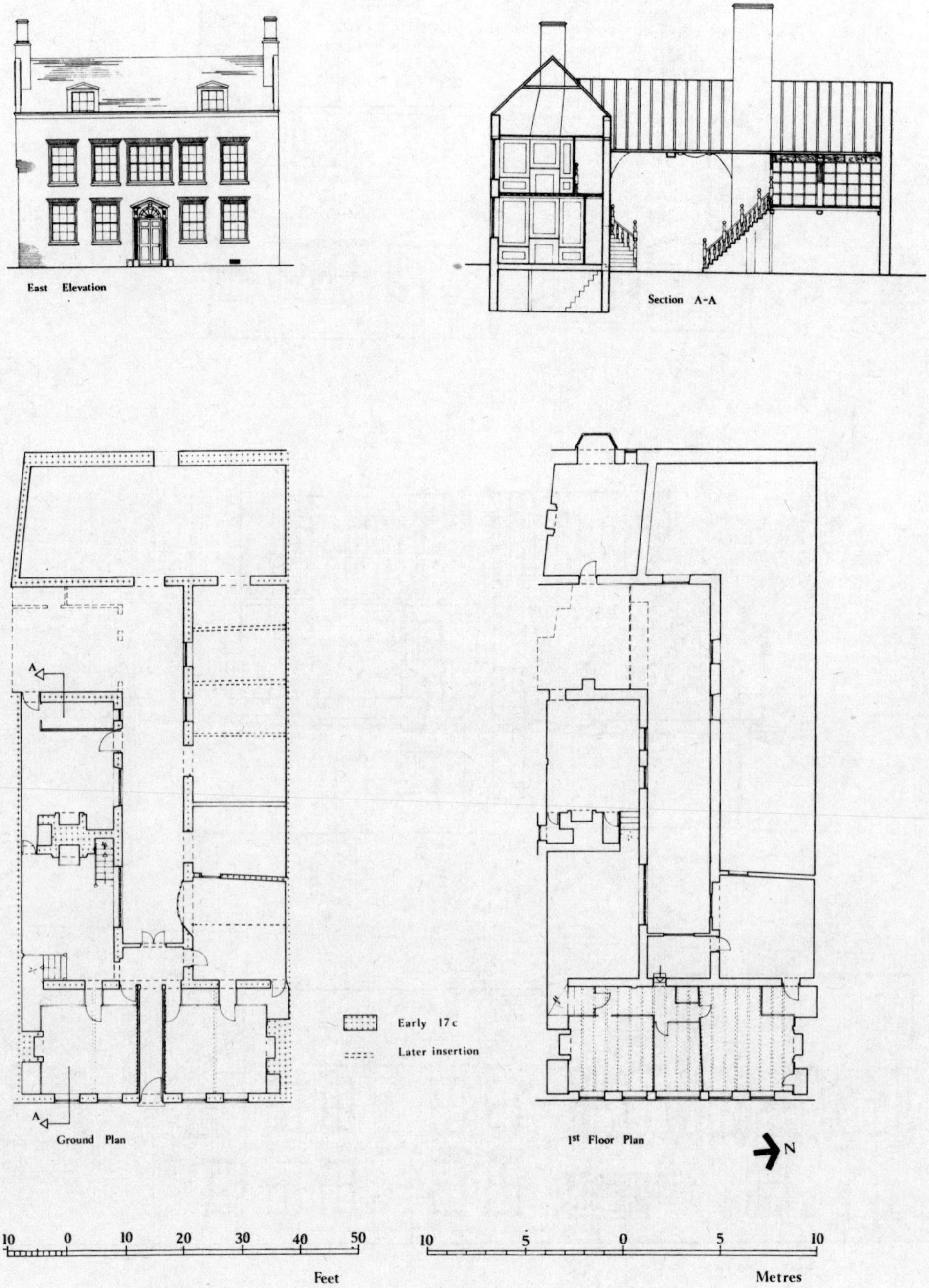

Fig 40 *No. 29 Queen Street: plans, sections and elevations*

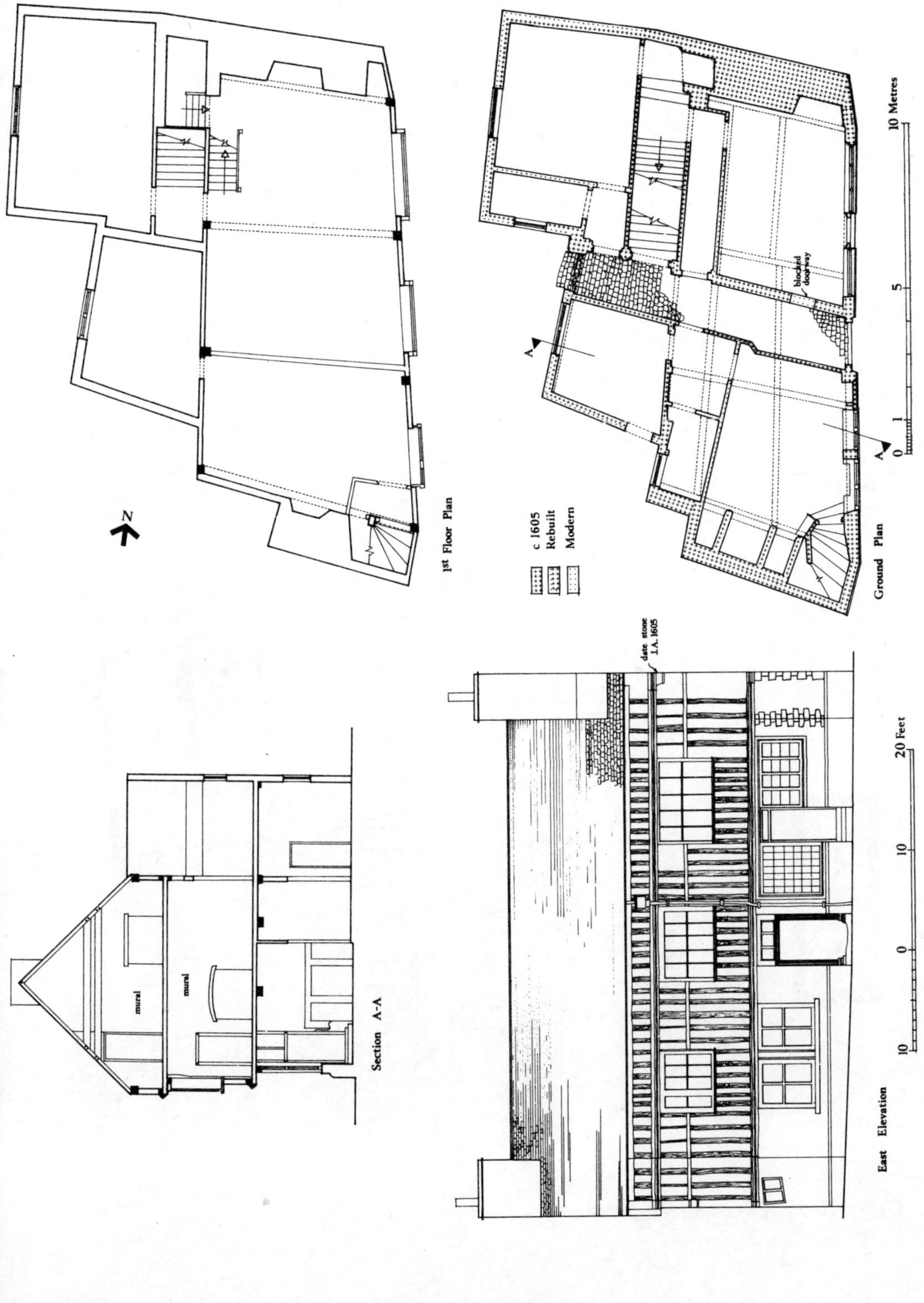

Fig 41 *Greenland Fishery, Bridge Street: plans, sections and elevation*

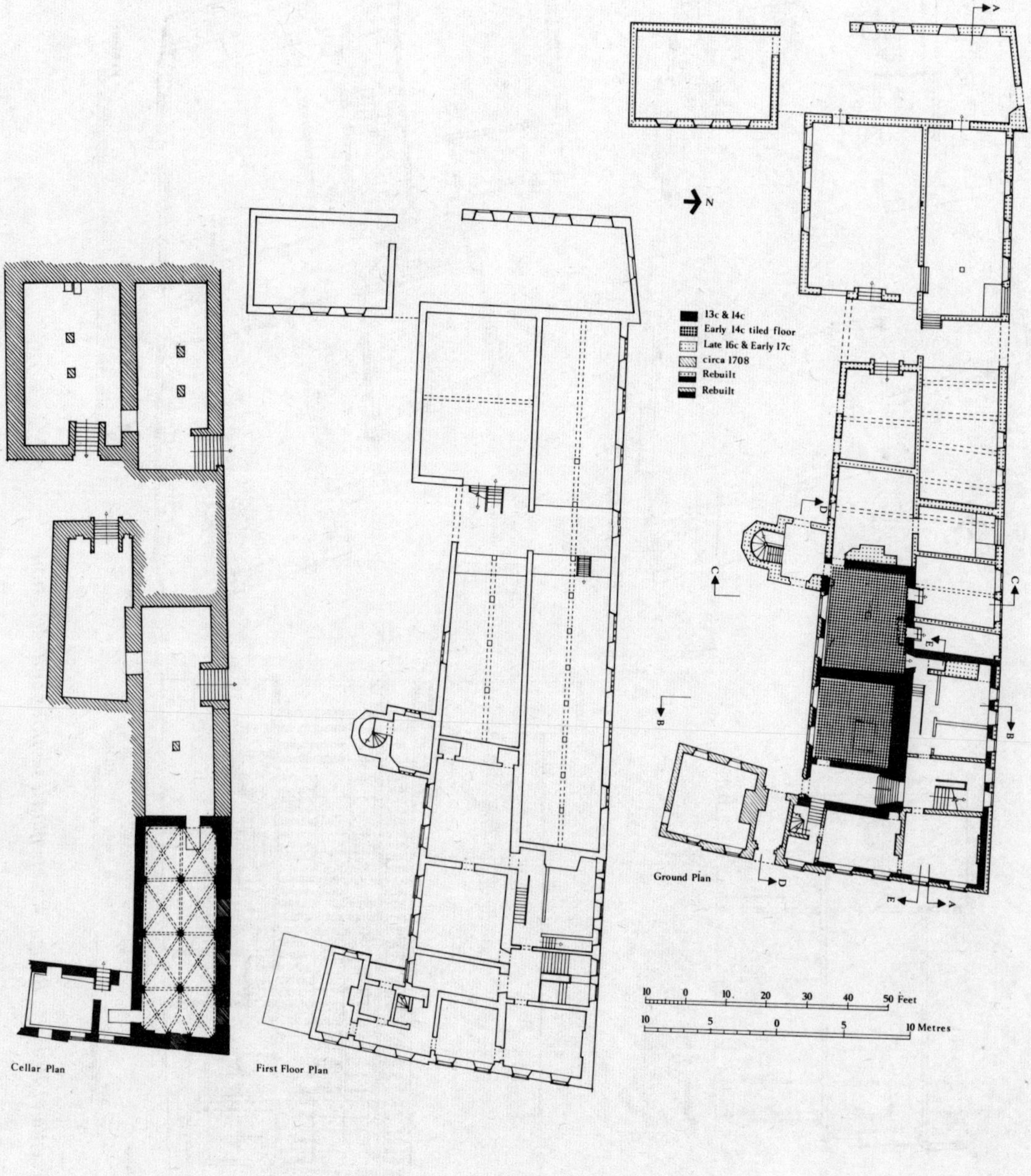

Fig 42 *Clifton House, Queen Street: plans*

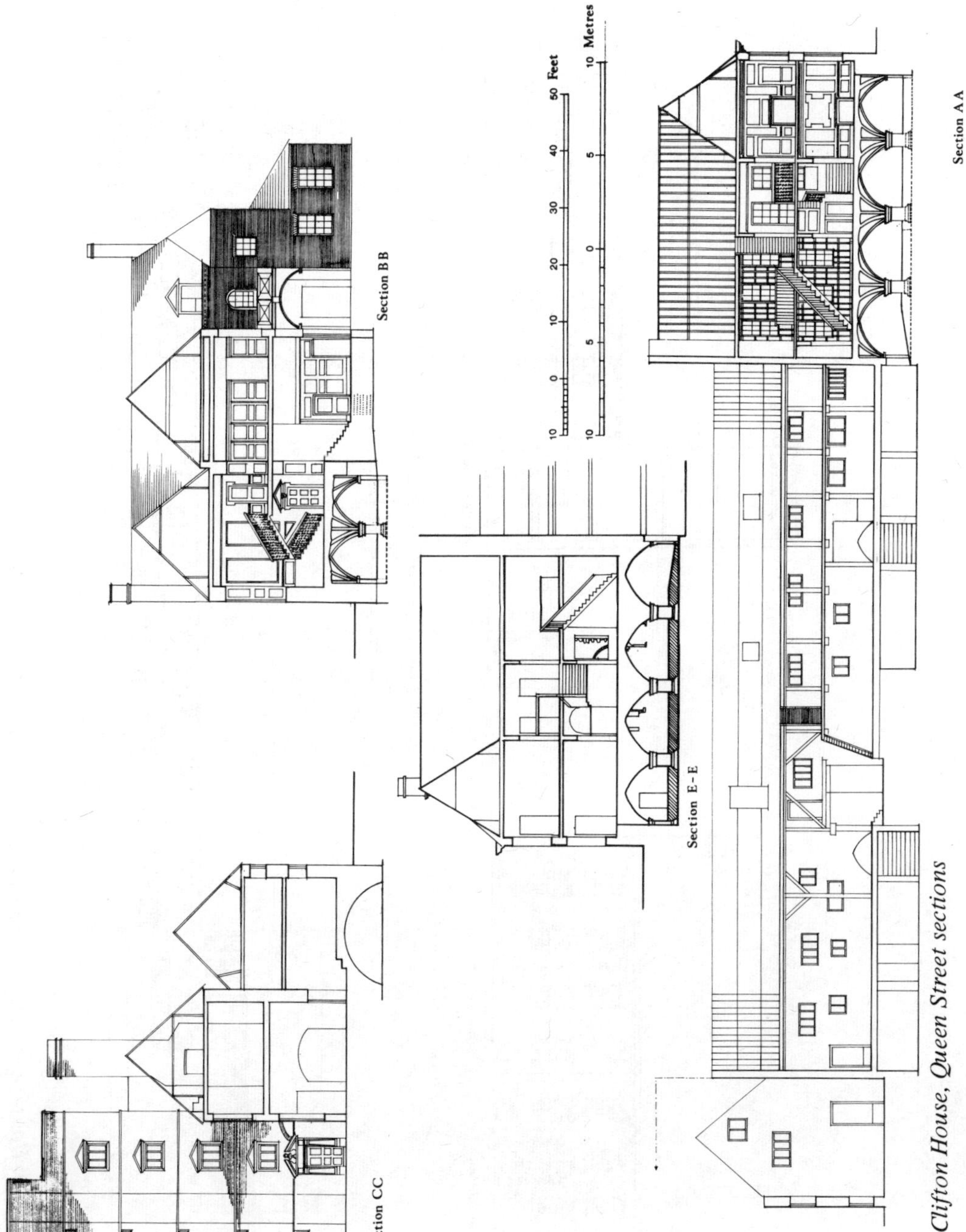

Fig 43 *Clifton House, Queen Street sections*

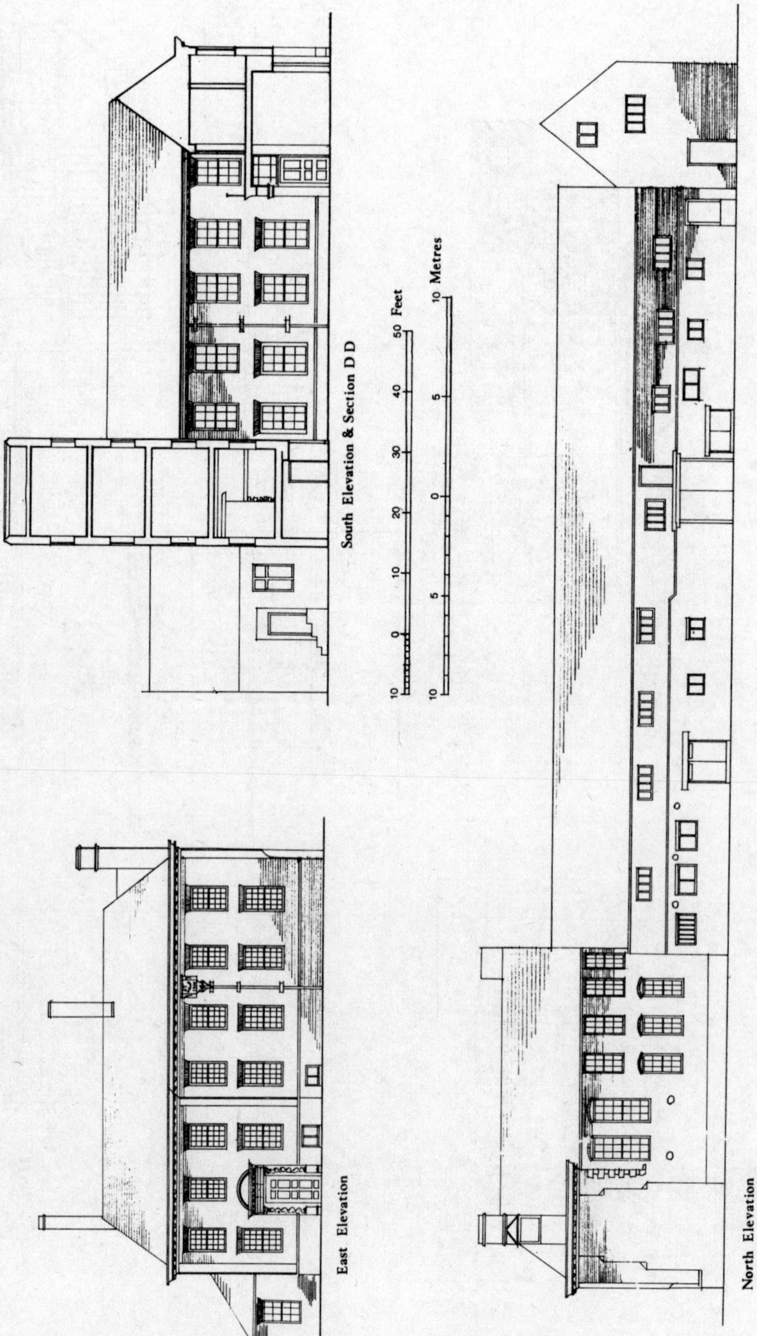

Fig 44 *Clifton House, Queen Street: elevations*

Street Names

Modern name	*c.1557*
Austin St	Hopmans Way
All Saints St	Coldhirne St
Baker Lane	(Old) Wyngate
Blackfriars Rd	mentioned but not named
Blackfriars St	mentioned but not named
Boal St	the Ball
Bridge St	Coldhirne St
Broad St	Webstar Row St
Chapel St	Lystar St
Church St	Stonegate St
College Lane	College Lane
Common Staithe La	Common Staithe La
Common Staithe	Common Staithe
Ferry Lane	Thimble Lane
Friar St	All Saints St
High St (S)	Briggate
High St (N)	Mercer Row
High St (n)	Cook Row St
Kettlewell Lane	Lane to Kettlemills
King St	Checker St
King Staithe Lane	King Staithe Lane
King Staithe	King Staithe
Littleport St	Littleport St
London Rd	not made
Market St	Pillory Lane
Millfleet	mentioned but not named
Nelson St	Lath St
New Conduit St	Fincham St
Norfolk St (W)	Gressmarket
Norfolk St (E)	Damgate
North St	Dowshills St
Page Stair Lane	Page Staithe Lane
Paradise Lane	Spinner Lane
Pilot St	mentioned but not named
Priory Lane	Priory Lane
Purfleet St	Purfleet St
Queen St	Wyngate
St Anns Fort	St Anns Gate
St Ann St	North End St
St James St	Skinner Row
St James Rd	mentioned but not named
St Johns Terrace	mentioned but not named
St Margaret Place	Bull Stake
St Margaret Lane	St Margaret Muckhill La
St Nicholas St	Woolmarket
Saturday Market	Saturday Market
Sedgeford Lane	Sedgeford Lane
South Clough Lane	Fuller Row St
Southgate St	not named
Stonegate St	mentioned but not named
Surrey St	Jews Lane
Tower Place	Codling Lane
Tower St	Basingley Baxters Row
Tuesday Market	Tuesday Market
Union Lane	Mad Lane
Union St	mentioned but not named
Valingers Rd	not made
Water Lane	Pudding Lane

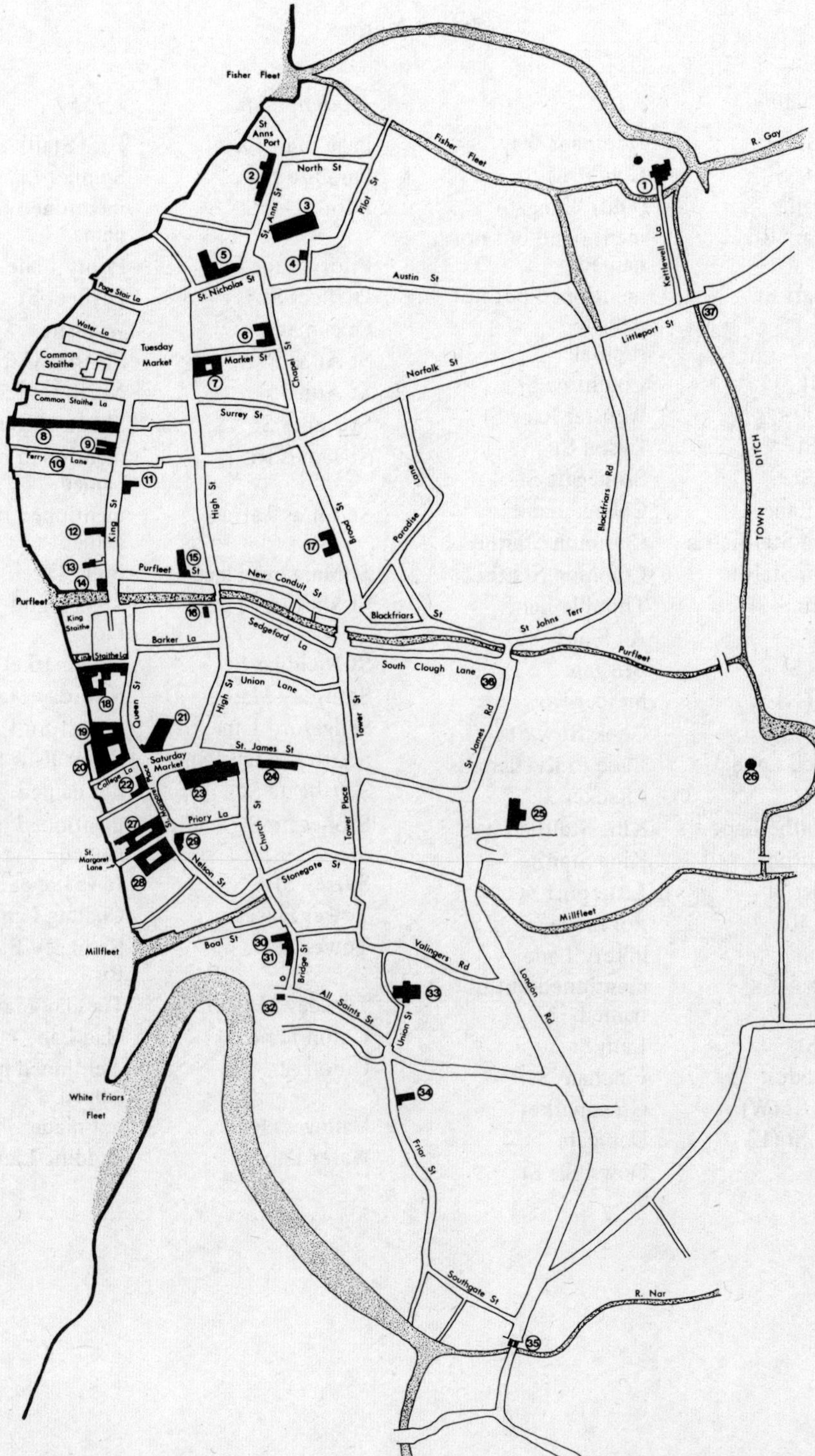

Fig 45 *Map of Kings Lynn from a Survey of 1830 showing the location of all the buildings and the main topographical features mentioned in the text.*

Key to Fig 45

1 Kettlemills
2 Ncs. 6-10 St Ann Street
3 St. Nicholas Church
4 Dutch Gabled Cottage
5 Nos. 9-11 St. Nicholas Street and St. Nicholas House
6 Nos. 31-9 Chapel Street
7 Dukes Head
8 St. Georges Gildhall
9 Nos. 23-5 King Street
10 Site of Michael Revetts House 1636
11 Nos. 30-2 King Street
12 No. 9 King Street
13 Hall of No. 3 King Street
14 Custom House
15 No. 8 Purfleet Street
16 Medieval Hall High Street
17 Nos. 21-3 Broad Street
18 Clifton House: Queen Street
19 No. 29 Queen Street
20 Thoresby College
21 The Trinity Gildhall
22 Site of Sparrow Hall
23 St. Margarets Church
24 Medieval Shops in St. James Street
25 St. James's Workhouse
26 Red Mount Chapel
27 St. Margaret House (Hanse Steelyard)
28 Hampton Court
29 Valiant Sailor
30 Greenland Fishery
31 No. 30-2 Bridge Street
32 White Friars Gate
33 All Saints Church
34 No. 13 Friar Street
35 South Gate
36 Site of the Almeshouse
37 Site of East Gate

Bibliography

Abbreviations:– Ag Hist. Rev., Agricultural History Review; Arch. Hist., Architectural History; Ec. H. R., Economic History Review; Geog. Jnl., Geographical Journal; Camb. Antq. Soc., Proceedings of the Cambridge Antiquarian Society; Med. Arch., Medieval Archaeology; Norf. Arch., Proceedings of the Norfolk and Norwich Archaeological and Antiquarian Society; Trans. R.H.S., Transactions of the Royal Historical Society; V.C.H., Victoria County History.

Allison, J.K., 'The Sheep Corn Husbandry of Norfolk in the Sixteenth and Seventeenth Centuries', *Ag. Hist. Rev.,* V (1957).

Anderson, G.H., *Inns and Taverns of Lynn* (Kings Lynn, 1933).

Astbury, A.K., *The Black Fens* (Cambridge, 1958).

Badeslade, T., *The History of the Ancient and Present State of the Navigation of the Port of Kings Lynn* (London, 1725).

Barbour, V., 'Dutch and English Merchant Shipping in the Seventeenth Century', *Ec. H.R.,* 1st Ser. II (1929).

Bardswell, M., 'Kings Lynn: Greenland Fishery Building', *Norf. Arch.,* XXX (1957).

Barley, M.W., *The English Farmhouse and Cottage* (London, 1961); 'A glossary of Names for Rooms In Houses of the Sixteenth and Seventeenth Centuries', Jope, E.M. (ed) *Studies in Building History* (London, 1961); *The House and Home* (London, 1963).

Bartlett, N., 'The Lay Poll Tax Returns for the City of York in 1381' offprint from the unpublished *Transactions of the East Riding Antiquarian Society,* XXX (1953).

Beloe, E.M., 'Freebridge Hundred and the Making of Lynn', *Norf. Arch.,* XII, (1895); *Our Borough, Our Churches* (Wisbech, 1871 and 1899); 'The Padders Way and its Attendant Roads', *Camb. Antq. Soc.,* IX (1895).

Beresford, M.W., *Lay Subsidies and Poll Taxes* (Phillimore, 1963); *New Towns of the Middle Ages* (London, 1967); and St Joseph, J.K. *Medieval England: an Aerial Survey* (Cambridge, 1958).

Bradfer-Lawrence, H.L., *The Merchants of Lynn.* Supplement to Blomefield's Norfolk, IX (Norwich).

Bridbury, A.R., *Economic Growth, England in the Later Middle Ages* (London, (1962); *England and the Salt Trade in the Late Middle Ages* (Oxford, 1955).

Brief and True Relation of the Seige and Surrendering of Kings Lynn to the Earl of Manchester. Unpublished manuscript (1643).

Burke, G.L., *The Making of Duth Towns* (London, 1956).

Carus-Wilson, E.M., 'The First Half Century of the Borough of Stratford-upon-

Avon', *Ec. H.R.*, 2nd Ser, XVIII (1965); 'The Medieval Trade of the Ports of the Wash', *Med. Arch.*, VI-VII (1963); *Medieval Merchant Venturers* (London, new ed, 1969); and Coleman, O., *England's Export Trade, 1275-1547* (Oxford, 1963).

Colvin, H. and Wodehouse, L.M., 'Henry Bell of Kings Lynn', *Arch. Hist.*, IV (1961).

Conzen, M.B.G., *Alnwick, Northumberland, a Study in Town Plan Analysis.* Institute of British Geographers Research Papers, No.27 (1960).

Cordingley, R.A., 'British Historical Roof Types and their Members', *Ancient Monuments Society*, New Series, IX (1961).

Darby, H.C., *Domesday Geography of Eastern England* (Cambridge, 1952); *The Draining of the Fens* (Cambridge, 1940); *The Medieval Fenland* (Cambridge, 1940).

Defoe, D., *A Tour Through the Whole Island of Great Britain*, ed Cole, G.D.H., (London, 1927).

Dollinger, P., *La Hanse (XIIe-IVe Siecles)* (Paris, 1964).

Dugdale, W., *The History of the Imbanking and Draining of Rivers, Fens and Marshes.* 2nd ed. (London, 1772).

Everitt, A., *Change in the Provinces: the Seventeenth Century.* Leicester, Dept of English Local History, Occasional Papers, 2nd Ser, I (1969); 'The Marketing of Agricultural Produce', Thirsk, J. (ed), *Agrarian History of England and Wales*, IV, 1500-1640 (Cambridge, 1967).

Fletcher, J.M. and Spokes, P.S., 'The Origin and Development of Crown-Post Roofs' *Med. Arch.*, VIII (1964).

Forster, G.C.F., 'York in the Seventeenth Century', *V.C.H. York* (London, 1961).

Fowler, G., 'Fenland Waterways Past and Present', *Camb. Antiq. Soc.* XXIII (1933) and XXXIV (1934).

Gras, N.S.B., *The Early English Customs System* (Havard, 1918); *The Evolution of the English Corn Market* (Harvard, 1926).

Hallam, H.E., *The New Lands of Elloe.* Leicester, Dept of English Local History, Occasional Papers, 1st Ser, VI (1954).

Harris, L.E., *Vermuyden and the Fens* (London, 1953).

Harrod, H., *Report on the Deeds and Records of the Borough of Kings Lynn* (Kings Lynn, 1874).

Hibbert, A.B., 'The Economic Policies of Towns', *Cambridge Economic History of Europe*, III (1963).

Hillen, H.J., *History of the Borough of Kings Lynn* (Norwich, 1907).

Hoskins, W.G., 'Elizabethan Merchants of Exeter', in Bindoff, S.T., Hurstfield, J., Williams, C.H., (ed) *Elizabethan Government and Society: Essays Presented to Sir John Neale* (London 1961); 'English Provincial Towns in the Early Sixteenth Century', *Trans. R.H.S.*, 5th Ser, VI (1956); *Local History in England* (London, 1959); 'The Rebuilding of Rural England', *Past and Present*, IV (1953).

James, M.K., 'Fluctuations in the Anglo-Gascon Wine Trade During the Fourteenth Century', *Ec. H.R.,* 2nd Ser, IV (1951).

Kerling, N.J.M., *Commercial Relations of Holland and Zeeland with England from the late Thirteenth Century to the Close of the Middle Ages* (Leiden, 1954).

Kestner, F.J.T., 'The Old Coastline of the Wash', *Geog. Jnl.,* CXXVIII (1962).

Kempe, M., *The Book of Margery Kempe.* Butler-Bowden, W. (ed) (Oxford, 1954).

Kingston, A., *East Anglia in the Great Civil War* (London, 1897).

Lavedan, P., *Histoire de l'Urbanisme* (Paris, 1926).

Lobel, M.D., *The Borough of Bury St Edmonds* (Oxford, 1935); (ed) *Historic Towns,* I. (London and Oxford, 1969).

Mackerell, B., *History of Kings Lynn* (London, 1738).

Margary, I.D., *Roman Roads in Britain.* 2nd ed. (London, 1967).

Martin, G.H., *The Story of Colchester* (Colchester, 1959); *The Town* (London, 1961); (ed) Gross, C., *Bibliography of British Municipal History.* New ed, (Leicester, 1966).

Miller, E., *The Abbey and Bishopric of Ely* (Cambridge, 1951).

Miller, S.H., and Skeatchly, S.B., *The Fenland Past and Present* (London, 1878).

Nef, J.U., *The Rise of the British Coal Industry* (London, 1932).

O'Neil, B.H.St J., 'Some Seventeenth Century Houses in Great Yarmouth', *Archaeologia,* XCV (1953).

Page, F.M., *The Estates of Crowland Abbey* (Cambridge, 1934).

Pantin, W.A., 'Domestic Architecture in Oxford', *Antiquaries Journal,* XXVII (1947); 'Medieval English Town House Plans', *Med. Arch.* VI-VII (1963); 'Medieval Inns', in Jope, E.M. (Ed) *Studies in Building History* (London, 1961).

Parkin, C., *Topography of Freebridge Hundred and Half, in the County of Norfolk; containing the History of the Borough of Kings Lynn.* Blomefield's Norfolk, VIII (London, 1808).

Parker, H., 'A Medieval Wharf in Thoresby College Courtyard, Kings Lynn', *Med. Arch.,* IX (1965).

Portman, D., *Exeter Houses 1400-1700* (Exeter, 1966).

Raftis, A., *The Estates of Ramsey Abbey* (Toronto, 1957).

Ramsay, G.D. (ed), *John Isham, Merchant and Merchant Adventurer: Two Account Books of a London Merchant in the Reign of Elizabeth I* (Northants. Record Society, XXI (1962).

Richards, W., *The History of Lynn* (Kings Lynn, 1812).

Riches, N., *The Agricultural Revolution in Norfolk.* 2nd ed, (London, 1967).

Rogers, K.H., 'Town Plan of Salisbury', in Lobel, M.D. (ed) *Historic Towns* I (London and Oxford, 1969).

Rye, W., *Index of Norfolk Topography* (London, 1881).

Savage, Sir W., *The Making of Our Towns* (London, 1952).

Schofield, R.S., 'The Geographical Distribution of Wealth in England, 1334-1649' *Ec. H.R.,* 2nd Ser, XVIII (1965).

Smith, J.T., 'Medieval Roofs: a Classification', *Archaeological Journal,* CXV (1958).

Steer, F.W. (ed), *Farm and Cottage Inventories of mid-Essex, 1635-1749* (Phillimore, 1969).

Stenton, F.M., 'The Road System of Medieval England', *Ec. H.R.*, old series, VII, (1936).

Supple, B., *Commercial Crisis and Change in England, 1600-1642* (Cambridge, 1959).

Taylor, W., *Antiquities of Kings Lynn* (London, 1844).

Thirsk, J., 'The Farming Regions of England' in Thirsk, J. (ed) *The Agrarian History of England and Wales,* IV, 1500-1640 (Cambridge, 1969); *Fenland Farming in the Sixteenth Century.* Leicester, Dept of English Local History, Occasional Papers, 1st Ser, III (1953).

Thrupp, S., 'The Gilds', in *The Cambridge Economic History of Europe,* III (1963); *The Merchant Class of Medieval London* (Michigan, 1948).

Tout, T.F., 'Medieval Town Planning' *Bulletin of the John Rylands Library,* IV, 1917-8.

Tingey, J.C., 'The Grants of Murage to Norwich, Yarmouth and Lynn', *Norf, Arch.,* XVIII, (1912).

Walker, N. and Craddock, T., *The History of Wisbech and the Fens.* (Wisbech, 1848).

Webb, J., *Great Tooley of Ipswich* (Ipswich, 1962).

Willan, T.S., *The English Coasting Trade, 1600-1750* (Manchester, 1938); 'River Navigation and Trade from the Witham and Yare, 1600-1730', *Norf. Arch.,* XXVI (1938).

Williams, N.J., *The Maritime Trade of the East Anglian Ports, 1550-1590.* Unpublished D. Phil. Thesis (Oxford, 1952).

Wee, H.R. van de, *The Growth of the Antwerp Market* (The Hague, 1963).

Wood, M.E., *The English Medieval House* (London, 1965).

Index
OF SUBJECTS AND PLACES IN KINGS LYNN

Index
OF PERSONS AND PLACES OUTSIDE KINGS LYNN

~~.73~~

73

73

.73

.73

73

24.

24.